Spire Books Ltd
PO Box 2336
Reading RG4 5WJ
spirebooks.com

CIP data
A catalogue record for this book is
available from the British Library.
ISBN 978-1-904965-16-9

Designed by Allon Kaye
Text set in Foundry Wilson and Galaxie Polaris
Printed in England by Alden Group Ltd.

for Hillel Helman

This book was written with the support of
the generous award of a Wingate Scholarship
by the Harold Hyam Wingate Foundation.

The cost of illustrating the book with both new
photography and reproductions from archival
collections was met thanks to generous
grants from The John S. Cohen Foundation;
Marc Fitch Fund; The Paul Mellon Centre
for Studies in British Art; The Pugin Society;
the Scouloudi Foundation in association
with the Institute of Historical Research;
Rupert Thomas and Alan Bennett; The Harold
Hyam Wingate Foundation; and The Society
of Architectural Historians of Great Britain,
which awarded a Dorothy Stroud Bursary.

Published in association with English Heritage

ENGLISH HERITAGE

Introduction

The story of the Victorian parsonage is part of the well-known history of the gothic revival. But the story of the early nineteenth-century parsonage is a different matter altogether.

From the 1810s onwards the governors of Queen Anne's Bounty, the Church of England fund established to assist poor clergymen, began to issue mortgages for new parsonages once an application procedure had been completed. This procedure required the parson's architect or builder to submit a full set of drawings and a specification for approval by his local bishop. As a result we have many hundreds of detailed applications in diocesan archives, a documentary treasure that has no equal on this scale with any other building type.

The documents themselves, of course, form merely part of a magnificent heritage that can so easily be seen in those many hundreds of parishes all over the country that still have early nineteenth-century parsonages or former parsonage houses. These buildings have become one of the most readily recognisable features of the English village. But it is thanks to the thorough nature of the mortgage application documents that we can really learn about them and appreciate them for their architectural value. We can begin to see how the style and layout of these houses changed over time, and learn the names of those who commissioned them and designed them. In fact the special value of the parsonage files in the county record offices is that they give us an unparalleled insight into the development of the smaller English detached house at a critical period in its history. In particular we can also see exactly how the gothic revival happened, because a great wave of parsonage-house building coincided with it. The elevations, plans and details of the houses of the period, many of them in the form of beautiful drawings that have lain hidden for nearly 200 years, are all there waiting to be discovered. For this we have to thank the clerks of the Church offices of the time, and in particular Christopher Hodgson, the long-time secretary to the governors of Queen Anne's Bounty, for insisting on the highest and most exacting standards from applicants.

The story is not, however, just about architectural style and language. The way in which parsonage houses from the beginning of the nineteenth-century onwards grew in size and quality provides a continuous commentary on the change in the social position of the rector or vicar. At the beginning of our period we encounter the 'squarson', the squire-parson, possibly an absentee with a second or

The rectory at Winterborne Came, near Dorchester, Dorset, a fine thatched house with an attractive verandah designed in the fashionable small country villa style by an unknown architect in the late 1820s.

even a third incumbency some distance away, and who acted like a member of the gentry and hunted and danced with them; with the growth first of the evangelical movement and then subsequently with Tractarianism he is replaced in time by quite a different sort of person – the high-minded Victorian priest living in the heart of his village. This story is familiar from early Victorian literature such as the novels of William Makepeace Thackeray or George Eliot, and it is beautifully illustrated by the development of the parsonage house over this period.

First of all, as our story opens most parsonage houses are in a terrible state of decay and quite unsuited for the second son of a member of the gentry who might by then have taken up his position in the parish: it was not unusual for many incumbents, like Mr Elton in Jane Austen's *Emma*, to be living in a house distinctly inferior in size and quality to that of neighbours of similar social class. Secondly, many more houses needed to be built from the late 1830s onwards because it became increasingly unacceptable, and eventually illegal in most cases, to hold more than one clerical incumbency. The long suffering and badly-paid curate who stood in for the local clergyman, living in very humble circumstances, was eventually replaced by a full-time parson who required a decent house near his church. And thirdly, the actual nature of the job changed: the earnest clergyman of the 1840s, whether evangelical or high-church, required a distinct type of house that could not be mistaken for a common dwelling-place or a minor country house. At the beginning of our period bishops would have objected to a parson building a private oratory in his new parsonage house; by the end, some encouraged it. And by 1860 too, both architects and parsons were writing explicitly about the architecture and significance of these houses in a way that they had never done before. Over our period the offices of the Church authorities who financed the new parsonages developed from a handful of clerks working in an old house to two substantial and expansively accommodated organisations with considerable internal bureaucracies. Building a new house is expensive – for most people, the most expensive project of their lives – and changes in patterns of construction consequently always indicate parallel social and economic developments. Unlike other economic indicators, however, the houses are often beautiful and memorable, and tell a story of their own. One of those stories is a clear demonstration of what people needed in their homes, and how they expected them to look.

And, as it happens, the early development of the Victorian parsonage coincides with one of the most obscure chapters in English architectural history. The architecture of the 1830s has been overlooked by architectural historians, coming as it does between the easily identifiable Regency style and the earnest buildings of the high gothic revival. Anyone who is not an expert in English architectural history might be hard put to identify an architect of note who was working between the ages of John Nash and A.W.N. Pugin, and the general impression is often that a kind of romantic and incompetent gothick style perpetuated by local builders lingered on until the Victorians put an end to it. In fact a close examination of the story of the parsonages shows that the real situation was a great deal more interesting and complicated. It soon becomes clear that the builders of the period are not anything like as romantic and incompetent, not to mention gothick, as conventional histories like to suggest. They are professional people working in an increasingly demanding professional atmosphere, and their work soon reflects their concerns: they need to accommodate a fast increasing number of specific technical spaces and equipment inside their new houses, and they are required for the first time to think hard about how exactly the parts of a building fit together and how exactly the thing is to be paid for. Coincidentally they have access for the first time ever to accurate drawings of the historical buildings of England, even if they do not quite yet know what to make of them, and that at a time when politicians and historians are engaged in a period of national introspection. The result was that the gothic, or more accurately Tudor-gothic, style of the 1830s is quite different from either that of the 1820s or the 1840s. There is a period of architecture here that has long deserved detailed treatment.

And on top of all that there is also the story of the birth of the true gothic revival, in many ways a different matter altogether and quite possibly as much to do with the national psyche as it is to do with architectural style. Pugin is the central figure in this second story. Very often he appears in architectural histories as either the end or the beginning of a tradition; alternatively he is treated primarily biographically, as a one-off who with his various peculiarities does not compare easily to other architectural figures of his generation. This study of contemporary parsonages aims to put Pugin back where he belongs – in the context of the architects of his time who faced similar problems. It was the extraordinary way in which he managed to provide an architectural imagery of great coherence and power exactly at a time when English religious society was searching for a way of projecting a vision of inspiration and control that makes him so important to any history of architecture; and it is the enormously rich supply of detailed documentation that the parsonage files contain that makes it possible to see exactly where it was that his work differed from that of his colleagues, and indeed how it was that the changes he made came to be echoed in the work of architects during the later part of the nineteenth century. Contrary to what is sometimes claimed, theoretical architectural principles cannot change the way we live; our houses have developed not because Pugin or anyone else made impressive statements but because artistic genius has allowed social conditions and preoccupations to express themselves powerfully.

We have in this country been very fortunate in our historians of the early nineteenth century, especially in relation to the Church of England: in particular, Peter Virgin, G.F.A. Best, Robert Hole and R.J. Smith have chronicled the 'Church in an age of negligence', in Virgin's memorable phrase. On the other hand, there has been until now almost nothing (and nothing at all currently in print) about the houses the parsons were building. No one has yet transformed the many intriguing details to be found in the later entries of Sir Howard Colvin's *Biographical dictionary of British architects* into a coherent narrative. What follows is based on a study of some 500 parsonages, to a great extent although not exclusively drawn from the diocesan collections now mainly located in county record offices. Further useful evidence has been found in many other places, including the records of Queen Anne's Bounty and the Ecclesiastical Commissioners, now at the Church of England Record Centre, and the Royal Institute of British Architects Library Drawings Collection at the Victoria and Albert Museum; but the true glory of this history is provided by the many hundreds of houses themselves, still standing, very often scarcely altered and waiting to be rediscovered, ready to tell their astonishing story of a great revolution in English domestic architectural history.

I have tried in this book to present a collection of different types of image to do justice to the story of the houses. Most of the drawings in archival collections consist simply of plans and elevations, and very often they are needed in order to present the facts of a particular instance in the clearest possible way. But I have also chosen to include drawings that seem to me to be unusual or attractive in order to give a sense of the delightful work that is hidden away, and also to give an indication of the geographical spread of the various collections where clergy house drawings can be found (which in one case shown here is as far away as Australia). I have also wanted to demonstrate how the style of the drawings develops along with the style of the architecture – partly because of the increasing professionalism as architects begin to replace builders and surveyors, and partly also because of the greater importance attached to these houses by their designers as the mid century nears. I have also included a selection from the published drawings that architects were looking at, particularly during the critical years of the 1820s and 1830s, in order to convey a sense of the interests and values of these far-away people. On top of all this, the magnificent photographs of Martin Charles convey so well the delightful and varied architecture of the houses that one could almost be standing in front of them. It is as much thanks to him as to my own researches that this neglected but important chapter in English architectural history will come alive before you in the pages that follow.

Chapter One
The 1820s: Between the villa and the cottage

It sometimes seems as if the times we are living in are reminiscent of the early decades of the nineteenth century. All around England people can be found building houses in an almost Tudor-gothic style, sometimes with huge chimneys over inglenook fireplaces, leaded window panes, oriel windows and great sweeping roofs. Many contemporary speculative builders are now running up 'Georgian' residences with meagre Tuscan porches fronting blank symmetrical facades, in quantities that would have been unthinkable when I was a child in the 1960s. The parallel is not limited to modest domestic architecture. Indeed, in pre-Victorian England the unprecedentedly huge Palace of Westminster was designed, to general wonderment and some scorn, in an unintelligibly idiosyncratic style that was said to be representative of Britain's history; today, in the late Elizabethan era, another vastly expensive parliament building has arisen above the pavements of the northern capital in an equally obscure style that has been described by its architects, with even less plausibility, as having new forms derived from Scotland's own ancient traditions. In many towns and villages, fine gothic churches are again being mutilated with gimcrack partitions devised for highly non-liturgical practices, and cheap lean-to additions once more deface the exterior of their ancient masonry. There is now, as then, much talk of the Anglo-Saxons and of the distinct peoples of Britain, and of their characteristics and customs; there is chatter in the newspapers and amongst the politicians of the rowdiness, the vulgarity, and the drunkenness of the poor people of the towns, and of the philistinism and decadence of the very rich. And there is now, not unlike then, a very Hanoverian heir apparent to the throne of the United Kingdom living with a lady who was until recently his mistress in a stucco house originally designed by Nash, a house gone over not long ago by a leading interior decorator, partly at the taxpayers' expense and no doubt also to their delight, in an opulent late eighteenth-century taste which now matches ormolu with wall-to-wall beige carpeting.[1]

What we do not know of the present day, as we know retrospectively of the end of the Georgian era, is whether we are in a period of decisive change. In many respects, the years from the 1820s to the 1840s created modern Britain. The post-Napoleonic settlement in Europe, the Great Reform Act, the establishment of free trade, the formation of two modernised political parties in England, and the beginnings of the

1.1
The offices of Queen Anne's Bounty in Dean's Yard, Westminster. Edward Blore designed no 3A, in shadow to the south (left) in 1846; the following year he added an extra storey to the house as well as the large office premises at no 3 with their imposing tall oriel (right).

process which created a structure of comprehensive government from parish to Empire all underlie subsequent developments in our history. New methods of analysis and the subdivision of 'science' provided the early century with professors, doctors and quacks in the developing fields of biology, botany, geology, mechanical and structural engineering, in medicine, sociology, phrenology, and much else.

In many ways, the private houses of this era are the touchstone for the great watershed which marks the Georgian era from the modern one that we took for granted until comparatively recently. The practice of architecture was revolutionised over a short period of time. It is from the early part of the nineteenth century that we first have the professional architect in the modern sense, presiding independently over the execution of a building contract that resembles the ones of today, questioning the stylistic rationale of his designs as he might do now, and specifying technical and mechanical apparatus such as the latest water closet and kitchen equipment like a modern practitioner. And it is during this period that specific building types that bridge the divide – most notably, the smaller private house – provide remarkable evidence of the changes that were occurring. The typical English parsonage provides an unparalleled window into a changing world, for it is a house-type that so many of us are familiar with, that can be seen in or beside almost every village, and which for many people has remained the quintessential English house, the one which at once conjures up a picture of a people and its landscape. Many hundreds were built at this time and, technically, it is the best documented of any contemporary building type; and yet ironically, in spite of that profusion of historic documentation concerning the clients, the sites, the materials, the elevations and the plans, there is next to nothing about the design of these houses in the academic literature, journalism or personal memoirs of the time, or indeed in architectural debate or personal memoirs. Furthermore, although Peter Hammond's *The parson and the Victorian parish* of 1977 included some very enjoyable descriptions of parsonages and parsonage life, there has been almost nothing written in modern times about their architecture, with the exception of passages in just two small books on the general history of the parsonage published in the early 1960s.[2] They simply are what they are, a remarkable collection of houses that represent the history of English domestic architecture at a critical period. These new houses reached into villages across the whole of England, from the south-west of Cornwall up to the Northumbrian coast. Of course they provide a remarkable backdrop to the stories of those that commissioned them, designed them and built them; but they also carry in themselves the germs of the new architecture: for there is no other building type that so accurately portrays the transition of English architecture from the symmetrical classical-Georgian to the colourful, sometimes rowdy, sometimes moralising, aesthetics of the mid-Victorians. And since the history of the medium-sized private house encapsulates in some ways the history of architecture as a whole, the clarity of the changes as they can be seen in the developing parsonage across the period is itself an invaluable guide to the hopes and vicissitudes of designers from all ages; for in spite of some bold attempts by pious architects of the 1840s to find a special character for them, the changing style and plan of the parsonage continued to reflect the general nature of the debate across the architectural profession. At the beginning of the nineteenth century nearly all new parsonages looked much the same. By 1850 almost every one was different. What had happened?

New laws for new houses

Early nineteenth-century English literature is rich with descriptions of parsons, and once one begins to look for them one soon finds clues as to the changing nature of their domestic circumstances. A most familiar example, from 1816, is Jane Austen's Mr Elton, the neighbour of her eponymous Emma. Emma is most careful to maintain social relations only with families of similar status, which largely means those with houses and servants on a scale comparable to the grand house in which she herself lives; and yet Mr Elton, though clearly socially acceptable to her and indeed in demand amongst the gentry for his company, lives in 'an old and not very good house, almost as close to the road as it could be'.[3] He seems to have very few servants, the most that his modest income and his small home can accommodate. If Mr Elton's house is to match his social aspirations, and if the little Eltons who will be born there are to enjoy the privacy and decency that would soon be expected of any respectable household, it is clear that the vicarage at Highbury is in need of substantial remodelling or rebuilding. And there were thousands of Mr Eltons with social pretensions living in comparably modest circumstances across the country.

It often seems that whenever in England the acquisition of property has become important as an indicator of status, a legal and financial framework has quickly grown up to accommodate the national passion for home ownership: and since the domestic circumstances of early nineteenth-century parsons were particularly inadequate relative to their social status, it appears, in retrospect, to have been only a matter of time before their needs were met. According to *The Church in an age of negligence*, Peter Virgin's fascinating study of the period, a very large number of parishes had no residence at all: as late as 1833, there were, he writes, nearly 2,900 parishes like this, and a further 1,700 had no fit building.[4] Many that were in use were ancient or dilapidated, and only slightly better than the houses of most working people; and those, by all accounts, were little better than hovels with one or two rooms. Mary Russell Mitford described some of them in her popular writing of the 1830s: of an unfortunate man called Tom Cordery she wrote 'Tom's cottage was, however, very thoroughly national and characteristic: a low ruinous hovel...tattered thatch...half-broken windows...one long, straggling, unceiled, barn-like room, which served for kitchen, bedchamber and hall'.[5] The great topographical writer John Britton, possibly exaggerating, wrote that the village where he had been born in 1771, Kington St Michael in Wiltshire, was 'so unlike Miss Mitford's that it might be regarded as belonging to a different part of the world, and occupied by a distinct class of the human race', by which he meant that it was a great deal worse. He too was brought up in a house where one room served for kitchen, parlour and hall. 'It was about fourteen foot square, by six and a half high'.[6] A typical parsonage of the era might have consisted of only a handful of similar rooms on the ground floor, with a couple of bedrooms above for the family, and one further one for a servant. Since some mortgage application drawings show an existing house, it is possible to see exactly how modest they often were: one at Woodbastwick in Norfolk, for example, had three small rooms in a row on each of two floors, and was a single room deep.[7] Jane Austen again provides a telling detail when Emma leaves Mr Elton in the room of his house 'that he chiefly occupied' and moves to meet his housekeeper in another room behind it 'with which it immediately communicated', for no small house of any quality built even as long ago as the beginning of the eighteenth century would have had a pair of communicating rooms in this fashion.[8] Until our period begins, a parson without his own income or the private means of a generous patron had no way of building himself and his family a decent new house. A substantial parsonage built privately from the Reformation until the end of the eighteenth century testifies to a comparatively wealthy family. To return to Jane Austen: the Reverend Henry Tilney in *Northanger Abbey* of 1798–9 is the son of the parish patron, and his new parsonage at Woodston, 'a new-built substantial stone house', was paid for by his father. As the latter accurately exclaimed, 'there are few country parsonages in England half so good'.[9]

By the end of the eighteenth century, the social nature of the clergy was changing in a process that Virgin describes. First of all, parsons received their income in the form of tithes, a tax on the agricultural produce of their parishioners: a vicar was one who received 'little' tithes, that is, a tax on produce grown *upon* the land, such as animals; whereas the rector was an incumbent who received 'great' tithes as well – that is, the income from crops grown *in* the land. They both profited therefore when farmers benefited from the wars with France that restricted foreign imports and pushed up the value of their crops. Secondly, as the national Church took upon itself new duties as an educator within the parish, the parson was expected to be an educated man himself; in some cases, he was in fact a don from Oxford or Cambridge who had chosen to marry and was thus required to leave the college, which used its patronage of parish livings to find him a home. The parson was also increasingly likely to be a magistrate at this period, and that in itself conveyed the status, if not the membership, of the gentry.[10] All these implied respectability, and as a result the clergy was boosted by those from wealthy or landed homes, who might also have made a sensible marriage. With a private income, social status, and a fine plot of land on the glebe on which to build, an incumbency in a quiet rural parish became more attractive that it might historically have been, and the second son of a landed family inevitably became an ideal client for an architect.

Furthermore, the politics of the Church of England were contributing to the demand for new parsonages by an increasing intolerance of pluralism – that is, the holding of more than one parish incumbency by a single parson. A parson appointed to two parishes required one residence only, leaving his other parish or parishes with neither resident parson nor usable parsonage, if any. Sir William Scott's Residence Act of 1803 required every incumbent to justify adequately his non-residence, and also every bishop to find out how many of their parishes had no resident incumbent – a significant duty given that each county had several hundred parishes and that the bishop himself, most probably old or very old, as Virgin so well describes, was busying himself at the House of Lords and in general not much given to travelling around country lanes.[11] In 1835, following a significant upsurge in support for disestablishment from Dissenters, two parliamentary commissions reported in detail on the finances of the Church, making recommendations for reorganisation and new diocesan boundaries.[12] Three years later in 1838 the Pluralities Act severely limited pluralism in the case of new appointments, permitting it mainly only in small benefices within a short distance of one another; that meant that in time almost every parish would have to find both parson and parsonage.[13]

In fact, the statutory changes needed to encourage the building of new and fitting parsonage houses had been enacted in the last quarter of the eighteenth century, but were still lying almost entirely dormant in the early 1800s. In the 1770s and 1780s the British parliament had been engaged in an unprecedented burst of legislation concerning building and in particular, the paving of roads: these new laws sit side by side in the statute books with those attending (with greater emergency, one imagines) to the political and military problems of the American colonies and elsewhere.[14] In the case of parsonages, the process started with an act passed by the British parliament in 1777, the first of two generally named 'Gilbert's Acts' in honour of their promoter, Thomas Gilbert MP.[15] This act, properly known as the Clergy Residences Repair Act, 17 Geo III cap. 53, was the first to allow the governors of the Church of England fund known as Queen Anne's Bounty to lend money for the repair and rebuilding of existing parsonages on the security of the revenues of the benefice, that is, their income from tithes (fig. 1.2). The Bounty, defined in the act as 'the bounty given by her late Majesty Queen Anne, for the augmentation of the maintenance of the poor clergy', had originated in taxes on church wealth called the first fruits and tenths which had been confiscated by Henry VIII from the Roman church. The first fruits, or annates, were a tax consisting of the revenue of the first year of a benefice after it became vacant, the incoming incumbent being expected to survive on his income from performing religious ceremonies rather than from the tithes; the tenths were a ten per cent tax on the whole of the church's wealth, originally imposed by Rome in the reign of Edward I to fund a papal campaign against the Holy Roman Emperor; the latter was raised sporadically and with discretion, and subject to restrictions imposed by the English parliament.[16] These taxes still provided an annual income although, following a long history of political and royal pressure, the number of people who had to pay them had been greatly reduced since the days of the Reformation.

As its preamble stated, Gilbert's first act proposed using the Bounty to improve living conditions because the lack of suitable accommodation was deterring clergymen from living in their own parish. The act contained instructions and restrictions pertaining to the mortgage, and also stated that a resident incumbent would have to return £5 per cent per annum of the principal sum borrowed; consistent with the act's declared intentions, an incumbent not resident for 20 or more weeks a year would have to return double that. Having borrowed the money, the incumbent would eventually pass on the debt (together with the repaired house) to his successor in the parish, the payments due being part of the remuneration package that came with the appointment; for the freehold of the parsonage was vested in the holder of the office of incumbent. Oxford and Cambridge colleges were also allowed to lend money for the purpose of building a parsonage house in parishes of which they were the patron. The original act merely allowed, rather than required, the governors to lend money, and in spite of a moment of generosity in 1779 when the incumbent at Kirkby Lonsdale received £95, in practice they did not do so before a number of revisions had been made. The second Gilbert Act of 1781 explained and amended the original legislation, and also corrected an impracticality relating to repayments, but it had no immediate practical effect; in a temporary triumph for the bureaucratic mind, however, it did emphasise the need for the applicant to use the standard forms of application included in the schedule appended to the original act.[17]

Eventually, however, new legislation originating in a broader desire for church reform made an impact on the provision of clergy housing. Scott's Residence Act of 1803, mentioned above, required bishops to

1.2
17 Geo iii cap. 53: the opening rubric to Gilbert's Act of 1777.

make an annual return to the privy council of the state of their benefices, which meant that the poor living conditions of much of the clergy soon became public knowledge at least to some extent;[18] and a second act that year, which ended restrictions on private benefactions to the Church that had been imposed by the Mortmain Act of 1736, allowed the Bounty to fund a new house where a benefice had been 'augmented' – that is, its income raised either in perpetuity or in the form of a one-off grant.[19] It was in connection with an application to refurbish and add to an old house at South Newington in Oxfordshire under this legislation that William Hony, representing the parish patron, Exeter College, Oxford, informed his bishop that the College 'did not apprehend any objection to this mode of applying the money, as the living certainly cannot be improved in any other way which shall be at the same time so advantageous to the Incumbent & to the Parish'.[20]

A third act, intended to permit the building of new churches by private benefaction up to the cost of £500, allowed for such benefactions to include 'ample provision' for 'decent and suitable accommodation of all persons, of what rank or degree soever, who may be entitled to resort to the same, and whose circumstances may render them unable to pay for such accommodation'.[21] This act concluded a period of legislation that had altered the relationship between the gentry and the Church: henceforth, visible benevolence on the part of the former to the latter became a way of enhancing prestige. The oldest complete files amongst diocesan collections date from this era: in Chichester, the Reverend John Cheale Green rushed to take advantage of the latest changes, and in 1804 received an augmentation of £200, which was spent on improving and enlarging his house.[22] In 1809 Sydney Smith, making the most of his personal connections, became one of the first people to make use of Gilbert's Acts, borrowing £1,600 for an ambitious remodelling of his house at Foston near York.[23] Then, in 1811, the governors of the Bounty decided (without, apparently, any immediate cause or incentive) that the existing legislation allowed them to start providing mortgage loans for entirely new buildings, and set aside £50,000 to be lent annually in mortgages;[24] and it is from now onwards that new parsonage building began in earnest. By the end of 1825, the Bounty had lent £362,129.11.5.[25] When, in 1838, the Parsonages Act allowed the old house and up to

12 acres of its land to be sold altogether, and a new house on a new site to be funded from it, the traditionally strong link between an incumbent and the mediaeval site of his parsonage was finally dissolved.[26] Finally, the Ecclesiastical Commissioners, originally established in 1835 by Sir Robert Peel and charged with the internal reform of the Church of England, decided in 1842 to make single grants of between two-fifths and half of the cost of a new parsonage house, requiring at first that an incumbent use the services of their architect, William Railton, and that in every case, each house to which the Commissioners gave a grant 'be erected and completed entirely under their direction and control'.[27] There were now four distinct paths to receiving public finance for a new or remodelled house: a gift from the parish patron or other private benefactor; a grant from the Commissioners; an augmentation by the Bounty; and, the most commonly employed, the offer of a mortgage under the provisions of Gilbert's Acts, which required the active support of the local bishop.[28] The procedures by which public money was raised for a grant or mortgage required new formalised administrative systems, and it is these which so vividly illustrate the processes by which rural Georgian England with its squires and parsons was transformed into the Victorian England of administrators and officials, increasingly introducing new public duties, new procedures, new approvals, new meetings, new standardised forms to be filled in, and new work for lawyers.

Plans and papers

It is the process of the awarding of a mortgage under Gilbert's Acts that has provided us with so comprehensive a picture of the new houses: indeed, the paperwork which must have been irritating and time-consuming for the architects and clients of the period has resulted in us having the most comprehensive record of any contemporary building type. In order to regulate both the application and the mortgage repayment procedures, the original act of 1777 itself included an appended schedule which provided the sequence and the wording for the various instruments used in this process. These varied slightly as legislation changed, but in all cases it worked as follows. The incumbent notified his bishop that living conditions were unsuitable in his parish, and this started the ball rolling. The bishop reacted by setting up a commission of enquiry, calling upon the incumbent's neighbours, clergymen from nearby parishes, to find out 'whether there is a fit house of residence within and belonging to' the parish concerned; what were 'the annual profits of the said benefice' (that is, the incumbent's income from tithes there); and 'whether a fit House of Residence can be provided'. These gentlemen would duly report that 'there is no fit house'; and they would confirm that land was available, which after 1838 could be other than on the existing glebe lands themselves. They would submit the details of the parson's parish income from tithes; a rector, with his higher income and mortgage-raising capacity, would be likely to be eligible for a larger mortgage, and thus a larger house, than a vicar, although a vicar in a prosperous part of the country would be likely to be at an advantage over a rector in a poor one. For the greater part of the clergy, income from the tithes varied between a few hundred pounds a year, and just over a thousand; from 1836, the process began whereby the tithes were eventually – over 35 years – commuted into fixed payments.[29] A curate, at the bottom of the ladder, might even after the passing of the 'Curates Act' of 1813 have an income of only £80 per year, received from the incumbent of his parish; but then his needs would have been less: George Eliot's Amos Barton, struggling to make a living in the mid-1830s, employed only 'Nanny' – 'nurse, cook, and housemaid all at once...the robust maid-of-all-work'.[30] The commissioners – those carrying out the enquiry on behalf of the bishop – were also charged with finding out whether an incumbent had already received funds from the Bounty for dilapidations on the original house, and they were required to state how much, and when, and whether the money had been properly spent.

The next process was the approval of the proposed architect, surveyor or builder, his plans, and his estimates. This person was required to sign an affidavit that asserted his competence – that he 'has been accustomed to survey and value and superintend the building and repair of houses and other buildings' or words to that effect. This affidavit summarises other declarations kept with the file confirming that he had surveyed the existing parsonage; that he was submitting a plan or set of drawings for a new house with a specification; and that he had properly estimated the cost of the new building.[31] He also gave here the value of materials from the old house that could be reused in the new one.[32] Further declarations provided the details referred to in the affidavit, including the survey of the old building, stating that it was unfit (or otherwise) for repair, and which materials might be reusable from it; and the signatory was required also to state whether there was timber growing upon the glebe land that might be employed in the new building (there almost never was).[33] Then followed the plans, specifications, and estimate themselves. Any further documents kept with these declarations and drawings usually concern the mortgage itself, for all or part of the building cost, stating the interest and repayment requirements; and the patron of the benefice would appoint an agent for handling the moneys that passed hands, which gentleman was required to keep a notebook containing the details of the transactions. The patrons themselves are scarcely referred to in the diocesan collections, although their approval was also sought. A rare example, for Soham, refers to an approval for a mortgage given by Pembroke College, Cambridge, nearby.[34]

According to the law it was the bishops that initiated, and by inference approved, the applications; and it was they that were responsible for the application procedure itself.[35] In practice, however, the governors of the Bounty as mortgagor set the conditions for approval and also seem nearly always to have approved the plan before it reached the bishop. Tracking the progress of the applications between the applicants, the diocesan bishop's court and the Bounty's offices in Dean's Yard, Westminster, is not always easy, because references in the minutes of the Bounty governors' meetings to specific applications and their approval do not always follow a consistent pattern. Part of the reason for this is that the governors, a group of usually eight bishops chaired by the archbishop of Canterbury, met at almost weekly intervals but only in the first half of the year, which means that the first session of the new year was a very long one and included lists of all approvals made in the second half of the year without further detail; and in any case, the governors were mainly merely ratifying decisions made at an earlier, undisclosed date by their secretary and his staff. Furthermore, there are rarely sufficient documents within the diocesan collections themselves to be able to ascertain to what extent, and when, an application was sent to and fro between the parties; but in a typical example where the information has however been retained on both sides, for the new vicarage at

Stalisfield in Kent, the governors approved the application on 1 May 1841; the commission was issued by the bishop on 26 October the same year, and the architect's affidavit was signed on 1 November: in other words, in spite of the wording of the acts which emphasises the role of the bishops, the real power of approval lay in the hands of the Bounty.[36] Plans were, however, sometimes submitted to the diocese before reaching the Bounty perhaps where an incumbent feared that a local bishop might prove obstructive; and some surviving correspondence implies that a parson felt obliged to justify his claim to a mortgage to his bishop rather than directly to the Bounty.[37] At any rate, it is clear that the bishop often launched his commission only when the results of it were a foregone conclusion, since I found no instance of a report advising against rebuilding: indeed, on many occasions the bishop evidently received his report from his commission of enquiry simultaneously with his signing of the paper for its appointment, and that the architect already had the necessary papers ready. At Biddenden in Kent, for example, John Walker of Maidstone completed his declarations on 21 March 1842, and the bishop launched his commission the following week.[38] Incidentally, the process by which parsonages were built with funds from augmentations granted by the Bounty followed a similar pattern throughout, even without the legislative framework of Gilbert's Acts. There was no need for the commission process emanating from the bishop's palace, but the Bounty demanded the same high standards of presentation from applicants, and the bishops signed the drawings with their approval; from 1840, the Bounty combined the two processes by requiring that applicants supplement their grant with a separate Gilbert's Acts application.[39] The patrons' approval for the project was also sought under this procedure, and unsurprisingly they seem to have welcomed the improvement.

Not all the records of such parsonage approvals have been retained, and not all surviving records are complete. Over the last half-century, the Church Commissioners, successors to the Bounty and the Ecclesiastical Commissioners from 1948, were supposed to have returned to diocesan archives papers relating to parsonages that had been sold; in practice this has not happened consistently, and, as mentioned above, there appears to be very little surviving correspondence accompanying the plans, declarations, and commissioners' reports. None of the dioceses appear to have kept many if any of the letters they themselves received at the time of the mortgage application, which means that there is almost no record of the notices of approvals that arrived from the Bounty, and whether these carried any conditions not stated in the Bounty's own minutes. Such few letters as do exist are those sent to the secretary of the Bounty or his agents: one occasionally comes across a letter written to a solicitor acting for the governors (the name John Dyneley, of Gray's Inn, London, crops up in several dioceses in the early decades of the century), asking for plans to be put before them. There is also considerable variation in the extent to which parsonage application papers have survived in the different diocesan collections. Survivals from the London and Rochester diocese are comparatively rare, and greatly split between different record offices, possibly reflecting the complicated history of boundary changes between them; there are many records for Norfolk parsonages at the Norfolk Record Office, but comparatively few for the same period for Suffolk in that county's three record offices, although both counties formed part of the same diocese, Norwich. The large and rich diocese of Durham has retained comparatively few records from the early decades. The archives of the diocese of Chichester at the West Sussex Record Office are an oddity: they have retained records only of approvals granted under the second of the 1803 acts described above, the one that allowed for new building as part of an augmentation; presumably the diocese simply did not retain records from approvals under Gilbert's Acts. Yet this augmentation procedure is rare, or unrecorded, in the surviving records in other dioceses. The Church of England's own parsonage records at their Record Centre in Bermondsey have remained uncatalogued and in practice largely inaccessible; they include some 3,000 files, and occupy almost 70 metres of shelf space; and they appear to include correspondence and documentation relating to approvals by the Ecclesiastical Commissioners, as well as to parsonages built under the augmentations procedure which have not surfaced elsewhere.[40]

But what there is in the various county record collections gives the most remarkable and comprehensive insight into the building world of the early nineteenth century.[41] The architect's drawings, of course, and his specification are themselves a record of professional changes; in the earlier years we have, mainly, builders drawing up what they have always built, but increasingly they are required to draw it competently and price it accurately. In the very earliest applications there is sometimes a glimpse of the traditions of what was already the distant past: in the Bath and Wells diocesan collection at the Somerset Record Office there is, for example, a crude drawing of a design for a rectory at Tolland which, with its mullioned oak windows and cast iron casements, resembles as much a house of 1712 as of 1812, its true date.[42] As time goes by, we increasingly see the apparatus of the growing professionalism of the architect's office – the carefully drawn and lettered plans, the standardised and thorough specifications; we see fewer people describing themselves as 'surveyor' or perhaps simply 'carpenter', and more who call themselves 'architect'. We see in some plans the work of well-known architects that was obliterated by subsequent alterations – the only place where any such record exists. We also see, of course, unknown builders, scarcely recognised by architectural history, producing beautiful drawings: in a remarkable plan for the new parsonage at Helmingham in Norfolk, we can see the position of the beer barrels in the cellar, each one carefully drawn as seen from above, the work of a sometime architect, auctioneer, timber merchant and crooked local politician called Benjamin Batley Catt (fig. 1.3); and likewise we see established London architects producing very lazy ones.[43] We can see the way in which technological innovations, such as water closets, new damp-proofing methods, and cavity walls, begin to make their first appearance, and thus establish when and to what extent they become standard practice in English domestic architecture. We see, for example, a hurried sketch, perhaps by the young architect George Edmund Street himself, inserted alongside the neat regular script of his clerk, to show a builder unfamiliar with the new principles of the gothic revival what an irregular stonework bond should look like (fig. 1.4);[44] and we see George Gilbert Scott illustrating what he means by 'cavity' wall.[45] A rather less well-known architect, William Edmunds of Margate, provided in 1836 a beautifully neat drawing which included a full water-supply and drainage layout for his new rectory at Little Mongeham in Kent (fig. 1.5).[46] Edmunds is best known to posterity as the constructor of the quay in his home town; perhaps it had been from that project that he had derived his knowledgeable interest in the movement of water.[47]

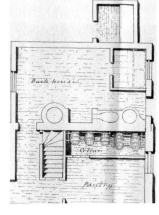

1.3
A detail of the cellar plan for Helmingham rectory (1812), north of Ipswich, Suffolk, by Benjamin Batley Catt – unscrupulous politician and part-time architect [*Suffolk Record Office, Ipswich, FF1/44/1*].

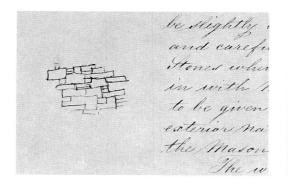 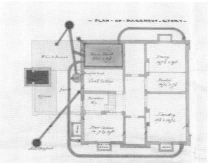

Not all the architects' specifications survive, but from the many that do we can construct an extraordinarily comprehensive picture of the building practices of the early nineteenth century. We hear about the bells for the servants, the styles of the fireplaces in the different rooms, the types of plaster required, the floor finishes, the decorative work, the crown glass (in the best rooms) and the common glass (backstairs). We can see plans for stable yards, fully kitted out *de rigueur* for the early nineteenth century; elsewhere, we might see that the incumbent's mortgage is in fact mainly for the purposes of bringing his kitchen offices up to scratch, and providing him with a dung pit (fig. 1.6).[48] We can sometimes see where land is bought for annexation to the glebe, to give the new incumbent a sense of living in the park like that of his father's grand house.[49] In some cases – notably in that of A.W.N. Pugin, who was otherwise too busy to prepare a full spare set of drawings and specifications of the buildings he designed – the diocesan application gives us the only surviving complete record of a practitioner's professional working method.[50] In addition we can sometimes see an accurate record of an old parsonage which the architect submits because he is remodelling and rebuilding it. Amongst the records of the Exeter diocese, held at the Devon Record Office, we can see something even more remarkable – a meticulous drawing of the plan, elevations, and site location of an old parsonage, probably sixteenth century, or earlier, a long, low building of ramshackle appearance, with merely a parlour and a kitchen downstairs, each with a large fireplace, together with wood house, cellar, and wash house; upstairs it had two bedrooms, a further servants' bedroom, and two lofts, one unfloored (figs 1.7, 1.8). One can easily imagine the excitement of the vicar as he looked at his architect's splendid proposal for a stately classical modern house,

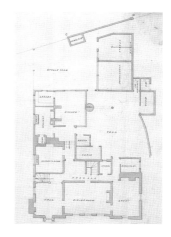

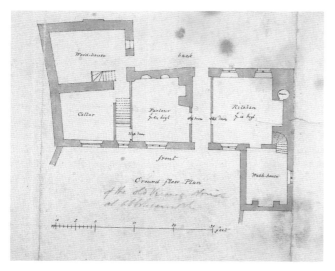

Survey drawings by S.H. Turner of the existing parsonage at Abbotskerswell, near Newton Abbot, Devon, included with the application documents for a mortgage to build a new house. The old one, which was typical of many, consisted only of a kitchen and parlour on the ground floor, neither of them much bigger than the cellar, wood house and wash house adjacent to them *[Devon Record Office: Exeter Diocese, Re-Building Parsonages file]*.

with its drawing room, dining room and study which were healthily large, modern, and orthogonal (figs. 1.9, 1.10).[51]

A record of England

But all this goes beyond a mere history of the designs and the construction of the new buildings themselves. The financial transactions, the signatures of the notaries who witnessed the affidavits, the dates on the documents which show us how much time elapsed between the applications and the approvals, and the actual construction itself – all these add up to a broad picture of early nineteenth-century life. It is possible to follow, through the careful minutes of the meetings at the Bounty Office, how the repeal of the corn laws and the drop in the value of agricultural produce that follows is adversely affecting the tithes, and thus is causing some parsons to have difficulty in paying their mortgage payments.[52] There are humble letters addressed to bishops at smart addresses in Mayfair, and we can wonder how concerned those prelates really were at the time with their incumbents' supplications.[53] There are, too, detailed reports of the conditions of churches and parsonages submitted by rural deans as part of the new legal requirement to compose full returns on the condition of a diocese and which provide so rich a picture of contemporary clerical life: a remarkably complete set dating from 1820-2 amongst the records of the Chichester diocese paints a favourable situation, in which one dean after another reports 'with great satisfaction' or with 'pleasure' that the parsonage houses in his

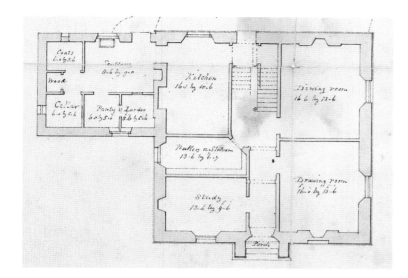

1.9, 1.10
Turner's design of 1837 for the new house on the site. This too is typical of its type, with three large reception rooms and a kitchen arranged around a neat central corridor and staircase [Devon Record Office: Exeter Diocese, Re-Building Parsonages file].

district are in good order, even if some are missing, but that 'the Vicarage Barn requires thatching in some places very much': the small number of approvals given in the early nineteenth century there implies that many of the houses were indeed sufficient for the time being.[54] Pevensey, where the existing house was 'a miserable Cottage, only just covered from the wind & weather' was an exception.[55] The many plans of existing parsonages, some evidently very ancient, typically long and low, with small irregular outhouses, that appear in such large numbers in the records from Bath and Wells bring alive for us the living conditions of the period; for where else were so many houses this humble recorded in such detail?[56] And why in Canterbury, the richest diocese, was there so much patching up of old buildings, when in Oxford, with two-thirds the number of benefices, but with a net income of so much less than that of Canterbury, there was a distinct preference for building anew?[57]

But most delightfully of all we see the fascinating intercourse between the great and the good, and the more humble people in their jurisdiction. Just as Queen Victoria is about to ascend the throne, established Leicester architect William Parsons is in trouble with His Lordship at the bishop's palace in Lincoln over his plans for a new vicarage in the Leicestershire village of Thurmaston: as the incumbent Reverend E. Hoare was obliged to put it, no doubt to his own chagrin, 'His Lordship desires me to acquaint you that considering the small value of the Benefice, the plans appear to be upon too expansive and too extensive a scale...he conceives that the Governors of QAB will not sanction a plan & estimate for a House upon such a benefice exceeding an outlay altogether of £700'. What had inspired Hoare's pretensions to a larger house than his status would suggest? A little over a fortnight later, he is able to report to the bishop that Parsons is able to get the cost down to £1,000; in the end, they compromised on £1,160, and the ambitious Tudor-gothic design went ahead (fig. 1.11).[58] These little spurts of pride are visible here and there all over the country, and each diocese provides a series of wonderful vignettes. Take Canterbury, for example, a comparatively small diocese geographically in spite of its prestige, where there are records of only 23 new houses between 1820 and 1840.[59] Here, in Hawkhurst, the curate Henry Cleaver tells the secretary of the Bounty that 'it is my intention to build my house in a more substantial manner than they are ordinarily built in this part of the county'; and he submits a stable plan with his application, surely a presumption on the part of a curate.[60] The Reverend John Boak, from Paston near Peterborough, writes anxiously to a lawyer at Gray's Inn to explain his hurry in submitting an application for a new rectory at his second incumbency at Swalecliffe, near Herne Bay: the house is for his new curate, the last one having resigned perhaps to attend to his own second parish; the only house available, which was currently tenanted, had not been lived in by clergy for the past 100 years.[61]

It is not only the incumbents that took pride in their station. An F. Brown, of Francis Street, Torrington Square, London, is unremembered by architectural historians, and yet undeservedly, for in 1841 he submitted a beautiful set of watercolours for his design for a small flint vicarage, at Stalisfield, between Ashford and Faversham (fig. 1.12).[62] At Stockbury, a young man called Hussey has in 1834 designed a bizarre asymmetrical house in (more or less) the prevailing classical–Georgian style: would anyone recognise here the latent talent that would yet turn him into a leading gothic architect many years

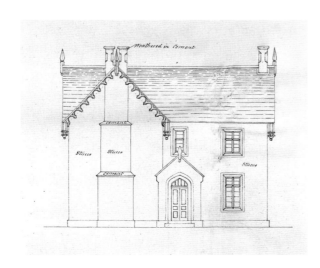

1.11
William Parsons' entrance elevation of his design for Thurmaston vicarage, near Leicester: a typical Tudor-gothic house of the 1830s, it was designed just over a month before Queen Victoria ascended to the throne [Lincolnshire Archives, MGA 220].

1.12
A charming application
drawing of 1841 by F. Brown
of Torrington Square, London,
for Stalisfield vicarage,
between Canterbury and
Maidstone, Kent [*Canterbury
Cathedral Archives, DCb/DC/
S28/1*].

later (see fig. 4.8)?[63] John Whichcord, a recognised local architect from
Maidstone, reports that the old rectory at Warehorne is 'ancient',
although £85 worth of materials from it are reusable in the new (and
rather crude) Tudor-gothic house he is proposing, about eight per cent
of the total cost of its rebuilding; so it is clear what became of that
particular 'ancient' structure.[64] We hear of the Reverend Mr Edge, at
Nedging; of the architect Hezekiah Marshall, at Romney Marsh; and
of George Langford building at both East Langdon and Langley.[65]
The occasional scene culled from the parsonage records of all types is
unforgettable. Henry Harrison, parson at the Beresford family's newly
and richly appointed church at Kilndown in west Kent, is having a row
with his architect and builder, an Italian of German origin called
Alexander Roos, who wants him to pay before the works are properly
finished, the oldest pretext in the world for a disagreement between
builders and their clients. As well as being incomplete, the house is
damp, and still uninhabited, and so Harrison is having to pay rent as
well as carry part of the cost of the new house which he cannot enjoy.[66]
The angry succession of inverted commas in his draft letter, perhaps
never sent, speaks for itself. 'With respect to "my opinion about the
Parsonage", which, "you regret to hear" – I simply said, that on looking

closely into things, I thought it a "cheap slovenly contract job"".[67]
At least three letters fly back and forth that week between the parties:
Roos, who has carried out work at Bedgebury Park, the Beresford
mansion, writes from that address implying his favoured status.
The row ends up on the table of the Ecclesiastical Commissioners,
who are contributing to the project and thus required to adjudicate,
and letters are soon flying in to London.[68] Unfortunately for Harrison
and the Beresfords, the architect Benjamin Ferrey, acting for the
Commissioners, has already attested that the work has been executed in
a 'good and substantial manner' with the exception of minor details
only.[69] Eventually, after almost three years of continuing attempts at
repair, the aging Viscount Beresford's stepson A.J. Beresford-Hope
decides to take the matter in hand and the up-and-coming architect
Ewan Christian is sent to have a look. A long list of complaints about
the layout of the house ('to the Dining room there is no good entrance
except through the Drawing room the other door being placed opposite
the Water Closet at the end of the passage into which the kitchen
opens. The staircase which is imperfectly lighted is far too precipitous
to be safe for young children. The entrance is mean and dark') is
followed by a crushing list of failures: the plaster in some rooms has
never dried out; the stable drains run through the house, to an open
and undersized cesspool just outside the dining-room window; and 'the
smell from the Water Closet on the day of my survey was very bad'.
The conclusion must have left no one in any little doubt: 'I think I have
never before inspected a modern built parsonage, the interior of which
was so devoid of all appearance of comfort and finish as that which
I have now reported on'.[70] It is a particularly wonderful picture of
architectural disasters and conflicting personalities, because it comes
at the crossroads of the gothic revival. On the one side we have
Lord Beresford, curmudgeonly Wellingtonian general turned
Regency politician, so different from his cultured, earnest stepson,
the quintessential young Victorian; and on the professional side,
Roos, after a successful career in which he has worked at Hadzor in
Worcestershire, at Aske Hall in Yorkshire, and at the Deepdene in
Surrey, and who has perhaps prided himself on his designs for delicate
Pompeian ornament, finds himself towards the end of his career
suddenly having to deal with three young men whose star is rising:
Ferrey, an established if uneven goth; Christian, who replaces Ferrey as

adviser to the Commissioners; and R.C. Carpenter, standard bearer for the Ecclesiologists, who is about to replace Roos as designer of the parsonage.[71] The fact that Roos' career as a fashionable and stylish Georgian architect was by now well in the past is suggested by a single poignant detail: Ferrey, on earlier checking Roos' plans for the house, had reported to the Commissioners that the proposed bedroom corridor was too narrow at a mere two feet, two inches wide; what had been sufficient for the slim frocks of the Regency would have been hopeless for Mrs Harrison, thundering downstairs in a broad-hipped dress of the 1850s.[72]

Even the differing style of the minutes of the meetings of the governors of Queen Anne's Bounty on the one hand, and of the Board of the Ecclesiastical Commissioners on the other, has something to contribute – remarkably so, since both consisted to a great extent of the same people, and were both usually chaired by the archbishop of Canterbury. At Dean's Yard, in the shadow of Westminster Abbey, the minutes recorded by Christopher Hodgson were brisk, lively, and business-like (fig. 1.1); whereas those of Charles Knight Murray, Secretary to the Commissioners at 5, Whitehall Place in the centre of government, were pompous, high-handed, occasionally fawning (where a grand family such as the Beresfords was concerned, for example) and desperately dry. The only humour these minutes provide comes in the form of the struggles for prestige between the bishops. An application for assistance from a humble parson may often be rejected out of hand for procedural reasons; but there is no end to the time and attention they will spend on getting a palace in order for a right reverend prelate. The early volumes of the minutes of the board of the Commissioners contain in some detail the process of ascertaining whether Stapleton House in Bristol and Riseholme Hall outside Lincoln would be appropriately grand to serve as residences for the local bishops; there is much to-ing and fro-ing between the Commissioners themselves, and the various architects acting on their behalf, as to the desirability and implications of their purchase, remodelling and refitting.

Viscount Duncannon, a lay commissioner and a well-known politician, personally made a list, recorded in the minutes, of all the fixtures in the various palaces which should remain the property of the sees after the incumbent has departed: 'Bins in the wine cellar;

Coal plates and Chains, in Coal Cellars; Scrapers; Knockers; Nobs for doors; Harness Pegs and rails; Saddle Trees; Cornbins'.[73] For a recent First Commissioner of the Board of Woods and Works, who had earlier dealt with such projects as the new Houses of Parliament and the National Gallery, this trifling with knockers and cornbins must have seemed a little absurd, especially since His Lordship, descended from both the Ponsonbys and the Cavendishes, was something of a Nob himself. The beneficiaries of all this fussing must primarily have been the new professional agents, the architects, surveyors and lawyers; it seems particularly funny that in the case of Stapleton House, the architect on site who profited most from the extra work provided by the vanities of these Anglican prelates was a man called Mr Pope.[74]

Walkeringham vicarage

This survey begins with a building which represents the typical appearance of the Georgian parsonage yet also in so many respects carries the germs of the changes that were about to alter the appearance of the type. In May 1823, in the fourth year of the reign of King George IV, the builder James Trubshaw designed a new parsonage for his friend the Reverend Joseph K. Miller at the village of Walkeringham, in the far north of Nottinghamshire by the Lincolnshire border, and just north of the road that runs eastwards from Sheffield and Rotherham towards the North Sea. The house was to be built on glebe land a few hundred yards to the south of the parish church of St Mary's, somewhat away from the circuit of tracks that made up the centre of the village – if it could be called a centre, since the houses at that time were for the most part strung out along the roads leading north and north-west. Miller needed to raise a mortgage for the construction of his vicarage, and he could do this through the legal mechanism established by Gilbert's Acts. He required the permission of the patron of his living, which was in this case Trinity College, Cambridge; and of course he required the services of a house designer and builder.

In the 47 year-old Trubshaw he found both these combined in one person. Trained as a mason at Haywood in Staffordshire, and with experience on a number of the prestigious projects of his day, he had established himself also as an architect from some point in the second decade of the nineteenth century.[75] He was first employed in building and making alterations to various large houses; and, having gained the confidence of his clients, began to design houses himself. Walkeringham was his first parsonage design, and he attempted nothing that would surprise his client.

The house that Trubshaw presented for approval was a two-storey one, symmetrical along the entrance front on its south side (figs. 1.13–15).[76] This was three bays wide, and the central bay was recessed a few feet into the building and contained the front door. From the outside the whole house was very plain on all sides. It was built of brick with no ornament at all except for thin pilasters which marked the divisions between the bays, and a decorative iron trellis around the front door, which was surmounted by a pretty balustrade in a Chinese pattern. There were identical nine-pane sash windows on the upper floors, and 12-pane ones below. A low slate pitched roof with deep eaves sat over the house and squat chimneys emerged over it. Trubshaw drew the west elevation of the main part of the house – ignoring the less attractive part to the north, which contained the back kitchen, the pigsty and the privies – but he did not bother with the eastern side,

1.13
The south front of Walkeringham vicarage, Nottinghamshire, designed by James Trubshaw in 1823.

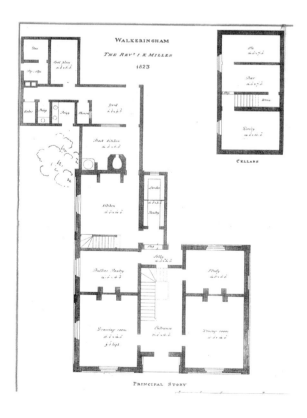

1.14 (above)
Trubshaw's design for the
south front of Walkeringham
vicarage *[Borthwick Institute,
University of York, MGA
1823/5]*.

1.15 (right)
The proposed ground-floor
plan for Walkeringham
vicarage *[Borthwick Institute,
University of York, MGA
1823/5]*.

which had nothing more than four blind windows on it although in effect it faced the garden.

The appearance of the house from the front door will have suggested its internal layout to the visitor. The house had what I shall call henceforth a central-corridor plan, meaning that there was a wide corridor containing stairs leading away from the front door, with a major room either side of it overlooking the front (fig. 1.16). At Walkeringham the drawing room was to the left, and an identically-sized dining room to the right. Behind the drawing room was a butler's pantry, and behind the dining room was the vicar's study. This might at first seem the wrong way round, but there was a logic to it. The drawing room was positioned on the south-west side to enjoy the best of the afternoon light, but the kitchen and its offices also needed to be to the west of the house in order to be closer to the road and away from the route across glebe lands to the church (fig. 1.17). A parishioner on the other hand could walk across to the house from the church and enter by the back door, and thus be hidden from the vicar's imposing entrance driveway and his front door. The main stairs were positioned in the corridor, rising straight up in front of the visitor as they would in any townhouse of similar scale. Upstairs there were two large bedrooms above the main rooms, and two smaller ones: one above the study, and the other above the front door; this latter one could enjoy the balcony with its balustrade. There were two servants' bedrooms on the same floor, and one more (lit by a rooflight) and a big storeroom in the attic. There were ale and beer stores in the cellar of the house, as well as a dairy, reached from the back stairs in the kitchen.

The Walkeringham parsonage was far enough away from the parish church to be considered in landscape or townscape terms to be almost entirely detached from it. It is true that Mr Miller could walk directly through his garden and across to the south-west porch of his church and avoid the public road, but his front door was on the south side of the house, the greatest distance away from it. In that respect it was entirely conventional, for parsonages then seem usually to have been designed in that way. The effect mimicked a country house in its park, although it should be added that there were then also new parsonages so grand that the drive up to them was as impressive as that of any minor aristocrat; after all, an early nineteenth-century parson might fancy himself as a squire, and eminently respectable.

1.21
Less 'calculated to meet the public taste', perhaps, than the alternative classical design, but nevertheless 'sober and dignified' and therefore 'appropriate for a rectory or vicarage-house'. A villa (plate 12) from the second volume of Thomas Dearn's *Sketches in architecture* of 1807.
In fact when Dearn did eventually design a parsonage, at Cranbrook, Kent, 15 years later, he chose to make it classical.

Cobbett rode around England for his *Rural rides* in the 1820s, and the country that he saw was exactly that which resounded to the carpenter's saw and the plumber's mallet on many an empty site on the glebe.

The classical-Georgian parsonage in a prosperous diocese

A part of the country that Cobbett frequently referred to is Norfolk, often reminded of it when travelling elsewhere.[82] In addition to the growing prosperity and status of parsons nationally, the draining of the fens had increased agricultural production throughout East Anglia, and consequently the parsons' income was increasing, too. There were 625 parishes in Norfolk alone, and, according to Virgin, there were proportionately more clerical justices of the peace here than in other parts of the country.[83] East Anglia was flourishing, and the Norwich diocesan records confirm it.[84] At least 16 parsonages there were remodelled or rebuilt before 1811, the date at which the Bounty began in earnest to process applications for new houses; these include a large and imposing house at Blofield of 1805, the cost of which was estimated at over £2,000.[85]

Because there are so many of these records in this area, we have a lively picture of the way in which architects, surveyors and builders profited by the new opportunities for work, and how they experimented by varying the standard layout of a central-corridor type house which was typified by that we saw at Walkeringham. In the 1810s, for example, a Suffolk carpenter who was also a versatile and picturesque architect called Mark Thompson had designed three buildings in romantic gothic styles, but in 1820 and 1821 he designed two parsonages, providing them with stern, plain fronts and central corridors. At Bures, halfway between Sudbury and Colchester, the drawing room and dining room were placed either side of a central door, divided by a corridor, and the study was at the rear; but the house faced the garden rather than the entrance drive; and the staircase was located in a back passage running across the house instead of along the central corridor that divided the main rooms (figs 1.22, 1.23).[86] This building cost £690 once the reuse of materials from the old house had been taken into account: these were worth £180, and so at a total of £870 the house was about £100 cheaper than Trubshaw's. At Hartest, south of Bury St Edmunds, Thompson built a much more expensive house, where the new rector, a Mr Maddy, had received substantial funds already granted for renovations from his predecessors.[87] The new house was to cost £1,420, with the reuse of some old materials, and after it was swiftly built Maddy was able to move into a six-bedroom house of some splendour. Here Thompson again varied the standard central-corridor type, but in a different way. The central corridor, this time with its stairs in the usual position, led into the centre of the house, but the two principal rooms were arranged to one side of it so that one faced the entrance drive and the other the garden. On the entrance side was a dining room, to the right of the front door on entering; and the drawing room was at the back, and had a grand apsidal end to it. In order to maintain symmetry on the front facade, there was but one window to the left of the front door, but this was split clumsily into two – one half lighting a small pantry and the other a storeroom. This was possibly an afterthought, with the two rooms taking the place of what ought to have been a study. The kitchen took up the final quarter of the main block of the house, at the back-left from the front door. Other examples across the diocese at this time show how architects made loose variations on the basic planning of the central-corridor house. An architect called George Maliphant designed a house at Worlington (half way between Bury St Edmunds and Ely) in 1819 which was again composed with a symmetrical front

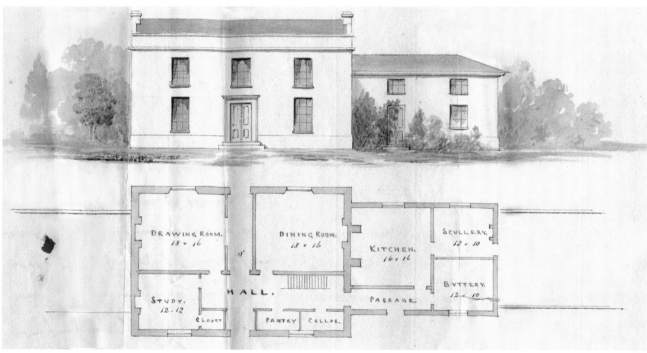

and a central-corridor plan, but he added a great deal of splendour by placing the stairs at the back of the house around an open well (fig. 1.24).[88] And in the following year, when the Bures house was under construction, a talented amateur architect from the cathedral close in Norwich, the Reverend Arthur Browne, altered an existing parsonage at Hepworth, north-east of Bury, which was different from the standard type in that the front elevation was asymmetrical: he placed the library to the left of the front door, but both the drawing room and the dining room (the latter reached by a rear corridor) to the right of it. His submission included a proposal for a charming cart lodge with rustic pillars, and a chaise house and stables with Diocletian windows (fig. 1.25).[89]

There is some evidence that the classical style was considered appropriate for parsonages even when other houses of similar status were moving into other styles. I have already mentioned Robert Lugar, as one of the authors of a villa pattern book of the 1800s. His literary career made a second start in 1823, when he republished both his *Architectural sketches* and a book of 1811 called *Plans and views of buildings executed in England and Scotland in the castellated and other styles*; and in 1828 he published his final work, *Villa architecture*. This last book provided readers with a perspective and plans of his

1.22 (opposite, above) The garden (south) front of Mark Thompson's 1821 vicarage at Bures, between Sudbury and Colchester, Suffolk.

1.23 (opposite, below) Thompson's mortgage application drawings sometimes included delightful watercolour drawings. This is his design for Bures. Unconventionally for a central-corridor or L-corridor house, the two principal rooms face away from the front door [*Suffolk Record Office, Bury St Edmunds, 806/2/4*].

1.24 (below) Worlington rectory, Cambridgeshire, 1819, designed by George Maliphant. The projecting bay in the middle of the house and lesene-like brick piers at the corners were a way of disguising the visual dissonance of a symmetrical elevation that has a narrow corridor bay at its centre.

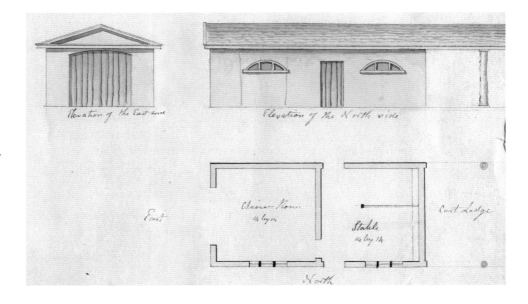

1.25
A detail from a design by the
Reverend Arthur Browne:
the chaise house and stable
at Hepworth between Bury St
Edmunds and Diss, Suffolk.
To the right, a rustic column
supports the roof of the 'cart
lodge' [*Suffolk Record Office,
Bury St Edmunds, 806/2/10*].

rectory of 1820-2 at Yaxham in Norfolk, the only parsonage he is
known to have designed (fig. 1.26).[90] His watercolour drawings can still
be found in the Norfolk Record Office, together with the more prosaic
details of the project such as its estimated cost: £1,876.[91] A grand
symmetrically-fronted house with an imposing Tuscan porch between
bays topped by 'Greek' gables, this is the only new large house in the
entire volume still in the classical style, for Lugar has otherwise moved
on to a castellated Tudor-gothic.[92] He derived this imposing front from
an earlier design of his for a house called 'The Ryes Lodge' at Little
Henny in Essex, which had appeared in his *Plans and views*.[93] Why did
Lugar persist in the classical-Georgian style for a parsonage, when he
had abandoned it for most other buildings? He was, after all,
an eccentric planner, devising contorted routes through his villas
probably to enhance their picturesque potential. His descriptions of the
house at Yaxham published in the book suggest that the style carried
implications of modesty and retiral appropriate for a clergyman:
'This style of house is suitable to the neighbourhood of a large town
or village, and may be accompanied by a paddock or small lawn, with
plantation and neatly dressed grounds. The outline of this Design is
sufficiently varied to divest it of formality, yet not so broken as to
deprive it of the character of a genteel residence, occupying a place in
style between the villa and the cottage.'[94] In the text facing the plan of
the house, he describes how the house is sheltered from the winds (and
from the church) thanks to the rich plantation round about,

commenting in conclusion that the setting 'promises in a few years to make this a very comfortable retired residence'.[95] In this last he was perhaps underestimating his client, the Reverend Dr Johnny Johnson, who soon decorated its rooms with racy murals by his old friend William Blake.[96]

Conservative planning

These examples from the Norwich diocese indicate the prevalence of the classical–Georgian style throughout the 1820s; this was typical of the country as a whole, and so was a very marked consistency of plan. There were only two significant alternatives to the central-corridor type, of which one was not much more than a slight tweak in the arrangement of the stairs. We have already seen that Thompson's house at Bures had been arranged so that the staircase was out of sight, tucked away to the right as one entered. When the rooms are arranged so that there are three major ones in total, two facing the entrance front and one behind, and the stairs are located at the side, behind one of the front rooms and at right angles to the entry corridor, we have what could be called the L-corridor plan (fig. 1.28). Parsonages arranged like this were rare at this date, finding broad favour only in the 1830s, perhaps as soon as it was recognised that they shield the upper landing from the vulgar gaze of those who happened to be waiting at the front door of the house. There are none in the Norwich diocese but for Bures (an oddity, since the house faces the garden rather than the entrance) until the 1830s, and even another impressive collection, that for Oxford, includes just one new house with this plan from the 1820s, at Forest Hill of 1827, by John Hudson, an Oxford builder (fig. 1.27).[97] Interestingly, it was an extensive remodelling of an older house that provided the other L-corridor arrangement in the diocese during the decade, at Swincombe by John Plowman and also in 1827.[98] The L-corridor plan is essentially an adaptation of a simple urban type to a more open and larger rural site, since it works best with a side window for the staircase, and with plenty of space at the rear, since at least one room will be pushed further back from the entrance front.

The more significant variation was one in which the three principal rooms were arranged in a row to form what was usually a symmetrical front facing the garden; there was a corridor linking them as a spine that ran along the back of these rooms, leading to the front door near

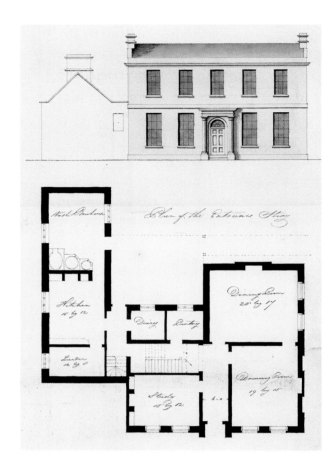

1.26 (above)
Yaxham rectory, near East Dereham, Norfolk (1820-2); Lugar's own illustration for his book *Villa architecture* of 1828 (plate 13).

1.27 (above, right)
Forest Hill, near Oxford (1827). This impressive project is doubly significant: it was the first new house recorded in the diocesan collection with an L-corridor plan; and its construction bankrupted its client, the colourful perpetual curate John Mavor [*Oxfordshire Record Office, MS. Oxf. dioc. papers b.103/2d*].

one end of it. This type, the 'back-corridor' type, had three major advantages over the other two layouts (fig. 1.29). One was simply that all three rooms could enjoy the best aspect, which might well be limited to one side of the house only. Another was that it could easily solve the problem of how to add a wing of new reception rooms to an old house: one simply ran a corridor between them. And the third was that this arrangement solved a perennial problem of the symmetrical, classically-inspired Georgian house. This problem was that a symmetrical front mimicking the classical tradition naturally suggests that the central bay of the main facade should be larger, or more dominant, than the two bays flanking it – and yet as we have already seen in so many examples, that central bay was occupied by a corridor which was narrower than the two rooms either side. There were several devices for getting around this problem. The most simple, and that generally adopted, was simply to ignore it, for the inner walls were hidden behind a flush masonry facade; only a builder or an architect, who would assume that the main room windows to the left and the

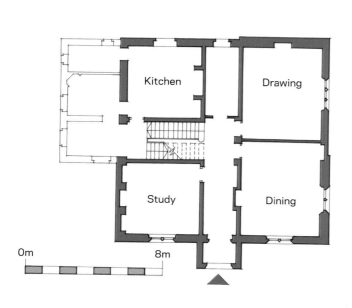

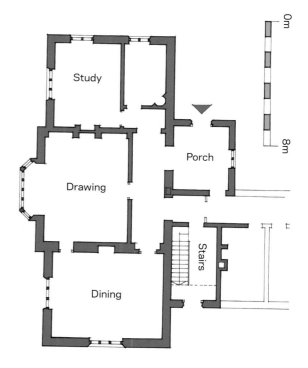

right were not necessarily positioned centrally in their rooms along the facade, would appreciate what was happening inside. This is what Thompson did at Bures and Hartest, and we are so used to it that it does not seem strange. But other architects were bothered by the discrepancy, and used various devices to cover it up. A broad porch certainly helped. At Worlington, Maliphant had gone one stage further, bringing the central bay forward slightly, and applying a simple projecting porch (see fig. 1.24). The result is that the three bays almost read as one combined broad bay at the centre of the house. Large projecting central bays are, curiously, rare at this time.

The back-corridor plan had been in use mainly for rather larger houses at least since the beginning of the nineteenth century: Nash used it, or variations of it, for several of his villas, including Cronkhill of 1802 and on a grander scale for his Royal Lodge at Windsor of 1811–20. Interestingly, he also designed a rectory in Ireland, at Lissan in County Tyrone, in this way in 1802.[99] The plan freed the architect to do as he wished with the main garden elevation of the house, and he could

1.28 (above, left)
The L-corridor plan type also has a pair of major rooms that faces the entrance or garden, but the stairs are tucked away to one side. There is usually, as here, a third room. This plan is based on the design by Henry Jones Underwood for Elsfield vicarage, near Oxford, 1836 [*Oxfordshire Record Office, MS. Oxf. dioc. papers b.103/2*].

1.29 (above)
The back-corridor plan type arranges the major rooms in a row facing the garden; the corridor, which runs like a spine behind them, is entered from one end. This example is based on the plan by James Pritchett for Bossall, near York, 1838 [*Borthwick Institute, University of York, MGA 1838/2*].

easily place the largest of the reception rooms – and thus its principal and central bay – in the centre of his facade if he so wished. But perhaps more significantly, as things turned out, the back-corridor plan resulted in the birth of the short side elevation, the one that had the front door on it at one end. Because of the front door, this elevation became an important one, and yet for the architects it must at first have been problematic. Alongside the front door was the side wall of the adjoining major reception room, whose windows faced the other way, along the main elevation. So the architect had a front door and a piece of blank wall to contend with. That blank wall might, however, have included the room's fireplace, so he had two major elements with which to try to build an elevation that would make sense with an otherwise classical, symmetrical house. At first, architects found this difficult: the fact that so few architects adopted this convenient layout in the 1820s must surely be a sign that they were reluctant to depart from the conventional plans of house building, as is the fact that they often treated their new freedom with caution; and when they did first attempt it, the results were not always successful. John Apsley, surveyor and builder of Ashford, produced an extraordinary design in 1836 for a parsonage at Kennington, in Kent, of which the symmetrical entrance elevation consisted of a central front door, a small landing window above it, and two pairs of blank windows either side giving a misleading impression of the rooms behind them (fig. 1.30).[100] Over at Winterborne St Martin in Wiltshire, in 1838, Edward Mondey used a combination of both blind and real windows, but still ended up with a peculiar facade (fig. 1.31).[101] Later architects, even comparatively accomplished ones, similarly failed to grapple with the potential of this new entrance front: John Whichcord, at Newchurch near Romney Marsh, also tried imitating on this side the traditional front elevation of a central-corridor house, and fared at least as badly as Apsley.[102] The garden front, on the other hand, was imposing. There are however two houses in Suffolk by the Melton architect William Bilby that demonstrate that by simply treating the effect of the plan as it was, rather than by twisting it into a symmetrical front, it was possible to arrive at some very fine effects. In 1836 he designed a vicarage at Bredfield with a bold entrance facade punctured only by a broad front door with a pair of pilasters either side of it, and a small window directly above it, all set to one side of the wall exactly as the plan would suggest.

The composition is further enhanced by the appearance on the entrance front of part of the kitchen offices, set back from the main front (fig. 1.32).[103] In a slightly later project, for Martlesham, he applied this approach to the remodelling of an existing building: the new house consisted of a pair of reception rooms; a corridor ran along the back of them, with a door at either end, and the old house provided the kitchen and office wing, which was clearly visible from the front.[104] These new entrance elevations have an interesting, style-less air to them, boldly admitting that they are different from the classical-Georgian composition along the main garden front, whilst being neither apologetic nor contrived.

Another approach was to build up a second symmetrical front for this entrance elevation, balancing the side wall of the reception room to one side of the front door with the side or main wall of the kitchen or offices on the other. This bestowed on the kitchen facade a grander role than had previously been accepted, marking a significant step towards its external expression. In one late classical-Georgian house, the urban vicarage at Tenbury Wells in Worcestershire of 1843, the architect Harvey Egerton dressed up the narrow side entrance elevation with a grand Ionic portico, thus achieving harmony on both elevations as well as a sensible plan, the best of all worlds (figs. 1.33, 134).[105] Some imaginative architects varied the plan, probably to reduce the effect of the long single-loaded corridor: at Hamble-le-Rice on Southampton Water there is a fancy helical stair at the entrance end of the corridor, altogether a surprising plan for as early as 1821. The designer was a builder called Martin Filer from Winchester,

1.30 (below, left) Kennington vicarage, near Ashford, Kent: an example of what happened when architects first tried to devise suitable entrance elevations for a back-corridor plan. By John Apsley, 1836. The house has been demolished [*Canterbury Cathedral Archives, DCb/DC/K3/2*].

1.31 (below, right) Edward Mondey's design for the entrance elevation of his parsonage at Winterborne St Martin, near Dorchester, Dorset (1838) shows that the back-corridor plan could throw up elevations that could almost be described as functionalist *avant le nom* [*Church Commissioners: CERC, QAB/7/6/E32*].

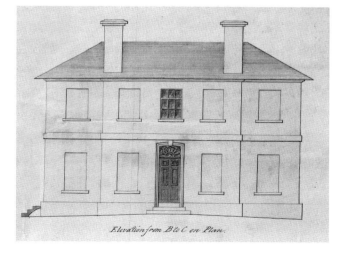

Elevation from B to C on Plan.

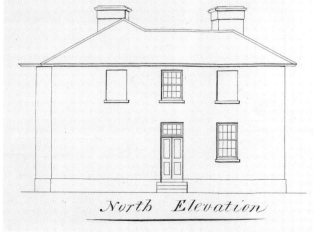

North Elevation

1.32
Bredfield vicarage, near
Woodbridge, Suffolk, 1836,
by William Bilby. An elevation
that frankly addressed the
requirements of a back-
corridor plan could produce
imposing results.

and his plan is unusually neat and logical in other respects, too.[106] Others achieved the same aim by dividing the long corridor route up into varying compartments: Maurice Davis junior did this at the curate's house he designed at Hinton St George in Somerset in 1839 (see fig. 4.29); and the London architect Edward J. Andrews was effectively doing the same at a much grander house a little later in the same county, the rectory at Compton Martin of 1841, where he created the rear route to the principal rooms from a series of widely varying spaces that started with an imposing entrance hall and continued via a narrow corridor to a stair hall at the end (see fig. 4.33).[107]

The back-corridor plan was then an interesting development that was yet to yield valuable results. For a stylistically ambitious architect it could be invaluable. William Donthorn is best known as a gothic architect, but amongst his many parsonage designs there are two schemes of 1831 in an Italianate style, in the Royal Institute of British

1.33, 1.34
Tenbury Wells vicarage,
Worcestershire, 1843,
by Harvey Egerton.
The remarkable overscaled
Ionic porch forms part of
a symmetrical facade that
turned a back-corridor
entrance elevation into a
suitable urban front.

Architects' Library Drawings Collection, for a proposed rectory at Moulton St Michael in south-east Norfolk. In his earlier plan, Donthorn provided the main part of his house with two symmetrical elevations. The first shows a pair of grand reception rooms facing the garden, with an octagonal stairhall behind them reached from a corridor that leads to a front door placed in the centre of the symmetrical entrance front (fig. 1.35). With only two rooms, it is essentially a central-corridor plan where the left hand part of the front is taken up with offices, and is not dissimilar to Thompson's rectory at Hartest. Unlike Thompson, however, Donthorn found himself juggling with blind windows to make his composition work, and in spite of the grand loggia on the garden side, and the promising staircase hall in the middle, the results are contrived.[108] It appears that it was James Wiggett, his client, who then sent him back to the drawing board, as he evidently now required a third reception room as well as more extensive offices. Since Donthorn could not provide a further room on the garden side without entirely changing the plan, he now

1.35 (right)
William Donthorn's first scheme for Moulton St Michael rectory, east of Norwich, 1831: this is essentially a central-corridor plan. If Donthorn had placed a third reception room at the front, on the other side of the entrance corridor from the dining room (bottom right) he would have had to push the many backstairs offices too far back [*RIBA Library Drawings Collection, Donthorn [Moulton St Michael]* 1].

1.36 (far right)
Donthorn's solution was to choose another of the three conventional house plans rather than try to come up with something original. The house is now a back-corridor scheme with an asymmetrical entrance front [*RIBA Library Drawings Collection, Donthorn [Moulton St Michael]* 4].

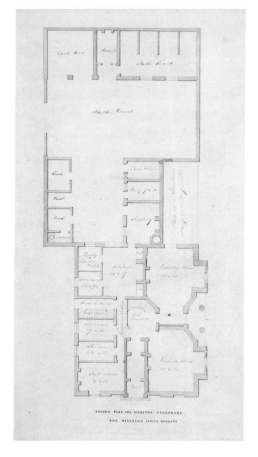

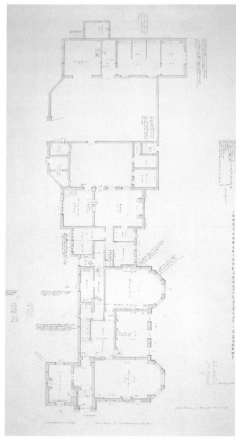

abandoned it and adopted the back-corridor type (fig. 1.36). The three major rooms face the garden in a row, and behind them is an even grander staircase hall, reached from a corridor which runs along the short side of the first of the three rooms. He balanced the front door with the tall narrow tower of a Tuscan villa to the left of it – a clever and logical move, because it signified the servant's room by the entrance, and therefore included the 'defensive' use a tower suggested; and he made a feature of the chimney of the reception room to the right by projecting it outwards and decorating it with a blind arch at each of the two floors, and then a real arch and a cornice at the top.[109] But for the unrelieved flatness of the Norfolk countryside, and, no doubt, the weather, the Reverend Mr Wiggett might well have fancied himself to be in Tuscany.

The back-corridor plan was useful and challenging to architects, and as we shall see, it was the only one of the three conventional corridor-type plans which entirely survives the upheavals of the period ahead. In the meantime, it will suffice to note that architects evidently came to like it, for it also survived their transition between styles. James Pritchett, for example, designed a substantial vicarage at Bossall in the North Riding of Yorkshire, costed at £1,150 in 1838, in Tudor-gothic style, with little ornamentation beyond hood moulds and a pointed front door, where a study, drawing room (in the centre) and dining room formed a symmetrical front along the garden (figs. 1.37, 1.38; see also 1.29).[110] When he designed a house on a similar scale but in the conventional classical-Georgian style three years later at Thornton in Pickering in the same riding, he designed a variation of the Bossall house, here continuing the spine corridor directly into the kitchen office wing and placing both staircases within it and along its axis, even though this left him with a clumsy front elevation which he lined with blind windows (fig. 1.39).[111] In general, the more modest provincial architects and 'surveyors' remained most loyal to the simplest versions of the three corridor-type plans, whilst their more sophisticated colleagues attempted slight variations; but even an ambitious and well-travelled London architect such as Matthew Habershon at the height of his powers was designing houses such as the parsonage at Rockland St Mary near Norwich on exactly the same type of L-corridor plan that was familiar to the humblest of builders (see fig. 2.53).[112]

1.37 (left)
The vicarage at Bossall, near York, designed by James Pritchett in 1838, clearly exemplifies the elevational advantages of a back-corridor plan. The arrangement at last allowed architects to make the central bay of the house the major one and thus escape from the pinched effect of the central-corridor and L-corridor types.

1.38 (above)
The corridor at Bossall, typical of similar houses, runs like a spine along the back of the major rooms.

We have seen that architects were occasionally required to modernise existing parsonages (some of which were mediaeval in part) by the addition of new reception rooms, and where possible they did so by applying to the house a new wing which imposed one of the three corridor-type plans. Eventually this was most easily done by attaching a new back-corridor type extension, but before this solution was generally arrived at there are examples of the attachment of a new block consisting of a central corridor with a new room either side: this was done for example at Galby in Leicestershire in 1829 (fig. 1.40), and at Dallinghoo (1832) (figs 1.41, 1.42) and at Nacton (1837) (fig. 1.43) in Suffolk, amongst many others; no doubt there are a great deal of other cases which were too minor to require mortgages and have thus

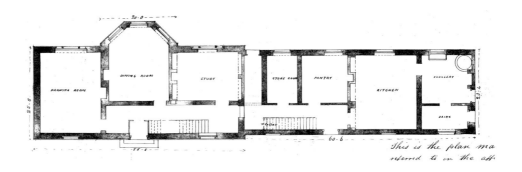

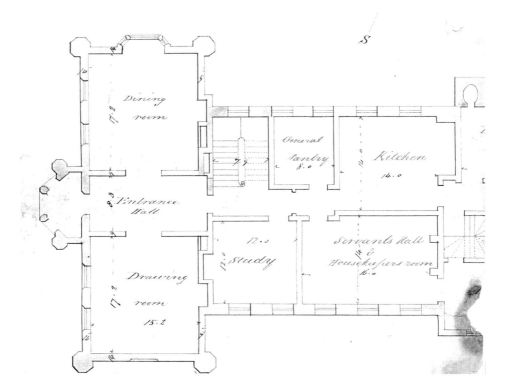

1.39 (above, right) Proposed ground-floor plan, Thornton in Pickering vicarage, North Riding of Yorkshire (1841). Another back-corridor plan from James Pritchett, this time less successful in appearance [*Borthwick Institute, University of York, MGA 1841/4*].

1.40 (right) Galby, east of Leicester (1829). William Parsons added this front block to an older house in a manner characteristic for the period. Two spacious rooms flank an entrance hall. Behind these, there is a new study, kitchen, and servants' hall as well as a more impressive staircase than the old one [*Lincolnshire Archives, MGA 153*].

gone unrecorded in the diocesan archives.[113] At Nacton the architect, John Whiting, also added a new staircase at the seam between old and new. In these three cases the old part of the house seems to have been Tudor or earlier – at Dallinghoo, there are roof timbers in the older part of the house which date back to the fourteenth century[114] – and at Galby and Nacton the architects chose to use a Tudor-gothic style which perhaps to their eye suited the historical remains.[115] The opposite also occurred: a simple classical-Georgian house was added to with a contrasting extension in new Tudor-gothic style: this is what the young goth Benjamin Ferrey did when he added a back-corridor addition to the rectory at Compton Valence, in Dorset, in 1839 (see fig. 2.59).[116] Thomas Rickman's expensive plan for extending the parsonage at Soham must surely be in a class of its own: the old house became the offices of the new, which was entirely conventional, but the grand main block of the new building with its big central pediment was attached at some distance by a wing, funnel-shaped in plan, that provided rooms for the footman and housekeeper.[117]

How different were these plan types to those of standard residential architecture? Not much, so long as the scale and status of the residents were similar. In fact there are amongst the diocesan collections records of a small number of houses that had recently been built for lay purposes but were bought soon after by incumbents for their own use; and, because a mortgage was needed, an application had to be made as if for a new parsonage. The original builder or another surveyor was thus required to draw up and present the plans of the house for submission, thus again leaving us with an unusually good record of it. On these occasions one can see the prevalence of the same basic house types. John Sarell, a surveyor from Montacute, proposed the purchase of a house at Ilchester in 1842, helpfully including the information that it had been built within the last six years; it is a standard L-corridor type plan.[118] An application in 1856 was made by Stephen George, carpenter, builder and surveyor, and shows a house in the parish of Linstead in Kent, located exactly a mile away (as George's site plan helpfully points out) from the door of the incumbent's church in the neighbouring parish of Teynham, for this was the maximum distance stipulated in the first of Gilbert's Acts.[119] He does not give its age, but he had almost certainly built it himself, and it is the simple central-corridor type.[120]

1.41, 1.42
Dallinghoo rectory, near Woodbridge, Suffolk, 1832, by Bilby. The imposing new symmetrical block was attached to an old low building to provide modern reception rooms and principal bedrooms.

But one can look to a more august source, a single plate in a book by John Britton of 1832, to see exactly how prevalent the basic plans were. This is an illustration of four of the villas designed by Decimus Burton from 1828 in his development outside Tunbridge Wells called Calverley Park (fig. 1.44). Three of the four representative houses shown are in the classical-Georgian style, with Italian touches: one has a tower like Donthorn's at Moulton St Michael, and another has pediment-like ornaments at the top of the chimneys; only one house is in a rarer, rustic-Tudor style. The three classical house plans are exactly those we are already familiar with. No 1 has a central corridor; no 3 has an L corridor; and no 4 is a back-corridor type. Only no 2, the Tudor house, is slightly different, a picturesque variation of the L-corridor type where the position of the stairs is brought in front of, rather than behind, the third reception room. Calverley Park was

1.43
Similarly, John Whiting's extension to Nacton rectory, near Ipswich, Suffolk, (in 1837) provided a formal front and new reception rooms to an old building. His mixture of Tudor and classical-Georgian styles on a single front is characteristic of the immediately pre-gothic revival years of the reign of William IV.

1.44
John Britton's detailed description of up-market modern villa architecture designed by Decimus Burton at Calverley Park, Tunbridge Wells, Kent, provides a point of comparison with similarly-scaled parsonage house plans. From *Descriptive sketches of Tunbridge Wells and the Calverley Estate*, 1832.

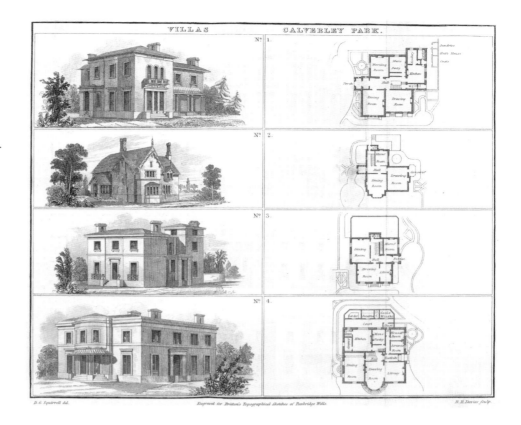

a speculative venture, and that means that the plans were likely to be conventional in order to attract as wide a market as possible; if that was indeed the case, it is clear that the basic types were established across the kingdom. A smart house in Calverley Park would thus have had the same plan as a modest parsonage anywhere else in the country. A clue as to the repetitive nature of house layouts is hidden in the pages of *Emma*: when Mrs Elton comes to patronise her smart neighbour with her dim conversation, she tells her hostess of the similarities between the Woodhouses' Hartfield and Maple Grove, the mansion of her brother-in-law Mr Suckling outside Bristol: 'And the staircase – you know, as I came in, I observed how very like the staircase was; placed exactly in the same part of the house'.[121] Of course it was: just about every house of the 1810s that was neither a palace nor a cottage was a variation on the same central-corridor plan; so naturally the stairs were visible to Mrs Elton immediately on entering both front doors.

It is important to mention that in none of the houses we have seen so far is there any kind of imposing staircase hall that constitutes a room in its own right. In a sense, the type of life these houses was designed for was a static one: receiving visitors or otherwise dealing with others in a clear hierarchical way according to social conventions; landed gentlemen would need a business room; a parson his study. Either of these that was a justice of the peace would require a suitable room in which to receive applications for poor relief and such like. In so far as the owner of the house could afford it, every activity had its own place, and the house provided a framework for these different and distinct activities. It is when the nature of daily social life begins to change that the plan changes too, for the plan is as it has always been both the generator and the reflector of social change. But in addition to those who either actively campaigned for, or reacted against, such architectural changes – and we will hear about them later – there were of course plenty of architects who ignored or who perhaps were even unaware of the changing landscape of their profession. Across the country, parsonages continued to be built in much the same classical-Georgian style, and with one of the three corridor plans, almost (but not quite) as far as the Queen Anne revival that started in the 1870s. The designers of these buildings were sometimes people who were already set in their ways. However, by 1840, less than ten years after Donthorn's splendid performance at Moulton St Michael, classical-Georgian parsonages were comparatively rare. The Oxford diocese seems to have approved one or two new parsonages a year, and in 1838 and 1840 it approved houses in this style by John Plowman, who was then in his mid sixties; he had been designing parsonages in the same plain classical style since his first for the diocese, that remodelling at Swincombe in 1827.[122] That at Launton, of 1838, was competent, plain, and asymmetrical (fig. 1.45); the second, at South Weston, was a small house with only two reception rooms and could hardly have been

1.45
Competent, plain, and somewhat lopsided: John Plowman's design for Launton, near Bicester, Oxfordshire, in 1838 [Oxfordshire Record Office, MS. Oxf. dioc. papers b.104/1].

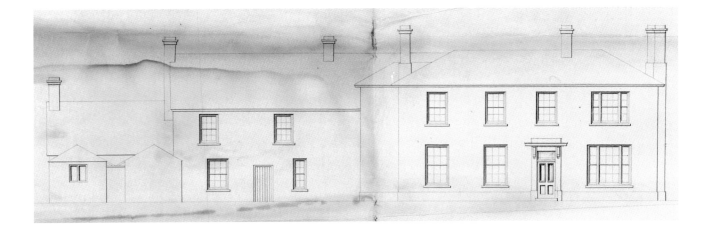

more conventional.[123] The same could be said of the house of 1843 at Caversham by Drake.[124] The last new classical-Georgian house in the Oxford collection for the 1840s is a very crude cottage of 1844 by a builder from Bicester called Joseph Clements, at Newton Purcell (fig. 1.46).[125] Finally, and interestingly, the very last appearance of the style in the diocese before the conscious revivals of the later century is an unambitious remodelling by the young William Wilkinson, in his mid twenties at the time, who cautiously added reception rooms to an old house along a new back-corridor at Broadwell, in 1846.[126] The early extinction of the classical-Georgian house at the Oxford diocese might well derive from the fact that in the 1840s it was at the centre of a religious upheaval in which architectural style played so major a part; in sleepy Hampshire John Colson, who had previously experimented creditably with the new Tudor-gothic style, designed in 1851 a Regency-style house for Newtown, between Soberton and Fareham, central-corridor and classical-Georgian, as if nothing had happened. And at £1,142 it wasn't cheap, either (fig. 1.47).[127]

In certain circumstances architects seem to have been resigned to add to a classical-Georgian house in a consistent style. In the 1840s this happened to a number of houses. Lewis Vulliamy, whose previous parsonages had been in new or eccentric styles, added a large wing to the rectory at Cottenham in Cambridgeshire in a classical style entirely consistent with the old building. As if bored by this, he submitted his new elevations drawn in a merely schematic way. Other cases of comparatively innovatory young architects resorting to the conventions of the past are less explicable. Why did Anthony Salvin, already the architect of many original Elizabethan-style buildings (including an idiosyncratic parsonage at Northallerton, demolished not many years ago) build so conventional a house at Denton, in Lincolnshire, as late as 1841?[128] It has a central-corridor plan, and the only unusual elements of it are that the front is asymmetrical, and the chimneys oddly monumental.[129] At nearly £1,750 it was expensive, too: almost double the cost of Pritchett's house at Thornton in Pickering, built the same year on a similar scale, and in the same style. Since Salvin was not one of those who reacted against the new architecture, and indeed had made his name with grand houses in Elizabethan and Jacobean styles, it appears that local tastes and traditions occasionally influenced the choice; maybe that was more than usually true in low-

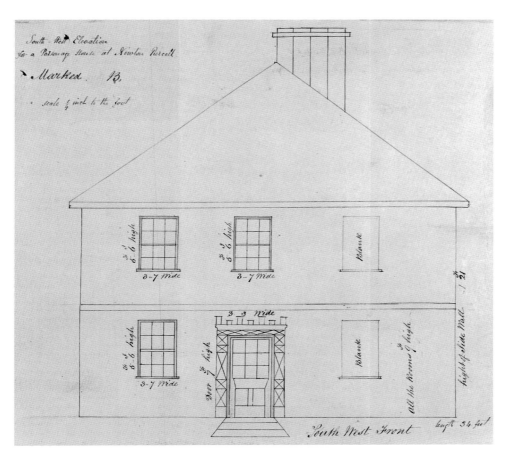

South West Elevation
for a Parsonage House at Newton Purcell

Marked 13.

scale ¼ inch to the foot

South West Front

length 34 feet

1.46 (left)
No gothic yet, and this is 1844.
Builder: Joseph Clements, at
Newton Purcell, Oxfordshire,
between Bicester and
Buckingham [*Oxford Record
Office, MS. Oxf. dioc. papers
b.104/5*].

1.47 (below)
Newtown, near Soberton,
Hampshire: John Colson's
entrance elevation from 1851.
The gothic revival had passed
him by too [*Hampshire Record
Office, 16M70/27*].

church Lincolnshire. Salvin brought forward the narrow central bay of the corridor, and gave it a little pyramidal roof; this unclassical treatment seems to have been his only consolation here.

Changes ahead

I have started with James Trubshaw's vicarage at Walkeringham because it seems to me that the house and the circumstances surrounding it contain the seeds of the revolution in domestic architecture that was so soon to come. In the first place the house is utterly typical of so many that were built at the time in its layout, its scale, and its understated classical-Georgian facades. On the other hand, Trubshaw had not really overcome the basic problem of a comparatively narrow central corridor having to do the visual work of the major bay of the main elevation, a design problem that lay behind many of the changes ahead. The rooms at Walkeringham were the traditional Georgian compartments; the spaces between them minimal corridors, intended only for accessing the rooms and not for any independent use. The flattish roof, the incongruous chimneys and the glum attics at Walkeringham may have suggested to younger and more ambitious architects that there are areas of domestic design which must be reformed if the resulting building is to do justice to the activities that go on inside it: the old Georgian shell will no longer suffice. Nor will the fact that a parsonage looks just like any other house. The extensive kitchen offices and the carefully planned courtyard around it indicate the increased sophistication of domestic life, and hint at the recent advances in the technology itself; their scale and position are at odds with the formal facades of the house. The pleasure of living at the house would have been derived from its attractive isolated setting, detached from the church and facing away from it on the very edge of the village, but that semi-detached relationship will soon be looked at again by those stressing a new association between the parson, his community, and his church; and the originality and charm of the house within would have been derived from its decoration and furnishing, rather than from some special character of the house itself. One imagines the Reverend Mr Miller toasting his muffins in the new fireplace, proud of the security and status his classical house has brought him; for there is very little in the social status of the parson of the time that should distinguish his daily routine outside the offices he performs at the parish church from that of his smarter and more relaxed neighbours. And as for Trubshaw himself, he was essentially a builder and an engineer rather than an architect, who went on to be an important bridge designer; and here he was acting as building contractor as well as architect; these distinctions are now becoming more critical as the various building professions start to go their own ways. At the start of his long career, Trubshaw's professional world was a simple one, and the new parsonages that he designed were likewise simple, with few different considerations to be borne in mind for each new job, similar to those for other houses of the same scale. For his next parsonage, for Ilam in Staffordshire, designed only a year after that at Walkeringham, he took a stab at joining the new fashion for the Tudor gothic; and with that he was to play a minor role in the first stages of the unfolding dramas of the birth of the gothic revival which were to reach into even the most far flung and the most small and inconsequential of the villages of England.

Chapter Two
The 1830s: How easy it is to be pleased

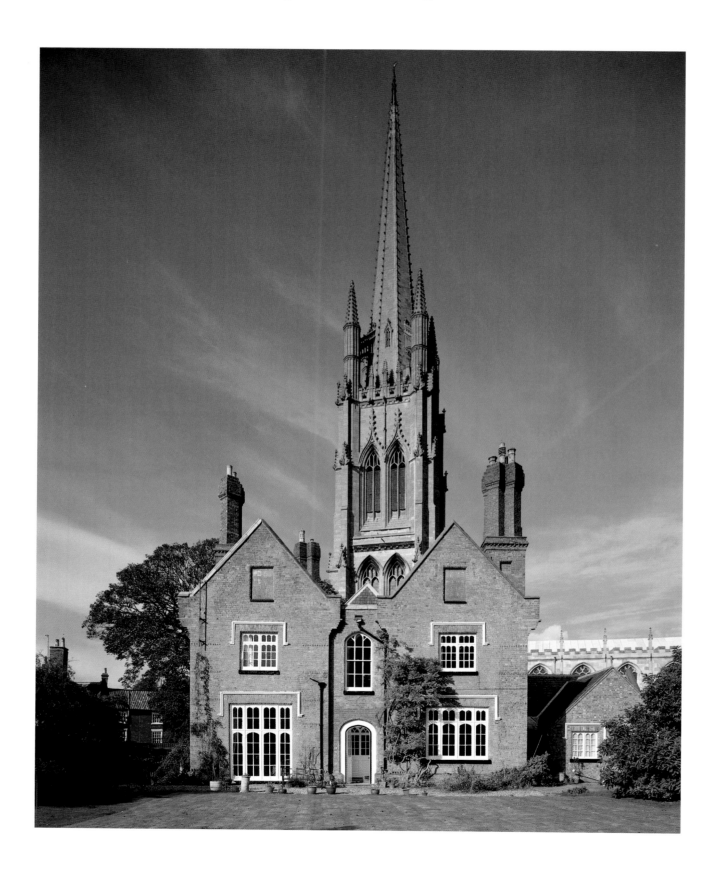

It is already clear that not all the new parsonages of the first decades of the nineteenth century were being built in the traditional classical-Georgian manner. New styles were, however, not at first necessarily applied to the whole of the house but more usually only to parts of it. The career of the Suffolk carpenter-architect Mark Thompson, briefly referred to in Chapter One, provides some delightful early examples. Perhaps inspired by his first significant architectural project, which was the conversion of Ormesby Hall in Norfolk soon after 1810 into a 'most desirable residence' in a severe castellated Tudor-gothic style, achieved with the application of a great deal of cement (see fig. 2.34), Thompson designed parsonages for two members of the family of the late Lord Chancellor Thurlow which happily mixed battlements and hood mouldings with sash windows and classical trimmings.[1] The small house designed in 1818 for Lound, for the Reverend Edward Thurlow, was a modest back-corridor type house with two reception rooms (fig. 2.2).[2] The garden façade was in an austere Tuscan style with unmoulded pilasters, tall casements, and a deep overhanging roof, but the entrance front had a gothic porch and pointed, traceried windows on the stair tower alongside. The tall chimney of the side wall of the dining room, which adjoins the porch on the other side from the stairs, is cleverly at once both Tudor and classical since it has very English

2.1 (opposite)
The vicarage, now rectory, at Louth in Lincolnshire, designed by C.J. Carter in 1832 during the reign of William IV. Compare fig. 2.45.

2.2 (below)
A design of 1818 for the rectory at Lound, near Lowestoft, Suffolk: one of two very different houses designed by Mark Thompson of Dedham that year which mixed motifs from both the classical and Tudor or gothic styles. Stylistic confusion became increasingly common up to the gothic revival in the 1840s. [*Norfolk Record Office, DN/DPL1/3/38*].

2.3 (below, left)
The castellated entrance front of Thompson's Boxford rectory, near Sudbury, Suffolk, 1818.

2.4 (below, right)
Little beyond the entrance elevation of Boxford rectory is Gothic: this is the staircase at the centre of the house.

shafts surmounted by a kind of entablature: it seems possible that faced with this chimney on his entrance front, as happened with back-corridor plans, Thompson used it as the inspiration for his gothic touches. In the same year, he designed a substantial new rectory at Boxford for Edward's cousin, Thomas, with approximately twice the budget he had been allowed at Lound, and the result is an imposing Tudor-gothic castle on the front side which turns into a classical-Georgian house with overhanging eaves on the rear, garden, side (fig. 2.3, 2.4).[3] The plan is unusual, and indeed portentous, for what is basically another back-corridor plan is varied by the inclusion of a grand staircase hall which provides a kind of hub for the three major rooms that revolve around it. Interestingly, Thompson's perspective showing the entrance front gives no hint this time of the more conventional style lurking around the corner (fig. 2.5). One is somehow reminded that 1818 was the year of Mary Shelley's *Frankenstein*.

There is another more modest and perhaps more typical example in Surrey. The architect Samuel Ware, with the builder William Moberly, designed a small two-reception-room rectory for an urban site in Guildford, and they applied Tudor-gothic trimmings to the front, consisting of hood mouldings, and a piece of fancy bargeboarding curiously laid horizontally under the gutter; but the rear – the 'back front' as they called it – was left as a plain classical-Georgian facade (fig. 2.6). This was in 1826.[4] Most other examples before the end of the

2.5
Thompson's application perspective of the gothic front of Boxford rectory: there is no hint here of the classical-Georgian style of the back of the house [*Suffolk Record Office, Bury St Edmunds, 806/2/3*].

decade have similar characteristics. The addition of an expensive new wing with an ornamental and symmetrical principal entrance facade to Galby rectory in Leicestershire has been mentioned: it had a projecting porch with four-pointed arches, low and high-level balustrades composed of rows of lancet-shaped openings, tall octagonal-plan cement turrets with bulbous tops at the corners, decorative bargeboarding that projected both above and below the junction of the roof tiles with the wall, and ornamental crosses at the apex of the gables; in between all this, the windows maintained Georgian proportions (although the architect, Parsons, drew them as if they were casements). The greater part of the house behind, some of which had been there before, was in an altogether simpler and more vernacular style (fig. 2.7; see fig 1.40).[5] James Trubshaw's vicarage at Walkeringham of 1823 introduced us to the typical classical-Georgian parsonage; he designed another parsonage, at Ilam in Staffordshire, in the following year, this time using an unpretentious Tudor-gothic style; he inscribed on his drawing that it was 'finished at two o'clock Thursday morning'.[6] Engagingly, his ground floor plan drawings show a figure relaxing in the study, labelled 'not at home'. But it was too early for the true dawn of Tudor gothic. Until the end of the 1820s it was still unusual to build a house in an English village in other than a classical-Georgian style, and the results when anything else was attempted were idiosyncratic, unhistorical, and inconsistent.

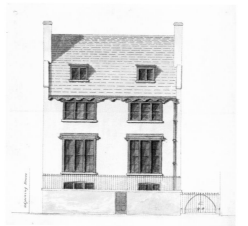

2.6 (right)
The front and 'back front' elevations of Guildford rectory, Surrey (1826) by Samuel Ware and William Moberly – another but much smaller 'Frankenstein'-type house consisting of favoured but conflicting styles grafted together [*Surrey History Centre, 472/12/1-4*].

2.7 (below, right)
Galby, Leicestershire: a fancy gothick front applied to a conventional classical-Georgian house by William Parsons in 1829. The facade has since been remodelled [*Lincolnshire Archives, MGA 153*].

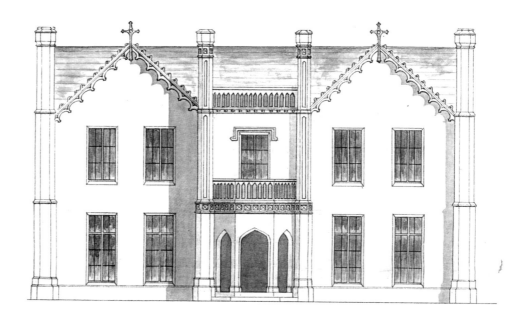

Since this situation ended very rapidly as the 1830s began – indeed, it has never returned – it is worth looking at the reasons why the traditional attitude to house design may have changed so much and so fast, and why these changes were particularly true of parsonage-building. The first reason was that over a period of about 20 years – the first 20 years of the new century – architects were beginning to look at the historical architecture of England in an entirely new light, a process which came about as a result of actually looking for the first time carefully and accurately at the remains of the mediaeval, Tudor and Jacobean architecture around them; and, inspired by this new scientific approach, metropolitan thinkers and writers were now able to turn their attention to the nature of Englishness in architecture, to question, and to experiment with it. In this light it is interesting, for example, that the school Lugar designed to sit alongside his classical vicarage at Yaxham in Norfolk was in the Tudor-gothic style, even though it was designed at the same time as the house (fig. 2.8). In his accompanying text he stressed the philanthropic efforts of the pastor and the 'Pastor's Lady'. The suggestion is that it was these that inspired the choice of the style, imitating the characteristically English almshouses of the past.[7]

The process by which Tudor architecture came to be widely associated with a broadly sympathetic political view of Old England in the era of Walter Scott is a well known one.[8] On the one hand it is illustrated by Joseph Nash and the popular illustrations of his *The mansions of England in the olden time* from the late 1830s (fig. 2.9), and on the other by literary descriptions of houses such as those by Benjamin Disraeli in his novel *Coningsby* of 1844.[9] But architects were more in the vanguard of this development than is sometimes realised. Crude attempts to copy old buildings were already rare by Nash's time. Architects who thought creatively about their work were by then on to something else: a much more analytical and informed if still often confused approach to the elements of Tudor-gothic architecture.

Rediscovering the past

For the process of the rediscovery of English architecture began not only with Walter Scott and the literary imagination but at least as much from the availability of accurate renditions of historical buildings for the first time; and the person responsible for this was

2.8 (below, left)
Although it was located close to his classical-Georgian rectory, Lugar's school at Yaxham, Norfolk, was designed in the Tudor-gothic style, which, with its connotations of Tudor almshouses, was considered appropriate for a charitable foundation. Compare fig. 1.26. From *Villa architecture* (1828), plate 15.

2.9 (below)
Joseph Nash's Merrie England, complete with jester: plate 4 from the second series of his popular *Mansions of England in the olden time* (1840), showing an imagined scene in the hall of the house in Kent now called Ightham Mote.

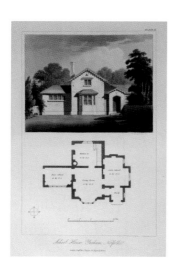

John Britton, the writer, draughtsman and publisher, who in 1807 inaugurated a series of volumes called the *Architectural antiquities of Great Britain represented and illustrated in a series of views, elevations, plans, sections and details, of various ancient English edifices: with historical and descriptive accounts of each.* Anyone who wanted to know what England's architectural heritage looked like could now do so relatively easily for the first time: Britton's books were intended for a far broader circulation than the previous publications for circles of connoisseurs.[10] As with his other ventures, the *Architectural antiquities* was sold to subscribers in the form of individual plates issued over a period of time and which were eventually completed with a letterpress; these could thus be bound into a book. This made it possible for many to build up substantial collections of drawings; and quite possibly, the process also encouraged them to study individual views with greater attention than if they had all arrived bound into a single volume and at one go, as they had for those who had been able to afford luxurious volumes of this kind.

And it was a long process. The *Architectural antiquities* emerged over 20 years, providing much evidence for the way in which the process of increasing and useful accuracy was achieved. The first volume, completed in 1807, consists largely of views rather than of measured drawings; the second volume (1809) has four times the number of subjects than the first, and most drawings are this time measured. The third volume (1812) re-presented the Cambridge churches of St Sepulchre and King's College chapel, because the editor had decided that they had not been accurately enough rendered in the first (fig. 2.10). The fourth volume (1814) notes the improvement in standards in antiquarian and topographical studies since the series was conceived, and announces that the forthcoming *Cathedral antiquities* will be in the form of 'a more regular and uniform style of excellence in drawings and engravings'; the volume is enhanced by a chronological table provided by John Adey Repton.[11] Finally, the preface of the fifth and last volume, completed in 1826, admits that although the series so far had been 'amusing and gratifying to students, [it] was not sufficiently scientific and systematic for others'; it has therefore taken some six years to complete.[12] 'It has been', Britton continues, 'my wish to guard against hypothesis and error, and to record nothing but undeniable fact, or inference from impeachable evidence'.[13]

2.10
From fantasy to fact: the third volume of Britton's *Architectural antiquities* (1812) included corrected views of buildings which had already appeared in the series in less accurate form. This is the revised depiction of the Norman church of St Sepulchre (the 'round church') in Cambridge. Engraved by William Woolnoth from a drawing by F. Mackenzie.

The plates are now entitled 'Britton's chronological history of English Architecture', and the entire sequence is concluded by a variety of scientific aids: an architectural dictionary; an alphabetical list of the architects and founders of the buildings; a chronological list of the architectural monuments, and finally an index to all five volumes.

It was through John Britton's publications that the historical gothic architecture of England was brought up to the level where it could be compared directly to the methods used in presenting and teaching the orders of classical architecture. Plates prepared by top-rate and innovating engravers such as John and Henry Le Keux were prepared from drawings by draughtsmen such as Auguste Charles Pugin, the French émigré, sometime assistant of John Nash, and pupil master of the illustrator Joseph Nash. The list of monuments that could be mined for historic details was prodigious. There were some 70 examples in the *Architectural antiquities* series alone. The great houses of East Anglia such as Oxburgh, East Barsham (then in ruins) (fig. 2.11), Blickling, Hengrave, Giffords Hall (fig. 2.12), and Audley End, along with Little Moreton Hall, Longleat, Wollaton Hall, Holland House, and Compton Winyates, amongst others, appeared in the second volume alone, and with the destroyed parts of the buildings restored to enable them to be properly appreciated. Britton repeated the process with French architecture, which after the defeat of Napoleon in 1815 was again available to the British topographer and architect, with his *Architectural antiquities of Normandy.* Here he covered ground already described by the French writer Charles Nodier, and by the Englishmen John Sell Cotman and Dawson Turner, but this time with crisp and accurate measured drawings by Pugin illustrating and reconstructing monuments that in practice were scarcely appreciable from ruination or neglect (figs 2.13, 2.14). The result of Britton's work was that it finally became possible for architects, some 20 years after the pioneering hopes of the gothic apologist and writer John Carter, to award the gothic style equal status with the classical. This had been Britton's aim. It is for example noticeable that at the outset of his career there were few technical names for many features of gothic buildings, in contrast to the extensive nomenclature used in the academies for the tiniest parts of Greek or Roman architecture. These had to be invented or distilled by antiquarians, and Britton's various glossaries occasionally refer to their originators and their sources.

2.11
At much the same time, the views Britton published of existing buildings either restored their original form or depicted them clearly enough for architects to use them as an authoritative source. East Barsham Manor, Norfolk, was at the time in an advanced state of ruin. A view of the south front from the second volume of the *Architectural antiquities*, 1809.

2.12
Giffords Hall, Suffolk was another highly regarded late mediaeval or Tudor building. This is the entrance gateway, also from the second volume of the *Architectural antiquities*.

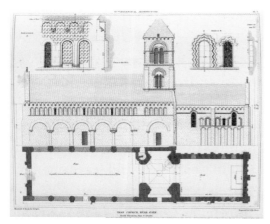

2.13 (above)
The Abbaye aux dames, Caen, from a drawing by A. C. Pugin and published in Britton's *Architectural antiquities of Normandy* (1828). The abbey was in a decayed state, and its floor level had risen to hide the plinths of the piers, but Pugin's drawing reconstructed it with unprecedented accuracy.

2.14 (above, right)
Thaon church, Normandy, from the same volume. The church is hidden in a valley some way from the village. There was something of a competitive, colonialising atmosphere in the way in which English draughtsmen found and measured ancient monuments in France after the defeat of Napoleon.

A feature common to both styles would be given a different name when applied to the gothic: for example, Britton's *Architectural and archaeological dictionary* coined the new gothic nomenclature of 'impost moulding' for the ornamental capital of a gothic pier; the book also gave considerable emphasis to words of Anglo-Saxon – that is, authentically 'English' – origin, and the Anglo-Saxon alphabet was used alongside the Greek and Latin ones (fig. 2.15).[14] The significance that Britton attributes to this process is illustrated by the fact that in his own autobiography he placed his *Dictionary* third in order of importance, following the much more widely known *Architectural antiquities* and his *Cathedral antiquities*.

At the same time, the accurate measured drawings pioneered by Pugin under Britton's sponsorship and the various published analyses of the setting out of different pointed arches, such as that which forms one of the last plates of the *Architectural antiquities*, would enable a parallel to be drawn with the regulated formulae of academic classicism.

House One
That England's historical architecture could provide a canon of grand houses to inspire admiration was clear; but whether it could also supply architects with practical information for their bread-and-butter commissions was quite another matter. What Britton singularly failed to do was to produce historical models on which a small modern house, such as a parsonage, could be based. He simply found almost none. The first four volumes of the *Architectural antiquities* include many manor houses as well as castles, palaces and abbeys, but nothing the size of a small private house with the exception only of a curious

timber construction in Islington (fig. 2.16).[15] The fifth volume, from
1826, was originally intended to be more concerned with castellated
and domestic architecture, and yet Britton found this impracticable;
and the only domestic building eventually referred to therein is
Winwall House in Norfolk which was 'considered the most ancient
and most perfect specimen of Norman domestic architecture in
England' (fig. 2.17).[16] The definition of a building such as this, the arch-
prototype for the modern gothic architect – House One, as it were –
would surely have been an important step in reestablishing the
principles of modern gothic architecture. Britton's preoccupation with
it and his belief that he had found it are underlined by the fact that
Winwall made a deep impression on him: 20 years after its 'discovery'
he included it in his own drawing illustrating the finest examples of
ancient domestic architecture, preceding a text by the Reverend
Charles Boutell.[17] During those two decades a long list of surviving
mediaeval work had been published in the third edition of J. H.
Parker's *Glossary of terms* of 1840, but Britton had evidently not been
convinced by any other candidate for primacy. His choice was a strange
one. An experienced topographical writer such as he surely cannot
have failed to see that Winwall House was a later formation from
the remains of a monastic building, as is evident from the lack of
architectural or practical relationship between the surviving features
of Norman architecture on it and the rest of the small farmhouse that
had been built around them.[18] As such, it was clearly not a surviving
Norman house. Perhaps its haunting and isolated location – in Gibbet
Lane, overlooking a path between two isolated villages – had had its
effect on him (fig. 2.18).

2.15 (above, left)
A typical entry from Britton's
Dictionary. In defining
terminology, he emphasised
Anglo-Saxon and Celtic origins
wherever possible in order to
establish the Englishness of
gothic architecture.

2.16 (above)
An old house in Islington,
just to the north of London:
the only domestic structure
that Britton included in the
first four volumes of his
Architectural antiquities
(from volume 2, 1809).

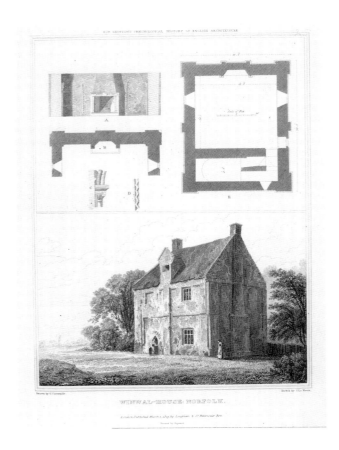

2.17 (above)
Winwall House, off Gibbet Lane, near Wereham, Norfolk – Britton's 'House One'. He considered it 'the most ancient and most perfect specimen of Norman domestic architecture in England'. This illustration by George Cattermole and John Le Keux of 1819 gives an impression which surely at the time must have seemed erroneous; in reality, the exterior east wall of the modern house is probably the interior west wall of a much older dwelling. *Architectural antiquities*, volume 5 (1826).

2.18 (above, right)
Winwall House, now Winnold Farm, in 1959 [*National Monuments Record, BB59/181*].

Boutell himself wrote of domestic architecture in the 1846 book that

the class of buildings which is peculiarly familiar to contemporaries, is precisely the one relative to which least is known in after times. Domestic Architecture is the most obscure chapter in the history of the art[19]

and he could give no surviving examples until the fourteenth century. Between the dates of the two Britton publications referring to Winwall House, 1826 and 1846, no writer can be found who gives a contrary opinion, mainly because the most humble timber houses of any kind were clearly beneath criticism.[20] Matthew Habershon wrote in 1839 that 'All writers who speak of this period agree that the lower orders especially were most miserably lodged'; and the encyclopaedist Joseph Gwilt wrote in 1842 that 'In London, towards the end of the twelfth century, the houses were still built of timber, and covered with reeds or straw'.[21] Furthermore, the phenomenon appeared to be universal: Turner's text to Cotman's *Architectural antiquities of Normandy* had noted in 1822 that 'the private residence of the more humble individual has, in no portion of the globe, been able to secure to itself any thing approaching to a durable existence.[22] He then refers to 'Winwal House in Norfolk, lately figured by Mr Britton in his Chronological and Historical Illustrations of the Ancient Architecture of Great Britain; remains that are calculated to excite no other emotions than regret, and to awaken, without being able to satisfy, curiosity. Nor indeed have Mr Cotman's extensive researches enabled him to meet with any of this description, all poor as they are, within the limits of Normandy'.[23]

Since there was no known historical model for a small house, architects had never had any better idea of how to go about designing a modern one in a gothic style than to choose what seemed to them to be the characteristic details of the large well-known houses and apply them in artistic fashion to conventional house plans. Britton's work was analytical in terms of style but much less so in respect of the other elements of architecture. For the great majority of designers who became interested in mediaeval architecture at this time, the results bore no more similarity to any actual mediaeval house than the various gothic trimmings applied to large houses on and off since the mid-eighteenth century had created any authentic neo-mediaeval architecture. In the case of these small houses however the clash between the pretentiousness of the decorative detail and the modesty of every other aspect of the house produced an entirely original effect, devoid of historical pedigree and very often too of common sense: there are gables sitting over parapets like a head over broad shoulders; flat or shallow roofs; a mixture of window types, from the castellated to the monastic; turrets; plaster decoration derived from flat tracery; a tendency to obscure, rather than express, constructional method; and a complete lack of coherence between the various elements of a building, even as if different parts of it had been executed by different hands. This was the Tudor-gothic style, an English compromise between the most easily suggestible elements of history, construction, politics, and art, and it flourished in the years following 1830.

All this seems the more remarkable because topographical writers did in fact refer to more likely and reasonable candidates for House One – the surviving mediaeval prototype for the modern architect – without being able to see them as such. The first volume of Pugin and Willson's *Specimens of gothic architecture* (1821) illustrates the Norman 'Jew's

2.19 (below)
The Jew's House, Lincoln,
photographed in 1969
[*National Monuments Record,*
BB64/5496].

2.20 (below, right)
An undated view of Moyse's
Hall, Bury St Edmunds, Suffolk,
showing the appearance of
the building before Victorian
restoration [*National*
Monuments Record, BB71/
4784].

House' in Lincoln (fig. 2.19): was it insufficiently 'English', or too extravagant to serve as a simple precedent for Britton? What about 'Aaron's House', that any visitor to the 'Jew's House' could have seen nearby; or 'Moyse's Hall' in Bury St Edmund's, recorded by Britton and Boutell in 1846 (fig. 2.20)? How did writers such as Britton or Willson fail to see that the monastic ruins around England which had been depicted over recent decades, and now with increasing accuracy, often had surviving residences attached which were little changed since their original detachment from the church at the Reformation. Muchelney, Wenlock, Lanercost, and many others: these were still there (figs 2.21–3). Furthermore, many of the applicants for mortgages from Queen Anne's Bounty were themselves resident in small mediaeval houses: they were now engaged in applying to demolish them.[24] The ability actually to see a small mediaeval residence as such eluded the older generation of early nineteenth-century observers, and yet in a sense this is not surprising, for it sometimes seems that so did the ability to look accurately at historical architecture at all. The parsonages that appear in the villa pattern books of the period do not carry any characteristics drawn from ancient examples in spite of claims made to the contrary. John Buonarotti Papworth, an active, experienced, well-travelled, and educated architect, had in 1818 illustrated 'a vicarage or farm house' in his *Rural residences* (fig. 2.24), as well as 'a vicarage house, in correspondence of the architecture of the neighbouring church' (fig. 2.25); but given the gothicky nature of Papworth's design, it seems very unlikely that it would have been

2.21 (left)
Muchelney Abbey, Somerset: view of the abbot's lodging from the south east [*English Heritage Photo Library K031314*].

2.22 (below, left)
The abbot's parlour at Muchelney, photographed in 1978. This room could well have provided A.W.N. Pugin and later gothic revival architects with the House One interior they seemed to be looking for. [*National Monuments Record, AA78/2607*].

2.23 (below)
The former prior's lodging at Wenlock Priory in Shropshire: one of the most remarkable and beautiful of all late mediaeval houses, photographed in 1954. [*National Monuments Record, AA54/4558*].

The 1830s: How easy it is to be pleased

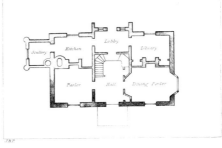

A GOTHIC COTTAGE.

Pub. at R. ACKERMANN'S REPOSITORY of ARTS 101 Strand, June 1818.

A VICARAGE HOUSE.

Pub.^d at R.ACKERMANN'S REPOSITORY of ARTS 101 Strand, June 1816.

2.24 (above)
J. B. Papworth's 'gothic
cottage'; he thought the design
suitable for a 'vicarage or
farm house'. Plate 9 from *Rural
residences* (1818).

2.25 (above, right)
Contrary to its designer's claim,
Papworth's 'Vicarage House'
was highly unlikely to have
resembled either any actual
old building or church. Plate 11
from *Rural residences*.

derived from the architecture of any real church.[25] In common with many other contemporaneous villa pattern-book writers, Papworth had not yet learned how to *look* at gothic buildings.

A younger generation, brought up with Britton, could begin to see their surroundings differently not least because of their greater interest in historical documents and their ability to look more accurately at historical building. As it happens, a chance event of 1822 provides something of a watershed, a date that marks the end of the wild stylistic fantasies of the villa pattern-book writers. A disastrous fire at Josiah Taylor's 'Architectural Library' that year deprived London of the publisher or seller not only of the works of Soane, and Stuart and Revett, but also of Malton (*An essay on British cottage architecture*, 1798), Richardson (*New designs in architecture*, 1792, and much else), Nicholson (many practical books on architecture from 1795), Lugar, Gwilt, Pocock (*Architectural designs for rustic cottages, picturesque dwellings, villas, etc.*, 1807), Dearn, Gandy (*The rural architect* and *Designs for cottages*, 1805), Aikin (*Designs for villas and other rural buildings*, 1808) and Plaw (*Rural architecture*, a bestseller from 1785 onwards, and *Sketches for country houses, villas and rural dwellings*, 1800).[26] Taylor retired from business thereafter; and in any case, an economic recession soon followed. The fewer books that appeared in the following years were noticeably more sober and more measured, and they also made more of an attempt to look at historical building and to evaluate the functions of its construction and its details, for Britton had evidently succeeded in raising expectations and standards. A move in a new direction is exemplified by T. F. Hunt, born in 1791, whose *Designs for parsonage houses, alms houses, etc. etc.* of 1827 intersperses some drawings of surviving Tudor detailing between his own proposals: 'the aim of this volume has been to select and combine characteristic details of the domestic architecture used in England during the fifteenth and sixteenth centuries; differing widely from, those in these times blended and confounded with, the ecclesiastical style, generally known under the denomination of *Gothic*'.[27] In fact the book includes only four plates of historical details, a 'curious old gable' from Well Hall at Eltham; a 'curious old chimney piece' from the presence chamber at St James's Palace (where Hunt was working at the time as a Labourer in Trust, a resident supervisor of building work); and then two further 'curious old gables' – one in fact a bargeboard,

2.26 (below)
A 'curious old gable' from Well
Hall at Eltham, Kent. From T.F.
Hunt's *Designs for parsonage
houses, alms houses, etc. etc.*,
1827 (plate 12).

2.27 (below, right)
'Almost the only remains of an
ancient mansion at Boughton
Malherbe, near Lenham in
Kent'. Another of the historical
views interspersed between
new designs in Hunt's *Designs*
(plate 21).

from Eltham Palace, and the last 'almost the only remains of an ancient mansion at Boughton Malherbe, near Lenham in Kent' (figs 2.26, 2.27). There were 14 designs on different scales, some incorporating these historical details in part or in full.

Hunt's book suggests a useful indication of the current state of understanding about late gothic or Tudor architecture amongst younger architects. Unlike many of his predecessors, some of the detailing and even, occasionally, the general form of his own designs, did in fact resemble those of ancient examples. His various references to particular historical buildings – such as to the old vicarage at Hackney, demolished a few years beforehand, another small old house which evidently Britton had overlooked – indicate that he saw that gothic was not a general term for an applied style, but part of a national tradition, the remains of which were all around: that in itself shows clearly the effect of the works of Britton, A. C. Pugin and others. He also used historical and topographical sources intelligently, for example quoting in one of his books from Whitaker's *History of Whalley* of 1801: '"of [quadrangular] form have been many of the most opulent parsonage-houses in England, emulating at an humble distance the monastic or collegiate style, to which the taste and habit of their builders would naturally direct them"'.[28] Furthermore, he had recognised that the character of these old buildings was derived from the expression of certain structural elements, in particular the chimney and the gable.[29] And yet he found it difficult to carry those historical and structural elements through to the creation of a logical way of building. He was at pains to emphasise that the interior of one of his

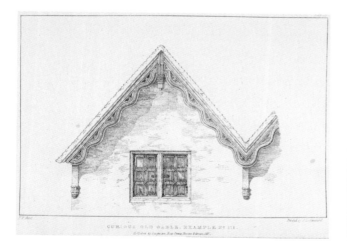

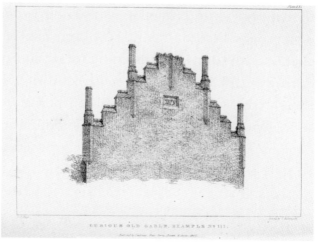

new houses would take on an uncompromised modern character; and, more surprisingly, he emulated historical forms in appearance but not in plan, for the proposal of his own for a modern parsonage *looks like* a building with a central quadrangle but in fact does not actually have one.[30]

Hunt persisted with the Tudor style, adopting a similar approach for his *Exemplars of Tudor architecture adapted to modern habitation*, of 1830, where he sharpened up this approach: he both stressed the importance of accurate historical detailing, and also the complete detachment of a modern interior from an historical exterior (fig. 2.28).[31] The younger Tudor-goths were moving in the direction of higher accuracy; they were also setting higher standards for designers in other styles, for some of the most imaginative of the new pattern books did have a higher degree of stylistic integrity even when their subject matter is eclectic. Charles Parker's work in *Villa rustica* of 1833, for example, is derived from particular Italian examples: a porch in plate 37 is 'copied from a farm house, situated near Florence'; plates 51–4 are based on an original building situated on the banks of the Tiber; and plates 60–2 have 'a correct example of an Italian Porch'.[32] It probably was (fig. 2.29). Two architects of note who designed parsonages in this particular style were both members of

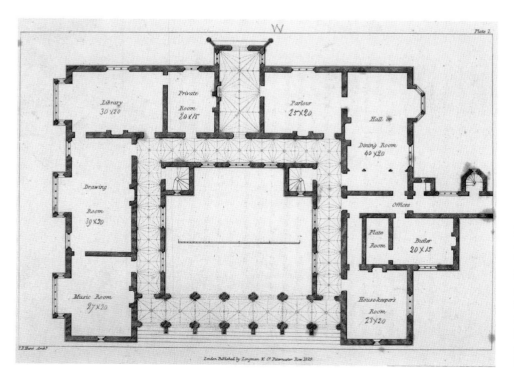

2.28
An attempt to combine 'modern convenience with the splendour of ancient quadrangular form': the opening plan from *Exemplars of Tudor architecture* (1830). Hunt has at last accepted that a cloister will only really look like a cloister if it is a real one.

the Hakewill family: Henry Hakewill designed one as early as 1820 at Exning, near Newmarket, a central-corridor design but with a grand central staircase; and his son John Henry, perhaps inspired by Parker's book, designed a much more picturesque example with a pretty porch with Roman pantiles, at Uphaven in Dorset in 1841.[33] This had an unusual plan – a combination of a back-corridor type with a stair hall. In the post-Britton era architects were at least striving for authenticity, even if they could not manage it.

G. Poulett Scrope reviewed Hunt's parsonage book with others in 1831 for the *Quarterly review*; and he addressed the matter of the national character of English architecture, and where it might be found:

> every country has an architecture more or less peculiarly its own; formed, like the character and language of its inhabitants, by the blending of various foreign ingredients which have at different periods introduced and naturalized themselves, but which have been also in turn modified by the original stock, as well as by the local peculiarities of climate, soil, social condition, and political history.

> This NATIONAL character attaches itself far more to domestic architecture than to that which is displayed in public buildings, ecclesiastical or civil.[34]

These comments are perceptive, and important: they are amongst the first suggestions of a theme that lay behind much of what John Ruskin

2.29
'A summer residence on the banks of the Tiber': a house drawn by Charles Parker for his *Villa rustica* of 1833 (plate 52).

was to say, and indeed what Hermann Muthesius was to preach to his German audience in the wake of English success over 70 years later.[35] Scrope, who was a geologist as well as an economist, was claiming that the style and details of architecture are best derived from the earth which dictates the physical nature of its building materials; and furthermore, that the resulting national character is best attached to the private home. All this was new to the 1830s.

The review did not, in fact, appear to be particularly sympathetic to the use of 'gothic' (by which Scrope appears to include the various Tudor-gothic styles) for new public works because of the lack of harmony with neighbouring buildings that would result; but the *'old English style'* is, he wrote, particularly appropriate to country buildings, and the effect is a fine one.[36] In a rare reference by any critic to the architectural style of the urban house, he says that 'we own that the glories of Brighton and Cheltenham sink in our estimation, and give place to a feeling of melancholy regret, whenever we pass the remnant of some ancient manor house, once the scene of comfort and joyous hospitality, now dreary and dilapidated'.[37] A writer who is not a designer soon slides back into descriptions of sentiment or emotion. The Elizabethan and Jacobean styles are particularly approved of, chiefly because of their 'effect'; they were 'a natural compound of the old and long respected gothic, with a new rival and opponent, the Roman'.[38]

Comments such as these carried considerable political weight, particularly since we are merely a year away from the passing of the Great Reform Act when the tensions of English politics were at a height.[39] It is not hard to join with Charles Hanbury Tracy, Sir Edward Cust, and the other promoters of a gothic parliament building in 1834–5 in seeing the historic English constitutional settlement itself in terms of a balance between the gothic and the Roman, the supposed earthy demotic of the Anglo-Saxon people versus the rationalism and authoritarianism of republics and empires, pivoted on the exclusively English fulcrum of the Reformation and the reign of Queen Elizabeth. But political philosophy is one thing: a practical way of translating the ideas into buildings is another. Even with a new, sharper eye for the architecture of England's history, architects and their parson clients would have been unable to make buildings from it without the work of a writer who could combine the interest in historical design and an came to domestic architecture, and by the close of that decade he was one of the best-known writers on the subject. By the time he eventually came to publishing his *Encyclopaedia of cottage, farm, and villa architecture and furniture* in 1833 he had so large a mass of information at his disposal that he required a thoroughly consistent and ordered way of presenting it. Using the best scientific method and providing a model for subsequent encyclopaedists such as Alfred Bartholomew, Joseph Gwilt, and Edward Cresy he ordered his text into parts, chapters, and numbered paragraphs.

The *Encyclopaedia* was intended to provide architects with a manual to modern design. Its author announced at the outset that: 'We have commenced our work with Designs, rather than with Principles, because in the analytical and critical remarks, with which we mean to accompany these Designs, we intend to develop, as it were, incidentally, and by little and little, all the Principles of Architecture'.[48] He continued:

> The great object of this work is, to show how the dwellings of the whole mass of society may be equalized in point of all essential comforts, conveniences and beauties.[49]

In other words, his approach was to be comprehensively analytical, critical, and empirical; and, in contrast to the advertising for work which formed a major motivation for the pattern-book compilers, examples are sometimes presented because of their failings.[50]

This analytical approach led to the sharpening up of a familiar old idea that a building could be beautiful if it was practical.[51] In referring to 'The beauty of fitness' Loudon was acknowledging the potential for picturesque massing that might follow from raising an elevation from a convenient plan.[52] There were certain functional features that he approved of: a central stair; efficient organisation of ventilated and lit spaces under a single roof; internal fire breasts (figs 2.30, 2.31). The plans provided by his contributors and illustrated in his book – for he himself did not design them – were generally dense, avoiding corridors; regarding propriety, chimney tops 'distinguish apartments destined for human beings from those designed for lodging cattle'.[53] The choice of style was itself not a matter of 'principle': judging by the examples given, he has a preference for Tudor or gothic, and yet in

The house in Exeter was also essentially designed in the manner of a parsonage but on a larger scale (fig. 2.36).[74] It has a symmetrical south front towards the close, with an off-centre entrance on the western side flanked by a broad, but shallow, chimney. The house is built of rough stone and is also castellated between the two gables that sit, Tudor-gothic-style, on shoulder-like parapets on the south elevation: it seems possible that Fowler may have been influenced by the largely fifteenth and sixteenth-century manor house at Cotehele nearby, which is built of the same stone laid similarly in places (figs 2.37, 2.38). As was always the case with these houses, any reference to a mediaeval house was at once offset by the architect's determination to give his house a civilised, disciplined front.

A grander and more influential project was soon underway in London. Much of the work by Edward Blore at Lambeth Palace,

2.36
The archdeaconry of Cornwall in the cathedral close at Exeter, by Charles Fowler in 1828, was a somewhat less elegant design than the same architect's Covent Garden Market in London of that year. Projecting masonry suggests that the building was originally rendered.

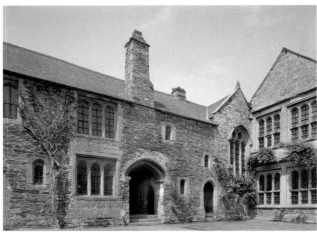

2.37 (above)
Cotehele, Cornwall:
the Jacobean tower in 1954
[*National Monuments Record,
AA54/5634*].

2.38 (above, right)
Cotehele; the courtyard,
with its logical, expressive
fenestration [*National
Monuments Record, AA54/
5641*].

later greatly derided by A.W.N. Pugin, was within existing historical fabric, but his residential wing was mostly new (fig. 2.39).[75] It is interesting to speculate to what extent Blore saw the house as being different from a country house project. The plan consisted of a main corridor running east-west along the length of the house, with major rooms to the north; on the south side there was a gatehouse tower which, contrary to historical precedent, contained a large two-storey staircase hall. From here steps led directly up to the corridor.[76]

Blore reused this design of 1829 almost immediately when making substantial additions, including a new entrance facade, at St Asaph in Flintshire.[77] He was here invited to double the size of an existing classical house, attributed to Samuel Wyatt, and he did this by building along the whole of the west side of the existing building, doubling its depth in much the same way as parsonage architects so often did when extending old buildings but here on a palatial scale.[78] He added a central hall with flanking major rooms to form a new west elevation, but he turned the central bay into a wide, major bay so that the double-height staircase hall was at least as wide as the rooms either side.

The stairs themselves led up through the centre of this hall directly to a gallery, which ran north-south through the house and provided access to the principal rooms either side; it seems likely that in commissioning the extension, Bishop Carey was interested in attaining an imposing entrance sequence. Externally, Blore used Jacobean elements to create an almost symmetrical front; instead of a projecting central tower he designed a broad, shallow chimney which rises from directly above the front door to provide a central accent (fig. 2.40).[79] The central part of the house has plain mullioned windows, but the bays either side were originally intended to have projecting angled oriels, again with Jacobean detailing, although these were dropped in execution. It is interesting to note that Danbury Place, another comparatively sophisticated neo-Elizabethan mansion of this period and designed by Thomas Hopper in 1832, was chosen 12 years later as a residence for the newly created bishops of Rochester. It has a bold asymmetrical entrance facade, and an unusual layout based around a great stair hall and a broad central passage that bisected the house (fig. 2.41).

Evidently, therefore, a number of very significant events were taking place which substantially changed the attitude of the educated public towards Tudor-gothic architecture by the early 1830s. Gothic architecture had been measured and drawn, and accurate representations of it were available; it could be seen as being thoroughly English; and Loudon was showing through the illustrations he published in his *Encyclopaedia* and elsewhere that it could be practical, expressive, and economical. Furthermore, the bishops were giving it their personal approval. After the *Encyclopaedia* a great deal more material was published throughout the 1830s which could in practice have assisted interested architects. The illustrations for A. C. Pugin's *Examples of gothic architecture*, which were issued from 1830 and which were published as a book in 1838 with a letterpress by E. J. Willson, included two Tudor parsonages: that at Great Snoring in Norfolk; and the 'rector's mansion', usually called the deanery, at Hadleigh in Suffolk. The list of subscribers for these volumes indicate clearly that significant London architects saw drawings from these series: the names published in the third volume of Pugin's *Examples* include Wyatville, Smirke, Barry, Railton and T. H. Wyatt, as well as Trubshaw (who bought two copies) and Carpenter and Sons, presumably the Islington builder and his talented son Richard. Following a visit to Hadzor in Worcestershire, the architect Matthew Habershon, a peppery, difficult person, published a series of plates entitled *The ancient half-timbered houses of England* from 1836, and these appeared with a preface and introductory essay in 1839.[80] He gave here examples of some substantial half-timbered constructions, some drawn years beforehand by his very young pupil, Ewan Christian, 'all estimated as being within 50 years of Queen Elizabeth'; his intention was to render

2.39 (above)
Lambeth Palace, London:
Edward Blore's new entrance
and reception wing designed
in 1829.

2.40 (right)
Blore's new entrance wing
to the bishop's palace at
St Asaph, Denbighshire.
Photograph by Geoff
Brandwood, July 2006.

2.41 (left)
The garden front of Danbury Palace, Essex, designed by Thomas Hopper in 1832 and later the residence of the Bishop of Rochester.

2.42 (below)
Hadleigh, Suffolk, with the Tudor tower to the right. The deanery was originally located there; the academic geologist and gothic enthusiast William Whewell assisted the architect Henry Harrison in the design of the new building in 1831-3. The house has been altered.

2.43 (below)
A plate from a drawing by a very young Ewan Christian illustrating an old house in Preston, Lancashire, for Matthew Habershon's *Ancient half-timbered houses of England* (1839, plate 3). It is fascinating that even architects such as Habershon who had a special interest in timber construction failed to draw any practical lessons from this type of historical English architecture with its expressed construction and continuous horizontal fenestration.

2.44 (below, right)
Part of the exterior west elevation of New Court (1823-5), originally King's Court, at Trinity College, Cambridge, designed by William Wilkins. As revealed by their vertical position relative to the other windows on the wall, the oriels are located at staircase landings in a most unhistorical way. A photograph of 1914 [*Trinity College, Cambridge, O.16.29*].

the examples 'scientifically useful' (fig. 2.43).[81] The expectation might be that these very few published examples of authentic old English design would have provided inspiration for the architects now engaged in the great wave of parsonage building launched by the application of Gilbert's Acts; but no: in practice architects continued to draw their details and forms from grander buildings, such as the ruined manor house at East Barsham which in 1830 was further illustrated by fine measured drawings showing its reconstructed form (in the first volume of Pugin's *Examples of gothic architecture*), or even from recent Tudor-gothic architecture such as William Wilkins 'King's Court', now New Court, at Trinity College Cambridge, with its solecistic bay windows on the half-levels of the stair landings (fig. 2.44).[82] Not even Habershon made use of the treasures that he had published: although he illustrated the 'Old House' in the Market Place, Preston, there is nothing in his own work which echoes that building's exposed structural skeleton and continuous horizontal bands of windows (see figs 2.52, 2.53).[83]

At least one of the published buildings, the Hadleigh deanery, may however have had a significant if indirect part to play in inspiring a model for a modern Tudor-gothic parsonage, because an extension was built up against it for an influential client. H. J. Rose, who personally knew leading members of what was to become the Oxford Movement, was appointed to the incumbency in 1829. None other than William Whewell, the Cambridge geologist and gothic architecture enthusiast, made sketches for the building, and these were sent to an established architect, Henry Harrison, for conversion into working drawings. The building, small and plain, went up between 1831–3; soon after its

completion it provided the backdrop to the decisive meeting of the Puseyites, where Froude, Keble, and Newman were all present in the wake of Keble's famous sermon on 'National Apostasy'.[84] Rose's house is certainly an early example of the new intellectual style applied on a small scale: no doubt his guests remembered it well, and its genuine Tudor neighbour (fig. 2.42).

New plans in the provinces

Outside such elevated circles the early Tudor-gothic of the 1830s is, unsurprisingly, somewhat on the coarse side. There is a stupendous example at Louth, in the Parts of Lindsey, Lincolnshire, by C. J. Carter, who then described himself as a surveyor, of Brereton near Rugeley in Staffordshire.[85] Louth seems to have been an exotic place: Humphry Repton described a visit to the Hermitage there in 1790 and declared that it was 'one of those things which no pen can describe'; the many exotic treasures of its interior included a 'magical' and 'supernatural' oratory, the floor of which was paved with highly polished horses' teeth.[86] The drawings of Carter's vicarage were prepared in May 1832, and sent for approval two months later. It was an astonishing proposal, and built not exactly as Carter had drawn it but certainly in a very similar way (fig. 2.45; see fig. 2.1). The plan was a simple central-corridor type, with the principal elevation on the garden side, and Carter designed it so that two tall gabled bays jutted out irregularly either side of the gothic door with its pinnacled ogee mouldings and hooded, pointed stair landing window in the centre. The two masonry gables were projected outwards at the eaves with no visible means of support either in the drawing or in reality; and because they projected out much further above the central bay of the house than they did at the outside edges, the apices of the gables were shifted towards the centre of the house so that they were no longer at the centre of the outer bays. Since however the windows themselves were at the centres of these bays, the whole house was given a peculiar twisted appearance. Carter added deep and rich bargeboards, quatrefoils, lancets, carved corbels and much else, and produced a building of quite unrivalled grotesque appearance; in his favour, however, it should be added that on the entrance side he achieved with irregular bays and projections an effect which successfully mimics the appearance of an old house that has been added to a number of times at different periods.

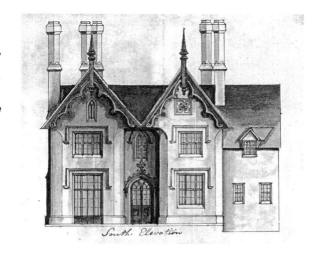

Carter's design was unusual, but the new style was fast adopted in
spite of its oddities and, presumably, its unfamiliarity because of a
number of basic advantages which would have been clear to anyone
who had read Loudon's *Encyclopaedia*. One was that the Tudor-gothic
style was better suited than the classical-Georgian variations to solving
the perennial problem of the central-corridor type, the conflict between
the symmetrical facade and the narrow central bay. A Tudor-gothic
house neither had to be symmetrical, nor have a wider central bay:
indeed, for those that had investigated the matter, it was clear that there
were many examples of symmetrical or almost symmetricalElizabethan
houses with a projecting narrow central bay. Some of these buildings
must have been well known to architects and antiquarians – Hopper,
for example, had reconstructed the interior of a paradigmatic house of
this type, Kentwell Hall in Suffolk, in about 1825–6.[87] Many parsonages
were indeed now built with a conspicuously narrower central bay,
in the form of a projection topped with a gable not unlike a pediment.
The form suited larger houses, and was used by Thomas Jones around
1830 for his deanery at St Asaph.[88] The combination of the Tudor-
gothic central projection with the classical-Georgian formula and
symmetry accounts for the stylistic confusion at Hardingham, where
Joseph Stannard, Wilkins' contractor for his new buildings at King's
College Cambridge, produced in 1833 a gothic central bay to a front
elevation otherwise entirely classical; this was presumably an afterthought, as the mortgage application drawings show a conventional
straight-headed classical-Georgian front door (fig. 2.46).[89] Something
similar on a smaller scale was done at the house we have seen at Nacton,

2.46 (left)
Possibly inspired by his recent work at King's College, Cambridge, Joseph Stannard decided at the last moment to add a pointed arch to his rectory at Hardingham, Norfolk, in 1833.

2.47 (below)
A rustic design of 1840 for the rectory at Sutton, on the edge of the Norfolk Broads, by Peter Thompson, who had been an unsuccessful competitor for the design of the Houses of Parliament five years earlier [*Norfolk Record Office, DN/DPL1/4/58*].

also in Suffolk, where Whiting's extension of 1837 did the same (see fig. 1.43).[90] In Tudor-gothic parsonages, and also in picturesque-Italianate ones, the central bay could be recessed, like Carter's in Louth: this seems to have been popular in particular with houses with a more rustic look, for example at Sutton, Norfolk, by the 'ingenious but dubious' Peter Thompson in 1840, and where the romantic detailing was probably inspired by illustrations such as Hunt's (fig. 2.47).[91] In one form or another this pattern continued for years, producing an example at Swilland in Suffolk, by the dull Oxford architect Thomas Greenshields, more than ten years later in 1843 (fig. 2.48).[92]

2.48 (below)
The Elizabethan narrow
central bay eventually evolved
into a convenient method of
dealing with the requirements
of conventional plans. This is
a late (1843) but typical
example from Swilland,
between Ipswich and
Stowmarket, Suffolk,
by Thomas Greenshields
[*Suffolk Record Office,
Ipswich, FF1/85/1*].

2.49 (below, right)
The gable-and-bay type
elevation, shown here against
the background of the rectory
at Boxworth, near Cambridge
(see fig. 2.54).

However, the greatest freedom allowed by the adoption of Tudor-gothic was the fact that a principal elevation need not be made symmetrical at all: it is because of this that it is all the more remarkable that the central and L-corridor plans, and variations of them, were retained. The most prominent non-symmetrical type had elevations composed of a gabled end wall of two storeys and with an adjoining two-storey elevation whose gable was perpendicular to the first, referred to below as a 'gable-bay' elevation (fig. 2.49). There were two varieties of this elevational type: in one, it was used as an entrance elevation, with a front door adjacent to the base of the gable-end wall, that is, in the centre of the elevation and allowing a central-corridor type plan. In others it was a garden front, with a garden door, and with rooms served by a central corridor that ran along their rear from the front door at one of the two sides. London architects as well as provincial ones used the gable-wall composition in conjunction with central or L-corridor plans, and it was these combinations that were soon widely used across the country: indeed in places they spring up almost side by side.

There are a great deal of houses from the 1830s that illustrate the type at its most straightforward and most simple. A mid-decade example of an exactly typical house might be the parsonage at Elsfield in Oxfordshire, by Henry Jones Underwood who went on to become well known as the architect of J.H. Newman's church at Littlemore (fig. 2.50; see fig. 1.28).[93] His house of 1836 is a standard L-corridor plan

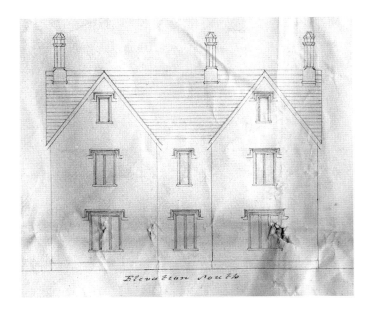

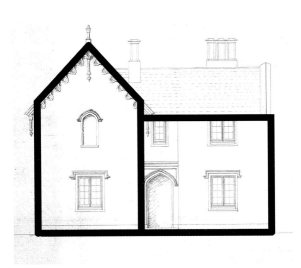

with Tudor-gothic detailing. Habershon had illustrated his own recent design for Aston Sandford parsonage, in Buckinghamshire, in his book of 1839; this small house was of this type too, and the style was Tudor-gothic with sash windows (fig. 2.52).[94] Chapter One referred to his rectory at Rockland St Mary in Norfolk in 1839 (fig. 2.53).[95] Both houses are standard corridor types: the smaller house has a central corridor, and the larger one the L-corridor variation. The prevalence of the latter type is illustrated by the fact that the following year another London architect, Robert Parris, submitted a plan of the same kind, for the nearby village of Rockland St Peter; Parris' stylistic treatment was, however, more authentically Tudor-gothic.[96] The entry elevation of all three of these houses relies on the juxtaposition of the chimney with the front door, an arrangement that could equally suit the back-corridor type. Tudor-gothic houses on standard plans of one sort or another appeared throughout the decade. In 1840, for example, Joseph Kay (who had once been the pupil of S. P. Cockerell, and no doubt could have done better) made no special effort at originality when he designed a standard gable-and-bay, L-corridor type house at Boxworth in Cambridgeshire in 1840 (figs 2.49, 2.54). The thin Tudor detailing is undoubtedly cleaner than that of his less distinguished contemporaries, or of earlier Tudor-gothic houses, and in execution it appears more sophisticated than in Kay's drawings, but the principles of the composition and layout are entirely conventional. From the drawings it appears that he added both the fancy barge-boarding and the lancet window in the bedroom above left of the front door as afterthoughts.[97]

2.50 (below, left)
Elsfield vicarage, north of Oxford, by Henry Jones Underwood in 1836: an exactly typical L-corridor house. See fig. 1.28. [*Oxfordshire Record Office, MS. Oxf. dioc. papers b.103/2*].

2.52 (below)
Habershon's design for the rectory at Aston Sandford, between Aylesbury and Thame, Buckinghamshire, in his *Ancient half-timbered houses of England*, was as conventional as any other Tudor-gothic parsonage of the period. A vignette from page 18.

ASTON SANDFORD RECTORY.

ELEVATION
of
Entrance Front

2.53 (above)
Rockland St Mary rectory near Norwich. In contrast to the atmospheric perspective of the Aston Sandford house from his book, this mortgage application drawing by Matthew Habershon emphasises the unremarkable character of his architecture. The plan was a conventional L-corridor type [*Norfolk Record Office, DN/DPL1/3/52*].

2.54 (above, right)
A conventional gable-and-bay facade: the rectory at Boxworth, near Cambridge, by Joseph Kay, a former pupil of S. P. Cockerell (1840) [*Cambridge University Library, EDR G3/39 MGA/44*].

Since the back-corridor plan seems to have been devised specifically to avoid the elevational problems of the central-corridor plan in classical-Georgian designs, it is not surprising that the plan type was less prevalent to start with in Tudor-gothic houses where the basic contradiction did not exist. Such early examples as there are tend to have a bleak appearance. This is true of an example from 1838 mentioned in Chapter One, at Bossall in the North Riding of Yorkshire (figs 1.29, 1.37, 1.38), and even more so of the grim residence at Black Bourton, designed by Greenshields in 1842. Both these houses have large central bays which would have exactly suited a classical house, betraying the origins of the plan form and appearing somewhat solecistic.[98] At Colwall in Herefordshire there is an early house by Samuel Daukes of Gloucester, which was a more inspired attempt at creating an historical facade to a highly typical back-corridor plan, but the detailing is crude and heavy (fig. 2.55).[99] Many other early examples are not much better: it seems that architects had to wait until the gothic revival started before discovering that the layout had a potential for separate expression of internal functions that was as yet unexploited. There are exceptions, of course. The Oxford diocesan archive has one particularly enjoyable example. An architect called Pritchard, building in 1843 at Wigginton in Oxfordshire, grasped the logic of the back-corridor plan and chose to put the study, the smallest of the three principal rooms, at the centre of his composition; he also made the bays either side of differing widths, put the main entrance at

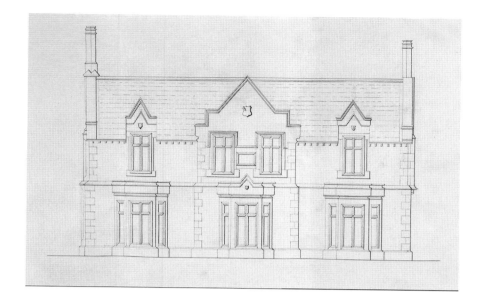

2.55
Colwall rectory, Herefordshire near Great Malvern, 1840. A typical back-corridor type elevation, this time by Samuel Daukes who later became a competent goth. See also fig 5.7 [*Herefordshire Record Office, HD8/15 1840*].

the back of the rear corridor beyond a stair hall, and added some eccentricities of his own, such as a hoodmoulding that rises and falls, and stops and starts, and thereby created perhaps for the first time a Tudor-gothic house that really did have something of the character of a vernacular building (fig. 2.56).[100]

Convivial confusion

There is therefore some evidence that a fashion for Tudor-gothic throughout England was influenced not only by the example of London writers and antiquaries, but also by the solutions that the style provided to the problems of designing a convenient house where the exterior matched the interior planning, as Loudon in particular was encouraging. Some new planning conventions were introduced alongside the old and elevations were given freer treatment; old plans took on more daring and more obviously antiquarian facades. As for the central-corridor plan, it now produced miniature versions, in the form of a projecting porch with octagonal turrets, of the narrow elevations of the chapel of King's College, Cambridge – all over the place: for example, at both East Bilney in Norfolk, and East Brent in Somerset, in the course of the same year, 1837.[101] Stylistic treatments conventionally referred to as 'picturesque' must be seen in the light of the fact that they afforded greater consistency between plan and elevation, and that was itself perhaps responsible for a degree of stylistic confusion: like the parsonages at Hardingham and Nacton,

An unusually successful
exercise in authentic
vernacular Tudor, by John
Pritchard at Wigginton,
south of Banbury, Oxfordshire,
1843 [*Oxfordshire Record
Office, MS. Oxf. dioc. papers
b.106/8*].

or the earlier buildings of Mark Thompson at Ormesby, Lound and
Boxford, they mixed different styles on different, or even the same,
elevations of the same buildings; or, they combined the massing of one
style with the detailing of the other. A house by William Mear at Little
Melton in Norfolk of 1833 is in a classical style but arranged around a
gable-and-bay elevation that was more familiar from Tudor-gothic
houses; an otherwise classical-Georgian house the following year, by
Whiting at Little Glemham, has like some other Suffolk parsonages of
the period what looks like a suggestion of a Tudor hood mould above
the sash windows.[102] At Brampton Bryan in Herefordshire there is a
delightful cottage-like wing of 1832-4 by Edward Smith that has
merely the gentlest suggestion of Tudor, with slight arches over the
windows on the garden side, and narrow projecting brick hood moulds
over them.[103]

A particularly interesting example of the more serious confusion
that now opened up can be found at Averham in Nottinghamshire.
William Patterson, a Nottingham builder, designed alterations in
1838 to a large rectory.[104] The existing house was in a plain, stuccoed,
classical-Georgian style; and on the garden, east, front Patterson
added bays in a matching fashion. On the entrance, west, side however
Patterson added an entrance tower which is in fact picturesque Italianate
in detail (apart, perhaps, from the gothic hatchment on a cartouche
above the door) but nevertheless distinctly Tudor in massing. Unlike an
Italianate tower in the manner of a Charles Parker *Villa rustica*, or for
that matter, of a recently executed example of one such as at Donthorn's
Moulton St Michael rectory, Patterson's tower is a narrow and minor
projection from the facade of the house, and it is flanked to the right

by a shallow projecting chimney on a blank wall in Tudor fashion (fig. 2.57).[105] The juxtaposition of a major chimney with the front door, here as with the back-corridor type classical-Georgian houses, was continuing to provoke architects into original compositions; it seems possible that it was, in fact, the only element of the whole design to which they came afresh each time.

In addition to these newly-designed hybrids there were a number of alterations to existing classical-Georgian houses in the new Tudor-gothic style. There are two interesting examples of these from the late 1830s. In 1838 William Parsons made an expensive (£2,503) remodelling of a three-bay classical-Georgian rectory of 1816 at Aylestone in Nottinghamshire.[106] Parsons had tried the Tudor-gothic style recently at Thurmaston where he had had to struggle to persuade the bishop to agree to a more expensive house than the latter had originally seen fit.[107] His enthusiasm had clearly not been dimmed by the incident, and at Aylestone he planned to remove an office wing which had predated the rectory itself by 28 years and build a grand new staircase hall which would lead on one side to a dining room and on the other to a large range of new offices. Above, Parsons added 12 new bedrooms to the existing three, which received dressing rooms. The style and some of the planning seem to have been derived from Wilkins' Trinity College building: there is here too an open arcade with pointed arches, and there is that solecistic staircase within a bay window. These new forms and the detailing – quatrefoil panels, big diamond-shaped lights in the gables, decorative hood-moulds and broad haunches at the bases of the gables – all happily ignore the style of the adjoining older fabric, and dominate the appearance of the house from the outside, in spite of the fact that in practical terms the new building was itself intended to be merely a subsidiary wing of the old. In some cases the rest of a house, or at any rate the front of it, was in fact refaced to match the new wing: William Moffat did this in 1841 at Teffont Evias, in an effective remodelling of the existing rectory (fig. 2.58).[108]

The following year saw an early work by Benjamin Ferrey who had trained as a draughtsman in the office of A. C. Pugin: he put his skills to work in the remodelling of the rectory at Compton Valence in Dorset. The old house here was a sober L-shaped building decorated externally with thin pilasters and with sash windows set within bays of

blind arches. Ferrey transformed the plan by adding rooms on three
sides: a large reception room with a bay window at the junction end of
the old L, a lobby and porch along the front, and a large office room off
the kitchen. The new crudely Tudor work sits alongside the old house,
an effect which seems to us today to have something of the engaging
picturesque falsification of a George Devey about it (fig. 2.59).[109]

Evidently some found the handling of the new styles difficult. The
great Charles Cockerell, eventually 'the most fastidious and the least
pedantic of English neo-classical architects' as Colvin has called him,
had a go in 1832, with a peculiarly untalented design for a parsonage
on the back-corridor plan at Enstone in Oxfordshire (fig. 2.60).[110]
With a low central gable like a pediment, and with a continuous string-
course above the upper-floor windows perhaps imitating the lower
level of a frieze, it was perhaps here that the future architect of so
many distinguished monuments in London, Oxford and Cambridge
resolved to become, in the main, a neo-classical architect; nevertheless,
his Seckford Hospital almshouses in Woodbridge, Suffolk, were
designed soon afterwards in an idiosyncratic Elizabethanesque style
and were a great deal more successful.

The 1830s: How easy it is to be pleased

For some, the style was an opportunity to try something entirely new – for the details of the Tudor-gothic style were so little known among the public at large that it was possible to get away with a great deal of originality. It is these houses, designed by minor architects who are little commemorated, which often come as the greatest surprise. In the early days, the fascination lies perhaps in the wilder gothick fantasies, such as the large vicarage and school at Stottesden in Shropshire, by a London architect called Robert Wallace for the Hon. Robert Plunket: it had a pompous entrance front like the west porch of a church (fig. 2.61).[111] Even when Wallace had calmed down a little, he still produced enjoyable original work: a later parsonage can be seen at Stourmouth, in East Kent (fig. 2.62).[112] The prolific Portsmouth architect Thomas E. Owen, little known outside his home town, designed in 1828 and early in his career a splendid castellated house for a curate at Bembridge on the Isle of Wight with an octagonal library that projects forward in front of the porch.[113] Robert Parris, whom we have seen at Rockland St Peter, designed in 1839 a wonderfully lively rectory for Attleborough in Norfolk, with very fancy Tudor-gothic pinnacles, gables, buttresses, string courses, and castellations.[114]

But in some cases the fun and the mystery is in quieter, minor work, made from simple materials and with low budgets, which all speak of the puzzlement and change of the era. They also very probably show the effects of having read Loudon and possibly Britton, and yet still being unable to make aesthetic sense of either. John Watson, who worked from Manchester Street in London and who is probably best known for his terraces of houses in the Paddington area, built in 1831–2 a vicarage at Norton, now on the borders of Letchworth

2.59
Benjamin Ferrey added a new central bay with a front door to the rectory at Compton Valence, west of Dorchester in Dorset, in 1839: there is no attempt at marrying the new Tudor-gothic work to the style of the earlier house [*Wiltshire & Swindon Record Office, D1/11/77*].

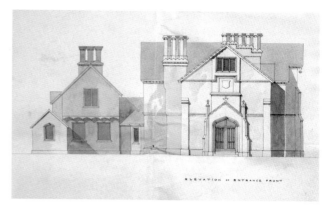

in Hertfordshire (fig. 2.63).[115] At first sight the house appears to be a two-storey, three-bay Georgian house, but the right-hand bay has been brought forward and given a shallow balustraded gable top with a brickwork pattern to it suggesting machicolation. A projecting porch has a pointed opening and a similar gabled top to it, but the chimney at the centre of the house has a monumental termination in the form of an arch linking two stacks. The only other decoration on this plain, grey-brick box is a diamond-shaped plaque on the front facade with a quatrefoil and the date on it. The house seems especially important because Watson's later parsonages were much more conventional: it tells a great deal about the interests and worries of its precise period. It is houses like this, stylistically unplaceable, somewhere between the old and the new, houses that sometimes seem to be in the middle of a transformation between two styles, that have a special fascination; they have never been properly recognised or recorded; and they are entirely English. In a way they have an engaging and sympathetic character which might be compared to that of the transsexual, moving silently between one form and another quite different one, with all the implications that carries for the well-worn debate about the femininity of classical architecture and the masculinity of high Victorian gothic. The fact that the famous Chevalier D'Eon, who was thought to be a woman dressed as a man dressed as a woman, but who was actually a man dressed as a woman dressed as a man, and who gave fencing lessons dressed in a skirt, was so popular a figure amongst London's Bohemians just before this period somehow nicely represents the character of the confusion.[116]

2.60 (above, left)
A design by Charles Cockerell, no less, at Enstone near Chipping Norton, Oxfordshire in 1832. A 'plain building' according to Robert Gardner's *History, gazetteer & directory for Oxfordshire*, 1852, which found the rectorial barn more interesting [*Oxford Record Office, MS. Oxf. dioc. papers b.103/2b*].

2.61 (above)
Robert Wallace's magnificent design for Stottesden, south Shropshire, of 1835: a gothic porch below a somewhat classical central bay. The block to the left is, interestingly, a prominent kitchen [*Herefordshire Record Office, HD8/10 1834-5*].

2.62 (opposite)
Stourmouth rectory, east Kent, by Wallace (1840): a large house, but a comparatively sober design for its architect.

2.63 (above)
The remarkable vicarage at Norton, now on the outskirts of Letchworth Garden City, Hertfordshire. John Watson's design of 1831 exemplifies an architecture in transition as designers struggled to resolve gothic ambitions with classical-Georgian traditions.

2.64 (left)
The massive chimneys at Norton: neither gothic nor classical-Georgian.

2.65

Shinfield vicarage, south of Reading, Berkshire, 1847, by Mallinson and Healey. This is very late for a Tudor-gothic central-corridor house, and the combination of this with sophisticated mid-century draughtsmanship seems surprising, but the partnership was also producing true gothic houses at this time. It is therefore more likely by chance than by foresight that this building seems to look forward to the relaxed styles of the later century. The house survives but sadly the roof and gables have gone [*Oxfordshire Record Office, MS. Oxf. dioc. papers b.108/3*].

As with the classical-Georgian types, architects could be found persisting with these Tudor-gothic designs well after the rest of the profession had moved on, although the detailing is generally more relaxed and the building's emphasis more horizontal, a harbinger of end of century free-style revivals. This is true of houses such as that by Mallinson and Healey at Shinfield in 1847 (fig. 2.65), and of a parsonage by a Buckingham builder called Edward Freeman at Turweston, of 1848, both in the Oxford diocesan archives; and even more so of another at New Radnor, by Thomas Nicholson of Hereford as late – or should one say as early? – as 1851.[117]

How much did this new generation of houses owe to Loudon, and how satisfied could he have been with the results in the busy building years following the publication of the *Encyclopaedia*? The debt was substantial, but the great man could hardly have been satisfied with what he saw. Very few of the houses have the internal fireplaces and the compact rectangular plan he espoused; and only the largest have the variety of well-ventilated, naturally lit and efficiently planned spaces in the kitchen offices which he believed should be within the reach of every householder. I found no examples of 'an economical staircase' – economical, that is, in space – such as he suggested.[118] By avoiding making a dogmatic stylistic intervention in the debate on modern domestic architecture, Loudon had actually achieved something else: a far greater awareness of the architectural

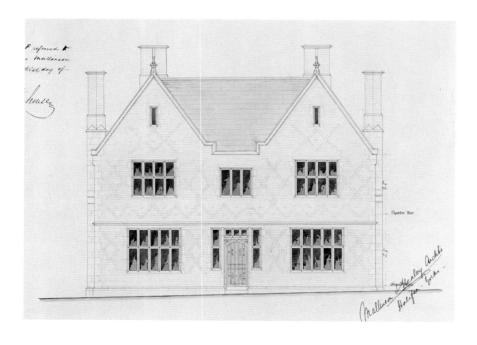

significance of the practical issues involved. The result was for the time being stylistic mayhem; but the new way in which the traditional layouts were now merged with elevations that suited and expressed them was a sign of the impact he was making.

At all events, a parishioner could no longer guess the eventual appearance of the new house under construction on the glebe. Throughout the 1830s many new parsonages went up, and it appears that just as many of them, or more, were in the Tudor-gothic style than in the classical-Georgian. Indeed, the whole story of the Tudor-gothic revival is told over these ten years, from the tidy and thoughtful house that Rose built at Hadleigh in 1831, to the extrovert display at Attleborough at the end of the decade. The blustering, crude character of the blocky massing, the convivial but clumsy detailing, and the unflattering and now peeling waistbands of cement mouldings has meant that this architecture, which should be especially associated with the reign of King William IV, has not aged particularly well and has been all but forgotten as a result of the radical changes of the decades that followed. Osbert Lancaster unforgettably but unfairly wrote of these houses that 'out of this innocuous and rather charming chrysalis would one day come blundering the humourless moth of Victorian revivalism' (fig. 2.66).[119] In fact, there was no connection between this romantic and picturesque Tudor gothic and what happened next: a complete overthrow of every conventional idea about architecture.

2.66
Osbert Lancaster's 'gothick': an 'innocuous and rather charming chrysalis'. *Pillar to post* (1938), page 51.

Chapter Three

The cusp: A peculiar character

The influence of Augustus Welby Northmore Pugin on English architecture from the late 1830s onwards has been so vast that it often appears that architectural historians have had difficulty in doing it justice. A rare exception comes from Andrew Saint: 'His true pupils', he has written, 'were the whole rising generation of English architects'.[1] And yet his influence came much quicker than is often thought, and was not limited to the gothic revivalists, or to his admirers late in the nineteenth century. Traditionally described as an eccentric obsessive, a driven visionary, and an ornamental designer of unusual talent, Pugin's reputation in architectural history has, ironically, been unsuitably served by those who present him primarily in sympathetic biographical terms: his own personality was so full of fascinating contradictions that the original, substantial nature of his achievement has been obscured. Most importantly, he must be seen in the context of the buildings he designed – the ones he really designed, not the many that are wrongly attributed to him – and, furthermore, those buildings must be compared with the conventional ones of his period. In the early 1840s he fed into the confused professional world of the early Victorian architect a whole series of coherent ideas, theoretical, practical, and visual. And as a result, by the end of his life in 1852, the picture described in the opening chapters of this book had changed altogether; for the ways in which the English parsonage is transformed across our period are precisely those which Pugin himself had introduced or suggested.[2] It is not merely the stylistically authentic Victorian church that owes its existence to him, nor even the rich free gothic styles and forms of the later gothic revival: it was the detached small family house that had no consciously applied historical style or inherited layout, but rather had been designed anew to reflect the period in which it was built. It was the first time that this had happened in English architecture since the late middle ages.

The extent to which Pugin is a problematic figure is reflected by the difficulty that even his champions have had in promoting him since his revival by Nikolaus Pevsner and his pupil Phoebe Stanton in the mid twentieth century. In 1943 Pevsner published an article in the *Architectural review* called 'a short Pugin florilegium' which promoted its subject as a functionalist.[3] Pugin had indeed determined, in 1841, that '*there should be no features about a building which are not necessary for convenience, construction, or propriety*' (fig. 3.2), and, furthermore,

3.1
Rampisham rectory from the south-west. Pugin's adherence to his 'true principles', a method described today as 'realism', did not generally result in pretty elevations, but this house is an exception. It survives almost exactly as the architect designed it.

3.2
The opening page of Pugin's
The true principles (1841).

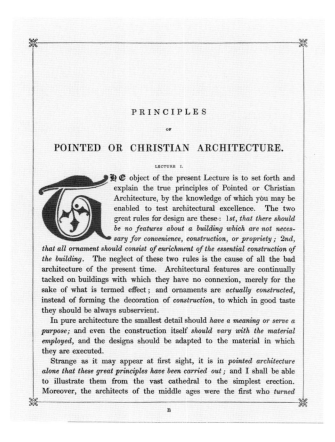

that 'the smallest detail should *have a meaning or serve a purpose*'.[4]
In *An apology for the revival of Christian architecture*, he rejected
historical copyism as 'absurd', and called for buildings to be designed
'in accordance with their actual purposes'.[5] And yet this was a man
who made many thousands of designs for historicising ornament and
mediaeval-style craftsmanship, in itself an activity quite unequalled
amongst English designers, and who covered most of the Palace of
Westminster with it – an activity so entirely removed from his
'functionalism' that it had to be marginalised into five short pages in
Stanton's *Pugin* of 1971 where it sat with the decorative schemes for
what she called 'rich men's houses' and was well separated from the
greater part of his architectural career.[6] There was, conversely,
a fashion a few years ago of presenting Pugin as a highly talented
designer of gold and silver ornaments, of glass, of fabrics, papers, tiles,
clothes, books and furniture, who happened also to be the designer of
some rather disappointing buildings which have neither the charm of
the Tudor gothic, nor the panache, nor the budget, of the high gothic
revival.[7] And then there is a recently revived idea from the 1930s,

which corresponds to the current fashion for seeing architectural terms as if they were a branch of literature, according to which Pugin the thinker and letter-writer seized upon the spirit of his time and uncontrollably expressed its romantic longings with towers and stained glass, a character quite unrecognisable from the proto-modernist of Pevsner and Stanton.

The only way to deal adequately, in so far as one can, with Pugin's work as an architect is to go back and look at the facts of his career, which as it happens is at its most original and remarkable in the field of ecclesiastical residences, large and small. In the first place, he overcame one of the basic impediments of Tudor-gothic architecture – the failure to look at and accurately record English mediaeval architecture. As a teenager he accompanied and assisted his father, A. C. Pugin, on drawing expeditions. We know for sure that he was an accurate draughtsman of real and imagined historical artifacts of astonishing ability, and with little or no parallel in English artistic history in terms of the extent of his output. Working without a break, from home or whilst travelling, he drew many thousands of details of buildings that he had seen, and he evidently had a phenomenal ability to recall them. When allied to the vigour with which he pursued the realisation of these decorative designs with the innovative craftsmen and manufacturers of his day, this accomplishment alone must surely be one of the principal reasons for the success of the gothic revival, because the coming generation of designers, in particular William Butterfield, made full use of them.[8] Until the mid 1840s, the English Tudor-gothic designer had a repertoire of perhaps 20 lame patterns, loosely based on mediaeval tracery; now he had more than he could conceivably use in a working lifetime, even if he chose a different one each day. Pugin's output as an architect working almost entirely on his own was immense; his total list of residential schemes, large or small, realised or not, amounts to over 80.[9] That is in addition to his well-known ecclesiastical architecture, his work for the Palace of Westminster which was continuous from 1844 almost until his death in 1852, and his writing, which together occupied every moment of his day from the early morning until the late evening.[10] He designed only two Anglican parsonage houses, but these form part of a set of six similar designs for small family houses which together were to have tremendous impact on English architecture; and he designed eight new Roman Catholic presbyteries, a new building type of his day, and a further two large clergy houses similar in scope to Anglican bishops' palaces. All this made him a highly prolific designer of priests' and parsons' houses in the 1840s, an important fact for our survey.

But in addition to his proficiency as a designer of ecclesiastical residences Pugin plays a pivotal role in the story of the English parsonage because in every respect he did things differently from his immediate contemporaries. His layouts were new; his choice of style and his attitude to Englishness was different; the scope of the architectural language he used was distinct and was applied to every detail of a house; and the way in which he set his houses into their landscape was different too. We have ahead of us the complex task of seeing how exactly these innovations spread across the country, and transformed the parsonage; but in order to do that we need to see in what way exactly Pugin designed houses that were entirely different from those he found all going up around the country as he started work.

That said, this study of Pugin does need to include some reference to the theoretical concepts with which he described his work, even if only to see how parsonage architects who read about him and his ideas might find concepts there that they would relate to and be interested in. His writing from 1836 onwards attracted wide attention well before his buildings did. His original use of these concepts is in itself interesting, and provides a commentary on how others of his period were preoccupied with similar ideas, and how they differed from him. Furthermore, it often seems that his success in altering the course of the development of English domestic architecture was, paradoxically, at first as much to do with the language he borrowed in order to present it as to do with the actual form of his buildings themselves. His new churches attracted attention; his houses, for the most part, did not. Hearing an appealing use of words and ideas, critics and potential clients may choose, as they have always done, an architect regardless of what his actual buildings look like. And it should always be remembered that Sir George Gilbert Scott, probably the most influential of Pugin's progeny, was converted to gothic architecture on reading Pugin's writings, rather than actually seeing a Pugin building.[11] In fact, much of Pugin's published technical theory and his various exhortations for reforming the way of building were not original, even if he expressed them in an engagingly novel and lively way; but in the end it was his consistency in applying them in his executed designs for houses that brought about the transformation in domestic architecture that faced the parsonage builders of the 1840s.

The beautiful and the true

Pugin's *The true principles* of 1841 famously ends with the cry 'Let then the Beautiful and the True be our watchword'.[12] The use of the word 'truth' and praise in terms of 'honesty' to justify architectural expression had evolved throughout the eighteenth century: although 'truth' has been traditionally considered more significant to Continental than to English theory, its appearance in contemporary English sources shows that by Pugin's time it had already become an established, if inconsistent, concept in architectural circles.[13] As early as 1821 Francis Palgrave had written in the *Quarterly review* that 'from architecture, the earth derives its moral physiognomy' perhaps meaning not only that architecture expresses morality, but referring to the truthfulness with which that form expresses the actual geological nature of the earth itself; and in Willson's letterpress accompanying the first volume of A. C. Pugin's *Examples* in 1831, the specimens represented in the plates are likened to 'collections of personal memoirs, original letters, wills, or other documents of genuine history; whilst books of modern architectural designs rather resemble fictitious narrative, or historical romances'.[14] Many architects must have become familiar with these concepts.

In introducing his technical manual of 1840 called *Specifications*, written at the time when Pugin had already launched his lecturing career as 'professor of ecclesiastical antiquities' at St Mary's College, Oscott, the architect and Hebrew scholar Alfred Bartholomew found specific biblical authority for the language of these moral arguments about architectural integrity and reproduced God's own awful warning to stuccoers in the original language. The translation familiar to his contemporaries reads 'One built a wall, and, lo, others daubed it with untempered morter' – an announcement explained, to those who looked it up in the book of Ezekiel, by its continuation: 'Say unto them which daub it with untempered morter, that it shall fall' (fig. 3.3).[15] 'Low, very low, is the abasement which the extensive use of external stucco has brought upon English architecture', Bartholomew added later; for he attributed excellence in architecture to purity of structure,

3.3
The opening epigrams from
Part 1 of Alfred Bartholomew's
Specifications (1840).
The Hebrew is translated by
the Authorised Version as
'One built a wall, and, lo, others
daubed it with untempered
morter' (*Ezekiel*, chapter 13,
verse 10).

PART I.

AN ESSAY ON THE DECLINE OF
EXCELLENCE IN THE STRUCTURE AND IN THE SCIENCE OF MODERN ENGLISH BUILDINGS ;
WITH THE PROPOSAL OF REMEDIES FOR THOSE DEFECTS.

" What" " Bath will become in a few years" " may be easily conceived." "These new mansions" are "built so slight, with the soft crumbling stone found in this neighbourhood, that I should never sleep quietly in one of them, when it blowed (as the sailors say) a cap full of wind : and I am persuaded, that my hind Roger Williams, or any man of equal strength, would be able to push his foot through the strongest part of their walls, without any great exertion of his muscles."—HUMPHREY CLINKER.

" Benche alcuni Architettori in diuersi luoghi d'Italia han fatte alcune fabriche di muro semplice, lasciandoui i luoghi delle pietre uiue, & da lì ad un tempo, poi ci han posto li suoi ornamenti : tuttauia per non esser tai cose ben legate ne' muri: ma quasi attacate con la colla; si uede in molti luoghi esser caduti de' pezzi, & ogni giorno minacciar ruina."—SERLIO, lib. iv. cap. 9.

והוא בנה חיץ והנם טחים אתו תפל
EZEKIEL, cap. xiii. ver. 10.

and stucco, notoriously, had been used to cover up jerrybuilding.[16] Indeed, the essence of his writing was the expression of the structural truth of a building in its form and method of construction. In revering Christopher Wren for the structural solution of the dome of St Paul's cathedral – 'Wren had more science in his head and heart, than a thousand Sir John Soanes in their whole souls and bodies'– he illustrated that he believed that a structural frame did not necessarily have to be visible, but it had to provide the governing principle.[17] He quoted with approval the Scots scientist John Robison: "the structure of a roof may therefore be exhibited with propriety, and made an ornamental feature...the roof is in fact the part of the building which requires the greatest degree of skill, and where science will be of more service than any other part" (fig. 3.4).[18]

This visible, structural purity is for Bartholomew the great advantage of gothic architecture: 'In Pointed Architecture, all is structural'.[19] Hiding the necessary parts of a modern building is an unnecessary dishonesty; of chimneys he wrote that 'All that expense which is frequently so absurdly, and with such ill-success, expended in the concealment of chimney-shafts, should be rather used in ornamenting, and in rendering agreeable, members so necessary to the comfort of domestic buildings'.[20] In his attitude to 'truth', Bartholomew provides us with a very clear example of how a general idea was beginning to claim for itself a series of particular scientific and rational definitions.

3.4
Part of a lesson in the value
of structural purity from
Bartholomew: *Specifications*,
chapters 66-7.

CHAPTER LXVII.

great trusses being required above the attic for the support of the roof, or for the binding together of the edifice, the covering of the building may be made in several small spans, supported from the great trusses below, not indeed rising higher than if there were windows in the frieze, and not appearing to crush the building with an overwhelming weight.

He who is weak enough to deform his buildings under any pretence whatsoever, with windows in their friezes, must, whatever be his ability, prepare himself for the repute of possessing bad taste, mean judgment, and want of ingenuity.

A. Best Chamber, &c.
B. Great Trusses.
C. Attic Story.
D. Low Roof over the Attic Story.
E. Frieze of the External Entablature.
F. Attic Windows.
G. Windows behind a Blocking-course.

Loudon had already been here. In 1806 he had written with his engagingly catholic approach to architectural styles not only that 'the principles of good taste...are always in unison with those of good morality' but had also made an explicit link between 'truth' and architectural design.[21] In the course of a discussion of his principles, he remarked that 'the opposite of symmetry is disparity or disproportion; which being inconsistent with use, fitness or truth, is always displeasing in the extreme'.[22] By the 1830s he had himself become more specific: astonishingly so, for the subject that inspired him was, of all things, the practice by architects of building technically redundant drip moulds above the windows of their gothic elevations where the depth of the mullions or eaves already provides sufficient shelter. He was moved to mention this untruthful practice twice in his *Encyclopaedia*.[23] The source he gave there for his choice of the word 'truth' was an unexpected one to anyone who had forgotten that Loudon was an agriculturist at heart: the *Epistle to Lord Lowther On Building and Planting*, for which he gave the date as 1776 – '"From truth and use all beauties flow"'.[24] Elsewhere he made general references to the 'honest' use of ornament: 'when a house is so small that it cannot be reasonably supposed to possess such appendages as a chapel and a dining-hall, it becomes a piece of contemptible affectation to finish its exterior with members which are naturally applicable to those appendages alone; and the only cause, therefore, which good taste can sanction in such a case, is, to treat the subject as what it *is*; writing an honest and obvious character with correct detail, and as much of the picturesque as circumstances will permit'.[25] Bartholomew's *Specifications* transformed these incidental observations into an architectural system, one that enlisted the precedent of gothic architecture, but which fell short of proposing any particular style.[26] Indeed, Bartholomew's avoidance not only of promoting a style but even discussing any of them in the ruminative philosophical terms of earlier decades was itself an important step towards accepting the influences of building method over a building's appearance.

From corruption to redemption

The Tudor-gothic styles of the fashionable housebuilders of the 1830s did not impress scientific writers like Bartholomew any more than their closely-related classical–Georgian predecessors had done. It was not until methods of professional practice changed, and proprietary technological improvements required a certain definite standard of specification and construction or installation, that new and more exacting building processes became commonplace. There was, for the time being, insufficient incentive for the architect to think through the structural and constructional implications of his design and its details. As Tudor-gothic houses spread across the country, however, their technical imperfections became better known, and by the end of the 1830s and the beginning of the next decade there is evidence of impatience with them. At the same time the style was increasingly decried by some architectural theorists for its impurity – and indeed for its pragmatic, compromising 'Englishness', the common basis for all styles from the Tudor through to the Jacobean. By 1843 the encyclopaedist Joseph Gwilt particularly disliked the Elizabethan style now popular for country houses; it contained, he wrote, an 'imperfectly understood adaptation of classic forms to the habits of its day in this country...[and it was] full of redundant and un-nerving ornament'; although, as far as its Englishness was concerned, 'Neither... are the English, as a people, susceptible of high feeling in respect of the production of art'.[27] For Bartholomew, it was a style 'founded in ignorance and corruption'.[28] Both critics were rallying against the widespread desire amongst house builders to amalgamate the comforts of modern living with the reassuring imagery of traditional English architecture which the Elizabethan style offered; it was only when popular attitudes to gothic architecture changed that their voices started to be heard.

At the Geffrye Museum in London there is a pair of Ackermann chromolithographed prints by John Absolon of 1840 entitled 'Marriage' and 'Single' (fig. 3.5). The latter shows a bachelor idling his time in agitated, fruitless fashion beside a fireplace in a windowless room. 'Marriage', however, shows the happiness of a young couple in a cheerful sitting room lit by a window which shows the spire of the mediaeval gothic church in the background. The conviviality of the grand Elizabethan style was almost impossible to portray at the scale of a small private house, so the artist decided to juxtapose the ancient in the form of a church and the new of the domestic interior to achieve a similar effect. In doing so, he was illustrating an idea which had already surfaced in the work of writers. The early novels of Charles Dickens, appearing at this time, and reaching a huge popular audience, include several significant uses of these images. The final chapter of *Oliver Twist* (completed in 1839) opens with the marriage of Rose Fleming and Harry Maylie 'in the village church which was

3.5
A pair of chromolithographed prints entitled 'Single' and Married', by John Absolon, published by Ackermann & Co in London in 1840. A distant view of a church, here seen through the window of the happy pair in 'Married', was at this period a convenient motif to express the reassuring and respectable qualities of traditional English architecture [*Geffrye Museum*].

henceforth to be the scene of the young clergyman's labours; on the same day they entered into possession of their new and happy home'; and Mr Brownlow, having adopted Oliver as his son, removes 'with him and the old housekeeper to within a mile of the parsonage-house, where his dear friend resided', thus gratifying 'the only remaining wish of Oliver's warm and earnest heart'.[29] *Nicholas Nickleby* (1839) is illustrated, by Phiz (Hablot K. Browne), with a scene of children playing in a churchyard, the church's old tower visible in the distance and apparently located at the centre of the final homes of all the novel's heroes (fig. 3.6).[30] And the penultimate chapter of the highly didactic *The old curiosity shop* (1841) describes not only the death of Nell's father upon her gravestone but also the fondness of the heroic old school-master for dwelling 'in the old churchyard' (the vile Quilp, the city dweller, was by comparison 'buried with a stake at his heart at the centre of four lonely roads').[31] In earlier nineteenth-century literature there had more commonly been an alliance between gothic architecture and gothic horror rather than a happy end for the spotless protagonists of an improving novel.[32] One is impressed by a feeling at around 1840 that the gothic church and the churchyard have been converted into images of comfort and decency, ones that are simpler, and purer, than the grand Elizabethan manner. The idea that the parson's house might be consistent with the style of the church is one matter arising here; it is another, and it is a new one, to suggest that the style itself bestows some kind of propriety on its inmates.

3.6
The rural idyll – again dominated by an old church tower – that closes Dickens' *Nicholas Nickleby* (1838-9). Drawn by Phiz (Hablot K. Browne).

The children at their cousin's grave

The coup de foudre

It seems likely therefore that at this time it was not only Pugin's theoretical emphasis on moral and religious rectitude (in his *Contrasts*) and structural integrity (in *The true principles*) that made him so attractive a figure. Others were discussing these issues too. But neither Bartholomew, nor Gwilt, nor any of the other writers who deployed these terms was a talented designer who could illustrate in practice, often with very small budgets, what sort of architecture might result from them. Pugin was different: he drew and designed incessantly; since he had been a child he had filled sketchbooks with imaginary views of palaces, cathedrals, castles and manor houses.

In 1833 he designed an imaginary 'Deanery', a scheme that is comparatively well known since in 1951 it provided Phoebe Stanton with the opportunity for a detailed analysis of his skill at the age of 21.[33] The house was set in the close at Salisbury, immediately to the west of the cathedral, and was supposed to have been built in 1471: the architecture of the building indicates Pugin's fluency in the appropriate English style (fig. 3.7). The plan is based around a corridor that takes the form of a T: the great hall is above the horizontal bar of the T, and this latter thus also acts as a screens passage (fig. 3.8). Some interiors were drawn in great detail; their main features were oriel windows and fireplaces. The kitchen, located between the great hall and the octagonal stair turret, took an English, medieval, form derived from the abbot's kitchen at Glastonbury.[34] Sleeping chambers are arranged either side of the corridor leading away from the screens; the dean has

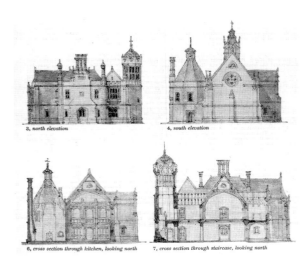

3, north elevation   4, south elevation

6, cross section through kitchen, looking north   7, cross section through staircase, looking north

3.7
A.W.N. Pugin's 'Deanery'.
Elevations from Phoebe
Stanton's 'Pugin at twenty-
one', *Architectural review*,
September 1951 (page 188).

his rooms above, although no first-floor plan was provided. No house Pugin had actually seen would have looked or been planned like this.

Two years later he had designed his own house, St Marie's Grange, at Alderbury on the Southampton road out of Salisbury, and there he had devised a house consisting on its principal floor of three inter-connecting rooms arranged in the form of an 'L': a parlour, a library and a chapel (fig. 3.9). The spiral staircase which linked the three floors was attached to the parlour, and there was no corridor, so to reach the chapel one had to walk through both the other two rooms. Although built on an open site alongside a river, with the potential for views north to the cathedral and town, Pugin designed the house in a remarkably introspective way with small windows facing the landscape. The best view, in fact, would have been from the water closet in a tower on the south side. In many ways this strange house is an architect's typical first home for himself, for it incorporates many strong ideas in their most literal way. The sequence of interconnecting rooms, each one giving way to another and having a different character, was very probably derived from the suite in which Amy Robsart is kept hidden at Cumnor Place, in Walter Scott's *Kenilworth* (1821), a story which

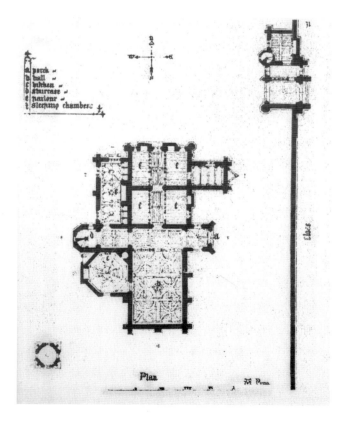

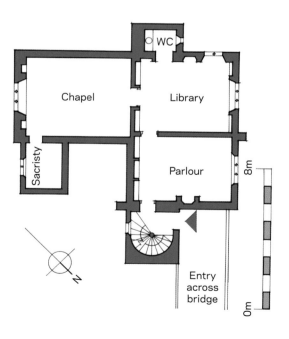

Pugin knew well, not least because of his having designed scenes for a ballet based on it in 1831.[35] Amy's rooms were quite claustrophobic in character, with no suggestion in Scott's description of them of any outside prospect; and the way in which one room is placed beyond the next gives, in the novel, an effective impression of a trapped human being whose choices are limited to variations in interior decoration. A second and more exotic influence was telescoped by Pugin down from the scale of castles and monasteries to that of a small private house. St Marie's Grange was entered through a drawbridge placed right up alongside the Salisbury road and which led directly to the stair tower: he seems to have copied this from a plate in one of his favourite books, his father's copy of the first volume of Charles Nodier's *Voyages romantiques et pittoresques dans l'ancienne France*, of 1820, which described in passionate and romantic language the surviving remains of mediaeval Normandy (figs 3.10, 3.11).[36] It is very likely that he was also influenced by other plates in the book. Several of Nodier's illustrations show scenes set in front of proscenium-like arches, such as one of the church at Caudebec-en-Caux, and another amongst the ruins of the abbey at Jumièges. Pugin copied the effect on a tiny scale in his own house by emphasising the openings between rooms, clearly illustrated by his sketch for his chapel, seen from the library.[37] Indeed, like much else that Pugin designed, the Alderbury house in its original form had

3.10
Pugin's watercolour of St Marie's Grange (c1835) as seen from the Salisbury road: entry was across a bridge to a door at the foot of the tower. This was the appearance of the house during his own residence there [*RIBA Library Drawings Collection, AWN Pugin V2/ 106B*].

A view of Chateau d'Harcourt at Lillebonne in Normandy from Charles Nodier's *Voyages romantiques et pittoresques dans l'ancienne France* (plate 32). The young Pugin participated in a surveying trip to Normandy like the one illustrated here, and he borrowed the idea of the narrow bridge for his own first house at Alderbury.

the same exaggeratedly vertical proportions that Nodier's illustrators had tended to emphasise in their work. He had accompanied his father on the trip to illustrate Britton's *Architectural antiquities of Normandy* in the early 1820s, and the combination of that visit with Nodier's romanticising plates had surely made a deep impression on him. The results at St Marie's Grange were so unconventional that Pugin soon left – it seems likely that his young wife found it inconvenient if not unhealthy – and indeed he was required to remodel it in 1841 when he came to sell it. What exactly he did to it then is unclear, because a further remodelling of the later mid-nineteenth century has largely obscured his alterations, but it seems likely that he built a stair hall in the crook of the 'L', thus solving at once the intercommunication problems.[38]

It was very soon after he had left the house for Chelsea that he designed his first presbyteries, in 1837 and 1838, not long after the publication of his famous *Contrasts*. Interestingly the commissions arrived just as he started his career as a country house architect, which began with an invitation to design substantial additions to the mediaeval hall at Scarisbrick in Lancashire (fig. 3.12). Here he had recently replaced Thomas Rickman and John Slater as architect for Charles Scarisbrick, a rich and reclusive collector of ecclesiastical and other mediaeval antiquities, and his style there was not dissimilar to the Tudor-gothic of many of his contemporaries – even if his draughtsmanship was undoubtedly a good deal better.

When designing to a small budget, however, Pugin was required to aim for a more simple kind of architecture. No doubt his first commission for a Roman Catholic presbytery, at Derby in 1837, brought him fast back to earth. His house was to stand immediately east of the new church of St Mary that he had designed at Bridge Gate, facing St Alkmund's Anglican church and just north of the city centre. St Alkmund's was itself about to be rebuilt by H. I. Stevens in a most unhistorical Tudor-gothic style; Pugin's St Mary's, on the other hand, designed together with his presbytery, was a convincingly authentic exercise in 'Perpendicular': a sensitive Anglican critic thought it was 'almost painfully beautiful' by comparison with Derby's other modern churches, the pain being that it was Roman Catholic, and not Anglican.[39] It is very probably the building that first established Pugin's reputation: after seeing the church as it went up, Wiseman described him as 'an architect of acknowledged merit', although by then he had in fact designed very little.

The church was oriented north-south with its 'west' porch at the southern end on Bridge Gate, and Pugin was apparently commissioned to design a pair of houses that would flank it along the street. To the left there was to be a large and richly ornamented but otherwise simple house, the purpose of which was always unclear, and which was essentially a central-corridor plan type consisting of a pair of major

rooms only on each floor. It was never built.[40] To the right, the east,
Pugin was to design his first presbytery, and on a budget that evidently
allowed for nothing more than a cheap brick finish and minimal
decoration. Indeed, it seems that even this modest house took some
time to materialise, because Pugin's builder, George Myers, was being
asked as late as 1839 to adapt an adjacent existing building for the
priest's use.[41]

The site for the house was extremely awkward – a narrow strip
of land scarcely 20 feet wide to the east of the church, which widened
to about 40 feet on a line approximately level with the second bay
of the nave. A conventional architect would have placed a central
or L-corridor house either at the very southern end of the site,

or alternatively back where the plot widened: in the former case it would have faced the street, like any generous double-fronted town house; and in the latter case it would have been protected from the noise of the street and have enjoyed a secluded garden front. Pugin chose neither of these obvious solutions. He extended the porch that emerged from the church's south-eastern corner into a winding corridor that reached the eastern edge of the site before turning south to reach Bridge Gate. In the crook of this L-shaped corridor he placed a parlour, a stair hall some ten feet square, and, at the street end of the corridor, a dining room. Beyond the corridor to the north he placed a study, and, as the plot widened, a kitchen and scullery (fig. 3.14).

The unusual nature of this layout cannot be stressed too much. In contrast to the plan of St Marie's Grange there was now at least twice as much circulation space than there would have been in a conventional house. The parlour window was jammed up against the south-east corner buttress of the church and the study faced towards the chancel,

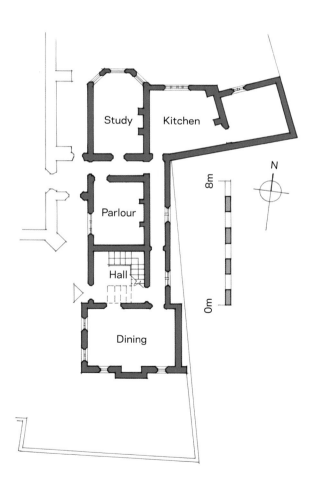

3.14
The ground-floor plan of St Mary's presbytery in Bridge Gate, Derby, apparently as executed and based on Pugin's own plan, now in a private collection. A conventional plan, by contrast, might have placed this house away from the road and in a garden made up from part of the churchyard, probably at its widest point to the east or north. Pugin's drawing was published in the *Architects' journal*, 4 July 1990, page 29.

but no room on the northern side of the house had any access to the adjacent churchyard; the kitchen and the dining room were almost as far apart as it was possible to be; and the dining room, the only part of the house that was easily visible from the street, was designed so that its long side wall, rather than the architecturally more important end wall, faced the street.[42] Nothing about its layout suggests any desire for conformity or indeed convenience. This odd building has long disappeared but there are perspective drawings and at least one good clear photograph – a luxury for those who search for records of Pugin's demolished presbyteries – and we can see that the whole of the house was faced in cheap brick with minimal stone dressings (fig. 3.15).[43] He designed a simple ogee moulding at the heads of the windows, and inserted a decorative cartouche into the dining-room chimney that faced the street. Elsewhere he used conventional Tudor-gothic styling, for example building out the dining-room gable that faced the church with broad haunches above the eaves line. One wonders how much exactly he had to do with the actual execution of this building as his diary and correspondence fail to mention it.

Before the 1850s there were no clear instructions as to how Roman Catholic clergy should conduct their households, and there is no record of Pugin receiving detailed programmatic instructions for the clergy houses he built: very few of these houses had been built since the Catholic Relief Act of 1791, an important legal turning point in the history of English architecture.[44] We can assume that those who paid for the buildings, rather than those who were to live in them, determined the architect's brief. In the case of many of Pugin's small presbyteries and other institutions the primary paymaster, or at any rate the major fundraiser, was his patron, the Earl of Shrewsbury; the earl required of his beneficiaries that Pugin got his own way in spite of the fact that at least one, Catherine McAuley of the Order of Mercy, disliked Pugin's buildings and often said so. We can assume that Pugin felt that he was here entering into uncharted territory – there was to be no nursery, no drawing room for the ladies, no extensive kitchen offices to facilitate entertaining – and furthermore grasped the opportunity of designing a house where the activities in it could be subservient to his romantic idea of how the restored Roman Catholic clergy should live.

3.15
A 1942 view of the presbytery from Bridge Gate, Derby, with windows taped as a precaution against blasts. The building was demolished after the Second World War, and parts of it salvaged to create a liturgical south-west porch for the church [*National Monuments Record, A42/875*].

Corridors and cloisters

It is a mistake, though, to think that this romantic idea led to a romantic type of house. What Pugin had done as early as this first presbytery was to turn circulation space from a necessity into a significant part of the design of the house as a whole – and it was exactly this that was to become the basis for the remarkable series of designs for presbyteries and parsonages that followed the house in Derby. He had, it soon emerged, a very small number of distinct architectural ideas, but they were entirely different from convention, and as time went by and he had more opportunities to exercise them, they began to take on a greater degree of sophistication; and it eventually became clear that whether or not he had intended it at the outset – and I would guess that to some extent he was aware of it, however subliminally – these design innovations not only turned out to echo other preoccupations of religious society but also to encourage and develop them. The use of long corridors is one of these.[45]

The evidence is everywhere. An intriguing sketch of the late 1820s, when he was still a teenager, shows a plan of a bedchamber with corridors running along two of its adjacent walls, the two meeting at the landing of a flight of stairs; one of the two corridors terminates in a spiral stair. It is an irrational amount of circulation space to serve a single room, and so both corridor and room must have been conceived of together.[46] Corridors, cloisters and complex junctions at their interstices were always for him the source of much enjoyment. An early imaginary scheme for 'the Hospital of Saynt John', dating from the 'Deanery' year of 1833, included a long covered way which he titled a 'cloister', but which was in fact almost redundant in terms of practical planning.[47] The 'Deanery' itself, as we have seen, had a most unusual circulation pattern; and the plan of St Marie's Grange essentially turned the rooms into sections of corridor. One wonders whether the fact that his patron Shrewsbury lived when in England at Alton Towers at Staffordshire, an enormous house then growing steadily larger on a somewhat organic plan involving lengthy promenades between formal reception rooms, might explain why he never seems to have objected to paying for Pugin's apparently wasteful planning.[48] We shall investigate later to what extent these corridor plans reflected Pugin's deterministic instinct in the design of the functions of his buildings. What is more significant right now, as the very young architect dreaming of turreted palaces is required to design cheap houses for the poor clergy, is what this new approach to circulation space can do for little money. He learned practical lessons from his work at Scarisbrick Hall, where he wrapped corridors and staircases around existing wings, soon discovering the richness of space that could be achieved very cheaply at the junctions between them; with the born architect's grasp of three-dimensional space, he experimented there with bridges and skylights, creating effects – particularly where the first floor corridor leads onto the gallery of the great hall – that have something nautical about them, recalling his own enjoyment of boats and the sea that he recorded in his sketch-books alongside his architectural drawings, if not of stage machinery (fig. 3.13).[49] A simple 90-degree junction between corridors can look impressive if each arm of the corridor is terminated in an arch; the more junctions, and the more arches, the better. The corridors soon develop a distinct architectural language of their own.

His early buildings soon illustrate how these ideas could be realised on a small scale. In 1838 he designed two very modest presbyteries, at Keighley in Yorkshire, alongside his church of St Anne's; and at Uttoxeter in Staffordshire, for his church of St Mary. Both houses have had considerable alterations made, but his drawings survive.[50] At Keighley he came closest to a conventional Tudor-gothic house, with an L-corridor plan and a gable-and-bay entrance elevation with big haunches at the base of the gable. Only the strongly vertical elements, such as the tall 60-degree gable and the attenuated lancet windows, mark these out from the work of the average Tudor-gothic architect. But inside the situation was rather different. The corridor marched back through a proscenium-type gothic arch not to a garden door but to a larder; and the staircase at right angles to it was comparatively broad and imposing relative to the size of the two-reception room house (fig. 3.16).[51] One can see from Pugin's drawing how much importance he gave to this tiny space. There was a large newel post between the flights of stairs. The position of the doors to the parlour and dining room either side of the front door is staggered, which means that to look out into the corridor from either of the two rooms is to be faced by a series of arched openings leading to spaces of different proportions. All these devices are on a tiny scale, and their effect is so small that they were almost negligible in reality; but the drawing unmistakably illustrates Pugin's interest in them.

At Uttoxeter the house is, essentially, a simple although asymmetrical central-corridor one turned on its side – the long axis of the two rooms faces the adjacent church, not the street, like the unexecuted grander house at Derby – but Pugin provided a little gothic corridor which he called a 'cloister' that linked the hall with the church (fig. 3.17). He also devised a back extension that would be reached through the rear of the two main rooms, providing a bedroom off the first floor library, in a device reminiscent of the plan of St Marie's Grange.

As time went by, Pugin organised his original use of circulation space into definable types. His two biggest clergy houses, at Birmingham (designed in 1840) and at Nottingham (probably late 1841) were organised around quadrangles. These were by no means a simple imitation of the circulation of a mediaeval cloister plan. On the very restricted urban site in Bath Street, Birmingham, Pugin designed his Bishop's House around three sides of a courtyard; the fourth side,

3.16 (right)
Even in early and small buildings Pugin exaggerated a theatrical sense of moving through a building by lengthening corridors and views which often terminated in some mundane part of the plan – here, the larder. Keighley presbytery, 1838 [*RIBA Library Drawings Collection, A. W. N. Pugin [73] 2*].

3.17 (below)
Pugin's presbytery at Uttoxeter, Staffordshire: a 'cloister' links a house that has an otherwise unremarkable plan to the architect's St Mary's church immediately to the right. This elevation has been greatly altered [*Research Library, The Getty Research Institute, Los Angeles, California (870366)*].

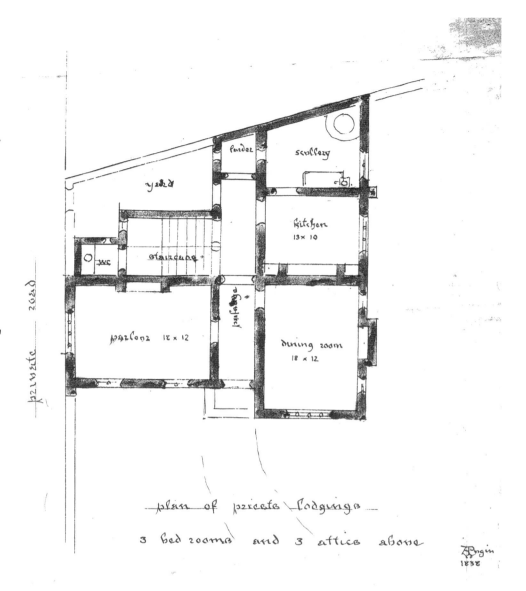

which was the street front, consisted of an enclosed corridor on the ground floor only with the entrance door. As a general form perceived from the street, this house thus resembled a fifteenth or sixteenth-century *hôtel* such as those Pugin saw on his annual sketching tours to northern France and Flanders, and went on drawing for the rest of his life (figs 3.18, 3.19). Those houses would have admitted the visitor directly to the central courtyard, whence he would have made his way directly or almost directly into the main hall. Pugin's Birmingham house did no such thing, even though the great hall was located immediately above right of the entrance door (figs 3.20, 3.21). Here the visitor wound his way up to the left, and then up again to the right, and thence right again into a tightly-wound stair that continued up in a turret to the floor above. Once here, he would continue to wind his way around the edge of the court along a corridor until reaching the great hall at the end of it. In other words, one walked almost as far as it was possible to walk across two storeys, passing the bishop's private and public chambers, and all along a corridor scarcely five feet wide, in order to reach the public room closest to the front door. Anything more different from the centralised, formal axial planning of the bishop's palaces altered and extended for example by Blore in the 1830s,

3.18
The Bishop's House, Bath Street, Birmingham, from the west, photographed in 1958 not long before its demolition [*National Monuments Record, AA58/4257*].

3.19 (above)
The north-eastern front of the Bishop's House. The bishop's private chambers were on the first floor of this side of the building; all visitors to the great hall at the front facing the cathedral were required by the layout of the building to pass his door. The restrained patterning of the brick and the design of the tabernacle with the saint at the far right-hand corner of the building illustrates how effectively Pugin could model simple and cheap materials [*National Monuments Record, AA58/4260*].

3.20 (right)
The Bishop's House, Birmingham: ground and first-floor plans (1840).

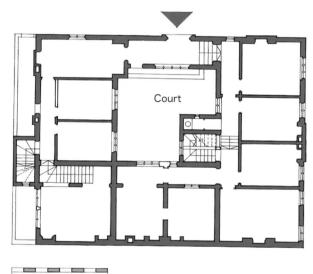

0m   8m

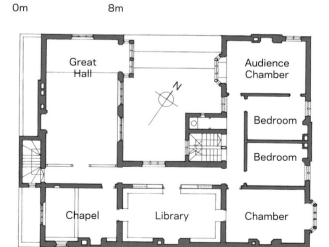

at Lambeth and St Asaph, with their grand central staircases leading directly to large public rooms, can scarcely be imagined. The demolition of this extraordinary building for road widening in 1960 was a scandal; the lessons it could have taught us about the changes in early Victorian architecture must be largely lost, since Pugin, needless to say, seems to have written next to nothing about his ideas for the building.[52]

The plan of his second large clergy house, attached to the southern side of his church of St Barnabas at Nottingham, was a great deal simpler: a corridor continued through the sacristy near the south-east corner of the church and wove its way around three sides of a small internal courtyard (fig. 3.22). In a very rare reference to one of his residential buildings, Pugin defended this house, which had been attacked by the *Ecclesiologist*, in a letter published in the *Tablet*. The *Ecclesiologist*, no doubt looking at the outside of the building rather than appraising its plan, had described it as 'mere builders' gothic', to which Pugin retorted that it was 'a simple, convenient residence without any pretensions whatsoever'.[53]

The Keighley house had made much of the junction between corridor and stair; a house that came a little later, the presbytery for his

3.21 (below, left)
The Bishop's House, Birmingham: the building's extraordinary layout required a visitor to wind their way through most of the building in order to reach the great hall which was located almost adjacent to the street door. Drawn by Francis Fawcett.

3.22 (below)
The clergy house, Nottingham: ground-floor plan (late 1841). The house was arranged around a courtyard which at the north-east end extended into the sacristy and church. See also figs 3.52-4.

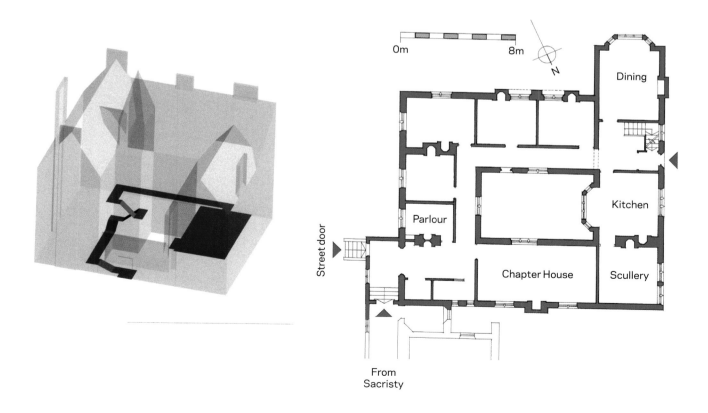

church of Our Lady and St Wilfred at Warwick Bridge east of Carlisle, made a great deal more of it (fig. 3.23).[54] Its very unusual plan exploited the potential of a pair of crossing corridors on a tiny scale (fig. 3.24). An entrance passage led inwards from the porch, and continued to a cross-passage running from north-west to south-east. The kitchen was divided from this passage by a timber screen, creating something of the effect of a screens passage on a miniature scale; the two principal rooms, a library and sitting room, were reached from this cross-passage to the right.[55] The cross-passage was redundant in practical terms, since it would have been possible to reach all the rooms by continuing the entrance corridor a few feet further into the centre of the house. It was thus there to create a tiny cloister, providing the priest with a framed view of the eastern end of the church, through pointed windows, every time that he left his library (fig. 3.25). Possibly Pugin considered a future covered link between the two.

His other later presbyteries are simpler, although not without their oddities. At Woolwich (1842), he designed a simple house of the Uttoxeter type, without the rear extension but with a long cloister route through to the sacristy beyond, at the liturgical eastern end of the adjoining church (figs 3.26, 3.27); and at Brewood in Staffordshire (1843) he designed a small and relatively conventional house on a tight central-corridor plan, but which was itself linked visually not only to his adjacent church but also to the little school and schoolmaster's house which were eventually built behind (fig. 3.28). In Rylston Road, Fulham (1847), he designed a small house around a pair of cross-corridors, which meet at the foot of the stairs; the house is perhaps most interesting because of the delicacy of its carved ornamentation, in the only residential project that Pugin designed for a woman patron (figs 3.29, 3.30).[56]

Pugin's first parsonage

In 1845 Pugin designed two Anglican parsonages which form part of a set of at least six similar schemes designed during the mid 1840s. In both cases he found his clients through his close friend John Bloxam at Magdalen College, Oxford, a member of a group of Puseyite sympathisers who had received Newman's Tract 90 enthusiastically but who were placed in an awkward position by their spokesman's defection to Rome in 1843. The first of these two, Frederick Rooke, was a graduate of Oriel College who was appointed curate at the parish of Rampisham with Wraxhall in Dorset in January 1843 and was instituted rector on 15th April 1845. A month later Pugin was in the village, attending to alterations to the church but also before long designing a new house for the incumbent who at 28 was five years younger than himself.

He had by this time designed at least one, and possibly as many as three, medium-size houses comparable in scale to Rooke's requirements. The first was his own house, which he called 'St Augustine's' but which after the completion of the adjacent church has always been called the 'Grange', in Ramsgate; the second was a house for the Liverpool merchant Henry Sharples, on the Woolton Road at Childwall, named 'Oswaldcroft'; and the third was an early scheme for Captain J. H. Washington Hibbert, at Bilton, south of Rugby in Warwickshire. The Grange was designed in the autumn of 1843;[57] Oswaldcroft very probably emerged from discussions with Sharples some time after the beginning of 1844,[58] and of the Bilton design it can only be said with any certainty that the surviving perspective, dated 1844, implies rather than proves this to be another similar house.[59] So the only clear precedent for Pugin's first parsonage was his own house in Ramsgate, and furthermore since he had moved into it in August 1844 he had had the better part of a year in which to assess the results before meeting Rooke the following spring. There is no period more critical for an architect to assess his own work than the first few months of living in his own house; and one is struck too by the fact that Rooke, like Pugin, went on to father a great number of children; the Rampisham house was perhaps also planned from the start to provide space for them. Interestingly, in a letter to Bloxam of October 1843, Pugin referred to designing a parsonage for the first time – it is not clear for whom – and his immediate reaction was 'I suppose the *nursery* must be a prominent feature'.[60] The presence of a crowd of children so greatly distinguishes a parsonage from the Roman Catholic presbyteries that Pugin had been designing up to that point that it was perhaps because of it that he seems to have rejected the types of plans he had devised to date for ecclesiastical dwellings. Instead, he reproduced for Rooke the plan of his own house with nothing but a small number of modifications.

3.23 (right, top)
The church of Our Lady and St Wilfred with its adjacent presbytery at Warwick Bridge, east of Carlisle, Cumberland (1840). The angle between the buildings reflects the type of scene that Pugin used to sketch from his imagination as a child. The presbytery door here is placed, characteristically, so that it could be seen from the church porch.

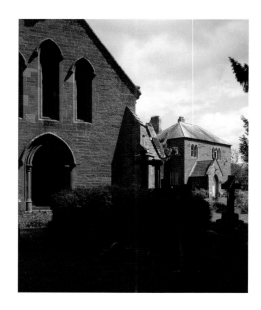

3.24 (far right, above)
Warwick Bridge: ground-floor plan (1840). Pugin exaggerated the amount of corridor required even in small houses such as this one. Here the cross-corridor that runs at right angles to the stair hall is redundant in practice. Its purpose must have been to provide a visual link between library and church. It also imitated in miniature the layout of his 'Deanery' scheme of 1833.

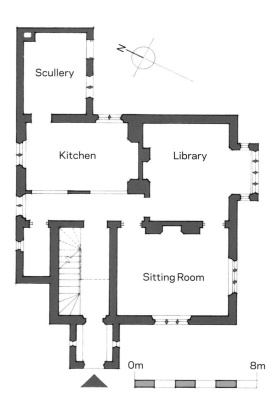

3.25 (right, middle)
Warwick Bridge: the view from the cross-corridor towards the east end of the church.

3.26 (right, bottom)
St Peter's presbytery, New Road, Woolwich (1842). The street front of Pugin's narrow house is now overshadowed by the substantial extension by E.W. Pugin to the north-east (left).

3.27 (far right, below)
St Peter's presbytery, Woolwich: ground-floor plan (1842). Much of the site is taken up by the long cloister running south-east from the street to the sacristy.

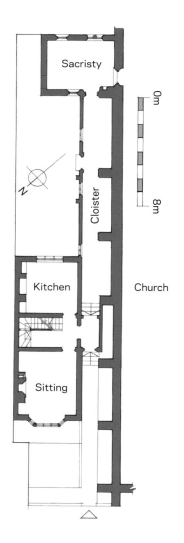

3.28 (left, above)
The school (left) and schoolmaster's house at Brewood, based on a drawing by Pugin but executed by others. Their location was very probably determined by the architect with the view from the back door of the presbytery in mind.

3.29 (left, below)
St Thomas of Canterbury presbytery, Rylston Road, Fulham, designed in late 1847. The lower right-hand window (to the study) has been blocked in, probably when the road was widened to remove a narrow outer yard.

3.30 (below)
St Thomas of Canterbury presbytery, Fulham: ground-floor plan. A late and conventional plan but one which echoed the Derby arrangement by having its main rooms parallel to the axis of the street and up against it.

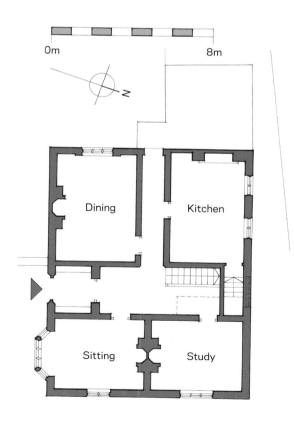

0m   8m

Dining

Kitchen

Sitting

Study

The Grange: introducing the pinwheel

At Ramsgate he had designed a remarkable home which was entirely different to the conventional house types of his day in several respects (fig. 3.31). The most important of these was the layout (fig. 3.32). A small porch on the north side of the house leads into a square staircase hallway, about 12 by 15 feet. Immediately ahead is a small fireplace.[61] To the right, a door leads into the drawing room; further along the same wall, a second door leads to the library, which was Pugin's study and drawing office. Off to the left, beyond the stair hall, was the door to the dining room. Each of these three rooms had its main axis at right angles to the adjacent one, creating what might be called a 'pinwheel' plan (fig. 3.33). Since the house was itself reached through a roundabout route from a side alleyway, and thence through a tiny gatehouse, and since the stairs continued the line of progress in an anti-clockwise direction, the whole of the house could be said to be forming part of a spiral-shaped route, with, as at the Birmingham Bishop's House, a circulation route like a tightly coiled spring.

We already can see that this was quite different from the houses of the 1830s that we have seen to date, although looking through the many houses going up at the time I can see that it is not absolutely without precedent. There were other houses with a hub formed by a staircase hall by 1843, although they are rare. John Whichcord, from Maidstone, had designed a house like this at Harrietsham in 1838: one enters under the staircase into a square hallway, and the three principal reception rooms are arranged in succession along the left hand side and straight ahead.[62] This might be called simply an L-plan type, as opposed to an L-corridor (fig. 3.34). At Elmstone, not far away, Edmunds of Margate produced a similar example in 1840, but with only two rooms organised around a stairhall.[63] There are further isolated examples throughout the country. At Steventon in Berkshire, Wallace designed a house very similar to Whichcord's in 1841.[64]

The L-plan house was not a new idea; but it seems at first surprising that it should be so rare, for in addition to the advantage of the spacious hallway there is the fact that one of the three main rooms is no longer cut off in that odd way in the crook of the entrance corridor and stairs. An L-plan house is in fact fundamentally a different type of house from the standard types we have already seen: its two main facades wrap around adjacent fronts, so it is no longer a house that has merely a 'back' and a 'front'. It illustrates a different way of thinking, one that comes as a harbinger of the Victorian mid-century, when a house is perceived as a three-dimensional object, carved from a single mass, as it were, and designed to be seen at angled views and not merely straight on. By applying it to their parsonages, architects were to some extent grasping at the characteristics of a large country house and telescoping it down to a tiny size. In the East Anglian collections there are isolated examples from earlier years: there is a very crude drawing for a rectory at Felsham in Suffolk from 1814, although this plan is slightly different in that the kitchen replaces one of the three rooms arranged in the L, and in addition there is a library isolated from the other principal rooms on the other side of the stair hall.[65] A house by Whiting of 1826 at Creeting is closer to a typical L plan: the three reception rooms are here arranged exactly in the L shape, but the staircase is brought into the depth of the house; although it is in the form of a generous spiral, it does not exactly create a staircase entrance hall. Interestingly, Whiting tried, not very successfully, to draw the outside of this house as if seen from the corner in the form of a perspective, so he was certainly aware of the implications of the L plan as far the general exterior massing was concerned.[66] By 1840, however, we have at Sutton in Cambridgeshire a typical house of this sort, designed by Joseph Stannard the younger.[67] In all cases, these novel plans were camouflaged by facades which suggested a conventional central-corridor or L-corridor plan within. Whichcord's was an asymmetrical classical-Georgian house; Stannard's was also classical-Georgian, but symmetrical and with a projecting central bay under a pediment. On the other hand Wallace, whom we have already seen at his most theatrical at Stottesden and Stourmouth, gave his Steventon house an understated Tudor-gothic front.

There is however a further early L-plan parsonage of the period in which Pugin was working which also has a facade that gives no hint of what is happening behind it, but which has something of a surprise within. This house of 1842, at Ruckinge near Romney Marsh in south-west Kent, is by an otherwise unknown surveyor of Dymchurch called James Elliott who produced a house with a

3.31
The south, garden, elevation of
St Augustine's, now called the
Grange, Ramsgate, designed
by Pugin in 1843.
Photographed shortly after
restoration in June 2006.

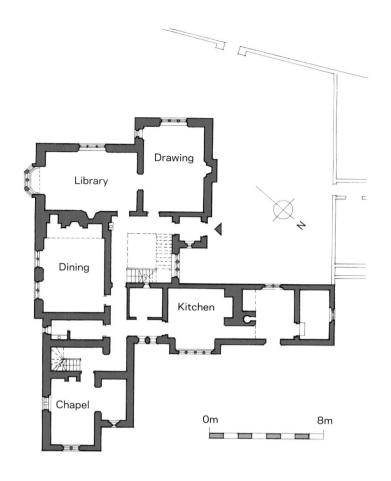

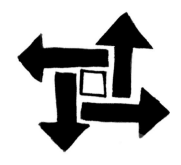

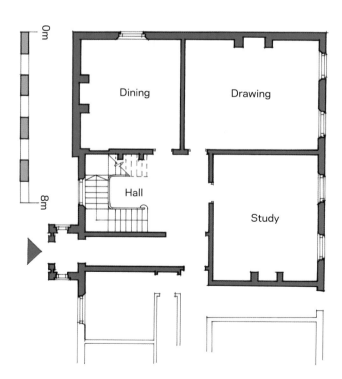

3.32 (left, above)
The Grange, Ramsgate: ground-floor plan (1843). This was the first pinwheel design. Pugin regretted that his library – the room in which he worked – did not project south beyond the plane of the dining-room wall. The dynamic layout is however already evident.

3.33 (above)
A diagrammatic represent-ation of the pinwheel plan type. Rooms are arranged in rotating fashion either clockwise or anti-clockwise around a central stair hall; the long axis of each room is at 90 degrees to that of the adjacent room, giving a dynamic quality to the house. Drawn by Assaf Krebs.

3.34 (left, below)
A typical L-plan house, based on the proposal by John Whichcord (senior) of 1838 for Harrietsham rectory, east of Maidstone, Kent [*Canterbury Cathedral Archives, Dcb/DC/ H8/1*]. Unlike a pinwheel, the L-plan type fits three principal rooms into a simple, usually rectangular, layout with no attempt to express the arrangement externally.

pinwheel plan almost identical to Pugin's (figs 3.35–8).[68] Elliott's drawings include a roof plan which further illustrates the fact that he had grasped that the organisation of the rooms in this way could also be expressed externally. And yet he did not do it. His house originally had a rather dim series of Tudor-gothic elevations, with one of those symmetrical and turreted central porches inspired by King's College chapel, and with no distinction made between the kitchen and store windows to the left of it and the dining-room windows to the right (figs 3.36, 3.37). There is little here to compare with Pugin's astonishing, almost brutal entrance at the Grange (fig. 3.39). We have no evidence that Pugin saw it, for he did not mention Elliott or Ruckinge in his correspondence, and his diary, which in any case is generally merely a laconic record of destinations, is missing for 1843.

So the pinwheel itself was not Pugin's invention and no doubt other examples can be found. A different and early plan using a similar device, for example, is that of the large and eccentric house at Boxford in Suffolk designed back in 1818 by Mark Thompson with a castellated Tudor-gothic front and a relaxed classical-Georgian back. This too has three pinwheel reception rooms, and there is a comparatively large stair hall, but this hall is not located at the hub of the rooms – and Thompson had gone to great lengths to hide these adventures behind his stern and almost flat front (see fig. 2.4). Pugin's house at Ramsgate is a fundamentally different type of house from any of these. The relationship between the plan and the front of the house is a clear example of how. We have seen how architects have played with entrance elevations; sometimes, indeed it was the only thing they did play with in their designs for these houses. Pugin's however merely presented to the visitor an almost blank aspect, decorated mainly by the large stair window but dominated by the windowless side elevation of the drawing room to the right, and the back of the kitchens to the left. This dramatic new unity between plan and form appears to be uniquely his. It allowed him to express on the outside of his houses not only the location of each of the principal rooms, but also to give that expression some constructional logic, in particular in the form of distinct chimneys and separate ridges to each of the three sections, a perfect illustration of the central messages of *The true principles*. It also created a dynamic interior in which anyone walking through a room and out into another would have to change the direction of their walk by

90 degrees, mid-perambulation, which means that even a small house provides a continuously changing vista; and of course the movement of people up and down the stairs at the centre of the plan intensifies this. It was this layout that he chose to repeat for his Liverpool house and possibly also for his early Bilton scheme, and then eventually for Rooke at Rampisham.

Rampisham

The former rectory at Rampisham is now the most complete survival of any of Pugin's houses, and it provides a wonderful opportunity to assess his approach to parsonage building. Because it is also a very beautiful house, and more expensively built (for £1,734, by his regular building partner George Myers) than his earlier presbyteries, it is an important landmark in his career and it cannot have failed to impress those of his professional contemporaries who saw it and admired him. Furthermore Pugin's mortgage application documents have survived in the Wiltshire and Swindon Record Office, the only example we have of a complete set of autograph drawings and specifications for any of his houses (fig. 3.40). [69] The plan is much the same as at Ramsgate except it is reversed, with the principal rooms running clockwise from the left-hand side of the entrance. The architect had by now experienced the pinwheel arrangement, and he liked it. He was evidently not deterred by the fact that the open character of the hall and its gallery above meant that noise from children or servants travelled easily across the house, even though people moving between bedrooms were exposed to visitors at the front door, precisely the problem that the L-corridor houses had solved. [70]

What was, then, in its favour? One advantage was certainly visual, and testifies to Pugin's training as a set designer and his youthful experience as a Covent Garden stage hand, which according to an observation in his 'Autobiography' had enabled him to acquire 'the thorough knowledge of the practical part of the stage business which has so materialy served me since' - a reference surely as much to his ability to manipulate effects of light and shade as to the construction of simple proscenium-type views. [71] At Rampisham Pugin made one important change from the Ramsgate plan and oriented the house so that the great window over the stairs faced south-east, rather than north-west. The pinwheel arrangement thus allowed the sun to

3.35 (above)
The ground-floor plan of Ruckinge parsonage, on Romney Marsh south of Ashford, Kent, based on the drawing of 1842 by James Elliot [*Canterbury Cathedral Archives, Dcb/DC/R14/1*]. This is unmistakably a pinwheel, even if the house has none of the three-dimensional coherence of the Grange.

3.36 (right, top)
Ruckinge, Kent, by James Elliot. The external appearance of the house, seen here from the south-east, does give some indication of its pinwheel plan.

3.37 (right, middle)
The entrance (south-west) elevation at Ruckinge. When the original decoration was complete it would have been more obvious that the porch is one of several of the period that was derived in a very general way from the chapel of King's College, Cambridge.

3.38 (right)
The entrance at Ruckinge: unmistakeably a real stair hall rather than a corridor.

3.39 (left)
The entrance front of the Grange, Ramsgate, now dominated by the post-1860 glazed corridor that replaced Pugin's original enclosed entry courtyard. Even allowing for the fact that the back-corridor plan had already produced functional elevations in contemporary houses, this was an entrance facade unlike any other. Visitors arrived alongside the back wall of the kitchen and scullery (far left). Photographed in June 2006.

3.40 (below)
Rampisham rectory, between Dorchester and Yeovil, Dorset: Pugin's drawing to accompany his application of 21 March 1846. It is thanks to the Bounty's methodical application procedures that this rare record of Pugin's work has survived; generally he made only a single drawing for a builder [*Wiltshire & Swindon Record Office, D28/6/11*].

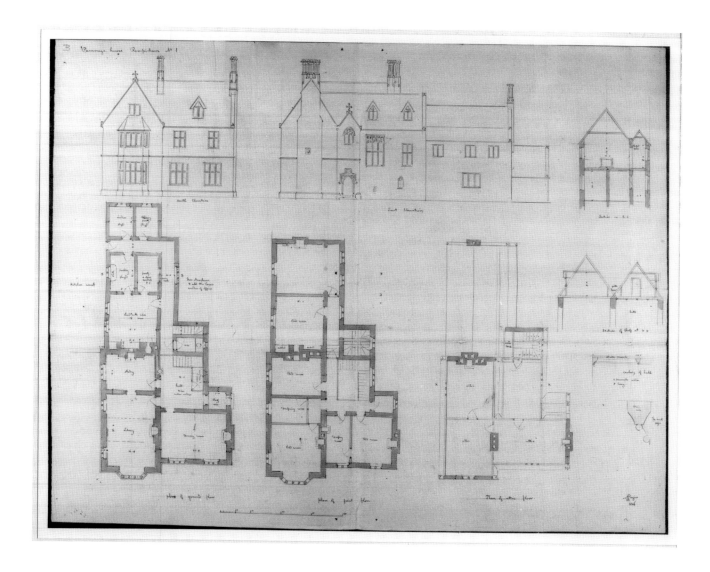

permeate deep into the house, giving the public parts of it a perpetually changing quality which has no parallel in the narrow corridor plans of his contemporaries, and which highlights the way in which the rooms lead off from one another, all of the doors and openings naturally lit and in different and varying ways.

But a more tangible reason for Pugin's adoption of the pinwheel form which he perfected at Rampisham was that it allowed him to express his ideas about construction in a coherent way at the scale of an entire house, so that the actual form of the building was as resonant of his ideas as were the mere details of it. The pinwheel plans allowed him to create distinctive wings out of each separate room, in accordance with his demand that 'An architect should exhibit his skill by turning the difficulties which occur in raising an elevation from *a convenient plan* into so many *picturesque beauties*'.[72] Moreover, this plan is actually representative of the details of its constructional method, in the sense that every part distinctly describes the way in which it is held together and forms part of the whole.[73] Each major space requires a separate roof which stresses the individuality of that room, or pair of rooms, from the outside; this is further emphasised by allowing each pinwheel room to break forward from the plan of the wall of the room that is adjacent to it, as evidently he wished he had done at Ramsgate.[74] On the other hand, by maintaining a continuous roof height his work is distinct from that of 'picturesque' architects seeking to differentiate various rooms for visual pleasure. By designing a disposition of windows on an entrance front that relates to the organisation inside – for example by giving unexpected prominence to the service stairs – it is possible to demonstrate externally the internal arrangements, and also to create a type of facade that is the product of the planning requirements of its era quite irrespective of historical precedent (fig. 3.1). And just as the constructional principle is telescoped up to the scale of the general form of the house, it is telescoped back down again to provide a key for designing the new details that are exposed in it. By preferring an overhanging eave to a parapet, the method of roofing is exposed. By creating decoration by cutting from materials, rather than by gluing or joining them, the physical nature of that material is revealed.

Furthermore, the open hall at the centre of the house provided a public backdrop to events within. A conventional parsonage was essentially a number of compartments linked by minimal circulation space; here the hall and the sequence of rooms leading off it gave a certain drama to the events of the day. There is no mediaeval precedent for a room of this type: a relatively small room used only as a double-height circulation space cannot be furnished for sitting or eating, and is not a modern descendant of a mediaeval hall. It is possible in this room to see how the pinwheel type was a development of Pugin's consistent preference for exaggerated corridor sequences. There had been a hint of it in the relatively large stair hall at Derby; and in other projects throughout the 1840s he inserted rooms like this, sometimes going as far as arranging the direction of the flights in order to lengthen unnecessarily the walking distances to upstairs rooms.[75] But in many ways it is the Rampisham rectory alone that stands at the centre of the whole of this book: it was the perfectly conceptualised new Victorian parsonage. The whole way of building had been thought out afresh and was here perfected for the first time: on the one hand the layout, the architectural language, the tectonic logic and consistency of its construction, the creation of an architecture which inspires the sometimes mystical experience of living in a building that responds to the changing day. On the other, there is the order and the completeness of the complex as a whole, with its pantries, its scullery and its larder, its coach house, its laundry, and its sophisticated water system (it had an underground tank fed from the roof): everything here suited exactly the moment it was designed for. The ideas for all these whether technological or philosophical were in the air in the 1840s; it took a genius to bind them together.

Pugin repeated the plan, or rather a slight variation of it, in the late autumn of 1845 for his second rectory, that at Lanteglos, the site of the historic parish church for the Cornish town of Camelford located a short distance to its north. The house is somewhat less interesting than that at Rampisham, not only because it has been badly mutilated, but also because Pugin relinquished control over its execution (fig. 3.42). It was too far away from London for Myers to manage economically, and as Pugin himself pointed out, it was cheaper for the rector to find local builders.[76] Here his client was Bloxam's brother-in-law, Roger Bird, who had become rector in 1845. Bird applied for and received a mortgage for the house from the governors of Queen Anne's Bounty, but the drawings and other application documents have disappeared.[77]

3.41
The stair hall at Rampisham.
The whole house is suffused
with delicate and varying
patterns of light.

On the other hand, Pugin's correspondence on the subject, which was directed to Bloxam rather than Bird, does at least throw some light onto his design intentions. He described the house as being 'very plain' but with a 'respectable character'; and he pointed out that he was locating the house on its site in 'the best position for warming and lightening the house with the sun': the staircase window now faces north again, and the principal rooms almost due south. Rather surprisingly, he also asked, apparently not sarcastically, whether Bird wanted the house built 'well or cheap'.[78]

Apart from reallocating the function of the three principal reception rooms, and providing an interior lobby to further separate the study, where parishioners would enter, from the private part of the house, Pugin repeated the Ramsgate-Rampisham formula. But because of the execution by local builders with, evidently, experience of conventional Tudor-gothic, what remains of the house has a disappointing quality: one can imagine what Pugin would have said about the blind windows and make-believe arrowslits (fig. 3.43).[79]

More about corridors and pinwheels

The long corridor routes and the connections between the different elements of them had clearly long been a dominant characteristic even of Pugin's small houses. In general, the corridor-plan types provided a place for procession: at the Bishop's House in Birmingham, the route from entrance door to great hall provided a lengthy processional way that was not only as long as possible, but also shielded the upper parts of the house from the street and unwanted attention. In institutional plans, such as the cloisters he designed for his convent at Handsworth and elsewhere, the processional way is the dominant part of the plan (fig. 3.44). At a convent of 1844 onwards alongside the Nottingham clergy house, his nuns were required to walk the entire length of the ground floor, rise through the stairs, and then walk the whole length of the floor back again to reach the most intimate part of the cloister which is, in fact, located immediately above their heads when they stand at the front door. The weaving of corridors around rooms also seems to express the different shapes and forms of construction in each room. Pugin wanted to make this happen.[80]

3.42 (above, left)
Part of the surviving fabric at Lanteglos near Camelford, Cornwall, a rectory designed by Pugin in 1846 but executed without his supervision. This is the east side of the house, showing the ground floor window of the study next to the entrance. The building has been substantially mutilated.

3.43 (above)
The kitchen chimney on the south side of the house at Lanteglos. It is hard to imagine that Pugin would have countenanced the inclusion of these blank, vaguely gothic windows resembling arrowslits.

3.44
The magnificent cloister staircase at the Convent of Mercy, Handsworth, Birmingham, is almost all that remains of Pugin's 1844 extension to his original building. It is remarkable that so much of his attention was concentrated on creating complex corridor spaces such as this one. Photographed by the author, February 2006.

His interest in religious processions can be demonstrated by his illustration of them in several of his published etchings: they can be seen in the mediaeval plates illustrating 'Contrasted parochial churches' and 'Contrasted college gateways' in both the 1836 and the 1841 editions of *Contrasts*, and in his view of Magdalen College, Oxford, in *The true principles* (figs 3.45, 3.46).[81] Figures in his views of modern urban scenes are, by contrast, in many cases seen to be standing about without purpose, or hurrying in an undignified fashion. The corridor schemes suggest that Pugin adopted the processional way as an architectural demonstration of Roman Catholic life, and the incorporation of long routes into buildings was therefore consistent with his call both for 'convenience' and for 'propriety'.

In the case of the pinwheel-plan houses, Pugin's practical aims are less evident. Perhaps he saw the pinwheel type as a way of impressing the processional form on domestic life: the need to walk across changing axes in these houses certainly complements the dynamic character of their graphic form. In his own house, the staircase balustrade mimics the pinwheel pattern of the plan; it is a form

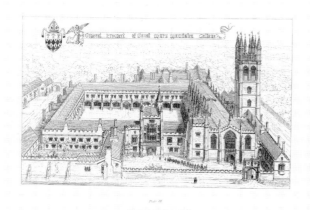

unmistakably suited to the architect's own almost boundless energy.
Pugin presided over little family processions to and from the house's
chapel, as well as between the hall and dining room, which he
described in letters to friends.[82] He clearly hoped that Rooke would do
the same. He provided his client with a tiny oratory on the upper floor,
decorated with a pointed gothic window, but carefully avoided
labelling this room on the drawings which he submitted to the bishop
of Salisbury for approval, presumably realising that the horror of
Puseyite heresies might damage his client's application for a mortgage,
if not his reputation (figs 3.40, 3.47). In common with Pugin's own
house in Ramsgate, the rectory at Rampisham has no direct door to its
garden: like the inhabitant of one of the Roman Catholic presbyteries,
Mr Rooke was evidently required to process the long way round.
The adoption of a suitable plan must surely indicate something new:
that the parsonage was, according to Pugin's vision, no longer merely
a comfortable home for a 'retired' cleric and his family, but a stage
for the public presentation of his role as the spiritual father of a
community. This must have been Pugin's aim at Rampisham and
Lanteglos.

Englishness

Inspired by topographical writers such as John Britton, Tudor-gothic
architects had grappled with Englishness, and tried to copy the distinct
decorative features of mediaeval churches. Pugin had a different
approach to it. It was not only the planning of his parsonages that was
consistently original. He employed for them a decorative style that

3.45 (above, left)
Contrasted parochial
churches, from Pugin's
Contrasts (1836 and 1841).
The plate shows Nash's All
Soul's, Langham Place, and St
Mary Redcliffe, Bristol.
Several of Pugin's book
illustrations contrast orderly
religious processions with the
aimless groups found in
contemporary streets.

3.46 (above)
Pugin's idealised view of
Magdalen College, Oxford,
from *The true principles*,
1841. Another procession
is under way.

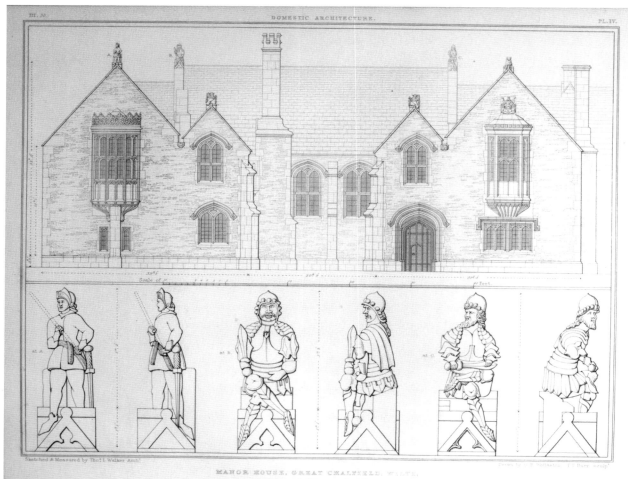

Pl. 30.   DOMESTIC ARCHITECTURE.   PL. IV.

Sketched & Measured by Thos I. Walker Arch.t

MANOR HOUSE, GREAT CHALFIELD, WILTS.

North Front and Figures on the Gables

London, Published May 1837 by the Author Thos I. Walker Arch.t at his Office 10a of Furnival's Street Holborn.

likewise had no true historic precedent, but which in this case testifies to his own deep appreciation of mediaeval work in different ways. We have seen many times how an architect might apply, very probably in Parker's Roman cement, or something similar, decorative details broadly copied from gothic tracery, at best glimpsed in a Britton publication, onto the face of their houses; and we have heard of the various imitations of King's College chapel. Pugin never did anything like this. In the first place, he used a very limited number of specific design features that he had derived from the accurate measured drawings that he, his father, and his father's assistants had carefully drawn, mainly during the 1820s. In the case of Rampisham, the two gables above its porch seem to come from the then-ruinous late fifteenth-century manor house at Great Chalfield, which was drawn by T. L. Walker for the third and posthumous volume of the Pugins' *Examples of gothic architecture* in 1836 (fig. 3.48). A further example comes from father's *Specimens* of 1821: in several houses from his 'Deanery' onwards and including the tower-like presbytery at the Alton Hospital (fig. 3.49), he designed a chimney reminiscent of that at the Jew's House in Lincoln. That in itself was interesting: this was the house that Britton did not consider to be a candidate for the oldest house in England and yet Pugin used it more than once, including for a presbytery in Reading in 1840.[83] And having seen the straight-headed, traceried windows with mouchettes at the mediaeval rectory at Marlow, by the Thames, on a visit in connection with Charles Scott-Murray, his client at Danesfield House, he started including these in his designs: the first one appeared almost immediately, for the stair windows at Oswaldcroft and Rampisham.[84] He often used a type of detail or architectural feature that other architects failed to see as important: the castles of Ludlow and Kenilworth provide many examples of mediaeval or late Tudor building techniques which found an echo in his own work. Many of Pugin's stone details such as battered stone bases, fireplace locations and mouldings, window details and window arrangements, can be traced back to these two buildings (fig. 3.50).[85] He was proud of his knowledge of English historical architecture, claiming he had 'not only visited every Cathedral and Abbey church in England and several thousand parochial churches, but [had] also inspected [not] in a cursory and superficial manner, but with deep thought, making careful drawings and notes of the same'.[86]

Opposite

3.47 (above, left)
The entrance (south-east) front of Rampisham rectory. The oratory is clearly identified by its gothic window – a rarity in Pugin's domestic architecture – but the architect was careful not to label the room as such on the plan he submitted to the bishop and the Bounty (see fig. 3.40).

3.48 (bottom)
The restored elevation of Great Chalfield Manor, Wiltshire, drawn by T. L. Walker for the third volume of the Pugins' *Examples* (1836–40; plate 30). The double-gabled bays of this beautiful late mediaeval manor house provided Pugin with the authority for his own use of the motif, at for example Rampisham.

3.49 (above, right)
The presbytery at Pugin's St John's Hospital (1839) on the Earl of Shrewsbury's estate at Alton, Staffordshire, was situated in a tower at the west end of the chapel. Its chimney, seen here to the right, rises from above a window in a manner reminiscent of that at the Jew's House in Lincoln (see fig. 2.19).

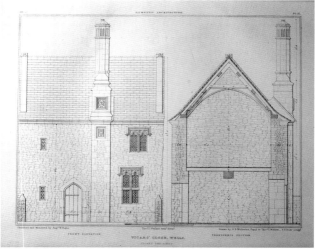

3.50
An engraving of details from
the hall at Kenilworth Castle,
Warwickshire, from the second
volume of the Pugins' *Examples*
(1831-6). The stone moulding
around the windows take the
form of a continuous bead with
a circular section. Possibly it
was the origin for Pugin's
distinctive door architraves
(see fig. 3.57).

3.51
The Vicars' Close at Wells,
Somerset, from drawings by
Pugin for the final volume of
the *Examples* (plate 2).
Few of these houses actually
resembled this restored view
at the time. They were very
probably the oldest small town
houses that Pugin saw in
England, and yet he never
copied their form when
designing a modern house.

So even where there is no direct evidence that he saw a well-known historical building, there is every reason to suppose that he may well have done. It was generally the geometry of the structural form rather than the decorative detailing that he copied, and the external expression of the pinwheel rooms, each defined by its own gable and ridge, allowed him to practice the modelling of simple materials at which he excelled.[87] These tall gables, so much taller than those of the Tudor-gothic architects, had the further advantage of making the attics considerably more spacious than they had been for those who had to sleep within them, and were therefore not only a functional solution but one which could be advertised on the front of every building. But for the most part, his decorative approach is indefinable historically. He never copied the external form of the houses of the Vicars' Close in Wells, which he loved and had drawn, although he could well have done if he wished for the comparably small houses on narrow sites at Uttoxeter and Woolwich (fig. 3.51).[88] If anything, his houses have about them the quality of the early seventeenth-century vernacular of the bay-windows of the terraced houses in the historic market town of Stamford. What all this shows is that Pugin had discovered a new approach to the search for Englishness that architects and critics yearned for: he imitated the inherent structural character of English historical buildings which was derived from their means of construction and some of their basic geometry, rather than their applied decoration or their elevations. Had one taken all of Loudon's practical advice but ignored everything that he had to say about style, one might have ended up as Pugin did – if only one had had Pugin's artist's eye for composition and his genius for abstracting the character, rather than the features, of historical building. It is what one would expect from the author of *The true principles*, who called for 'the decoration of *construction*' to replace the construction of decoration.[89]

Pugin had found Britton's illusive House One – not in a single historical house that contained the seeds of an authentic, reborn domestic architecture, but the essential spirit of the ancient buildings he liked as a whole, a spirit which also had in it something of an English character of restlessness, perhaps even something aggressive.[90] These buildings are, with the exception of the Rampisham rectory, never pretty. He turned this into a coherent style of his own devising, a vernacular language which instead of adopting the fancy-dress tones of historical ornament spoke in the down-to-earth tones of the late mediaeval workman. It is in fact hard to describe most of his domestic architecture as properly 'gothic'. It seems possible that this new kind of Englishness appealed to his contemporaries at more of a subconscious level than an immediate and obvious one. His irregular window patterns; his rows of gables; his wall buttresses that merge with the adjoining wall planes; these would have been familiar to those that looked at historical architecture without them knowing precisely where they came from. It is interesting that he himself drew remarkably few examples of English historical domestic architecture, especially in comparison to the volumes of drawings he brought back from his travels abroad. And even if his buildings have an Englishness about their general form (although it is often hard to say what, exactly), they undoubtedly have a Frenchness too, especially in their tall vertical proportions, influenced by the devices he copied from his beloved Nodier volume and that had made their first appearance in the Alderbury house. He himself said nothing about stylistic influence, preferring to draw the domestic architecture of northern France,

Belgium, Germany and Switzerland, and telling his friend Benjamin Ferrey that he was especially delighted with the domestic architecture of Nuremberg.[91] It was ironic that English domestic architecture was deployed in this new way by someone who had almost nothing to say about it: and it reminds us that architectural history is made by those who build, rather than by those who theorise.

Inside and out

These original planning and styling devices were by no means the only things that Pugin was doing differently from his contemporaries. His houses were always different from those of other architects because he used a comprehensive and consistent language of masonry and in particular timber detailing that was different from theirs. We have seen how much survived the transition from classical-Georgian to Tudor-gothic in the 1830s and 1840s. One element that remained constant was the external surfaces of walls: a homogenous brick, stone or plaster. Another was detailing of internal joinery. Here and there a more fanciful architect might decorate a door or a ceiling with a tracery quatrefoil or other supposedly gothic touch, but for the most part doors, architraves, skirtings, plaster cornices and ironmongery were exactly the same in the earlier classical houses as they were in the later Tudor-gothic ones. In the Lanteglos house, finished internally by local builders, one sees precisely the same classical-Georgian plaster and timber detailing as one would anywhere else in the country.[92]

Pugin did everything differently where these were concerned too. On his external walls he developed characteristic treatments which in themselves mark the transition from Georgian to Victorian. He almost never used plaster as an external wall surface, inexplicable exceptions being in the case of two service wings, one at Grace Dieu, the house of his friend Ambrose Phillipps, and another for his colleague, the Birmingham ironmonger John Hardman. He did not go in for decorative effects across the face of a wall, always preferring a single material of homogenous colour for the whole of the face of a wall, excepting only window mullions, frames and quoins.[93] He nearly always used English bond for his brickwork: I found no examples of English bond amongst the parsonages or indeed other houses of his contemporaries up to the 1840s. But most remarkably he derived the overall form of the external envelope of his buildings through the three-dimensional treatment of the basic materials he was obliged to use: not in a modelled, sculptural way but rather as if he had responded to the prophecies of men like Palgrave and Scrope, for his architecture was defined by the physical characteristics of materials drawn from the ground. At the Bishop's House in Birmingham, he arranged the chimney shafts and the corners of the buildings, the oriel windows and the projecting bays, into rich sculptural forms which belie the cheapness of the materials (fig. 3.19). No other architect seemed yet to have grasped how different the plastic quality of brickwork can be from that of shapes moulded from plaster or carved into stone.[94] At the Nottingham clergy house he returned to the idea of an arrangement of chimneystacks arching over a window first seen in the 'Deanery' scheme of 1833, marrying it to a tripartite form seen, for example, at the short sides of the mediaeval barn at Glastonbury (fig. 3.52). The resulting chimney projection forms a gable; the plane is cut back to admit two ground-floor windows. A further unconventional feature of this house is the pair of large mullioned windows in what must have been the scullery at the north-west corner of the ground floor: the northern one of the two directly abuts the crosswall, a very odd and unprecedented

3.52
A chimney on the south side of the clergy house at Nottingham, designed by Pugin in the early 1840s. Its design was perhaps inspired by details of mediaeval masonry such the tripartite buttresses of the barn at Glastonbury abbey.

3.53 (below)
The west and principal entrance front of the clergy house at Nottingham. The far left-hand ground-floor window seems to have been added as an afterthought, no doubt because of concern that the scullery within would be too dark. The result is almost a corner window.

3.54 (below, right)
A photograph by Samuel Bourne, taken sometime between 1870–80, of the south-east corner of St Barnabas, Nottingham: the clergy house is visible to the left. A cloister runs along the front, parallel with the street, connecting the sacristy and church with the house. This view demonstrates Pugin's skill at composing complex masses [*Nottingham Local Studies Library* and *www.picturethepast.org.uk*, *image NTGM010629*].

detail that to a modern eye shows a progressive sense of structure (fig. 3.53). All windows have plain square-headed lights; there is no decorative carving beyond hood moulds with label stops on the east and west front doors, and a monogrammed cartouche commemorating R. W. Willson on the chimneystack on the south side.[95] Internally, there is only one ornamental fireplace, and no finished exposed timberwork in the ceilings except in the corridor leading to the sacristy. A view of the house from the south-east side of the church confirms that this sculpted form is a coherent part of the compositional massing of the whole ensemble (fig. 3.54).

Pugin stated at the beginning of *The true principles* that '*all ornament should consist of enrichment of the essential construction of the building*'.[96] Enrichment, according to his description, means cutting away from the body of the structural work, expressing the physical nature of the material. The chamfering of the arrises of structural timber, derived from the use of the mediaeval (and later) adze for structural timbers, is the cheapest way of achieving an ornamental result in accordance with this principle; it does not require any lengthily acquired expertise; furthermore, he exposed the grain of the timber by avoiding paint.[97] He used chamfering patterns from the first, at St Marie's Grange: the major timber ceiling ribs are chamfered, and in one case, the exposed angle is further moulded with ogees; window embrasures are chamfered, and although it is difficult to gauge which are primary and which were added during alterations, some stone door stops may also have been. Chamfering provided the system of decoration for

every building that followed. The chamfering of the frames of timber windows first proposed for an unexecuted lodge designed for Scarisbrick, probably in 1837, was first realised a few years later in the convent he designed at Handsworth in Birmingham.[98] These have deeply chamfered edges along each of the external sides of the frame, and the chamfer is scooped upwards about half an inch before the joint: this produces a scallop shape. The same scooped chamfer appears at Handsworth on the structural members of timber doors, on banisters, the edges of fireplace surrounds and on the various members of the open roofs. Stone door embrasures are chamfered, the cut arris terminating towards the foot not in a scoop but in a pyramidal projection that reconciles the splay to the orthogonal plan of the base of the jamb (fig. 3.55). He used open roofs of different types – in some cases, for example at his 'St John's Hospital', his almshouses at Alton, he used a sequence of different types of ceiling along one of his corridor routes – and this too gave him an opportunity to demonstrate not only how a ceiling related to the actual form of the roof, but also how to express the decorative qualities of the materials used (fig. 3.56).[99] He often mirrored this along his corridor routes by providing different types of window all the way along. In his own house at Ramsgate, there are no two identical pairs of window jambs on the ground floor apart from the pair in the dining-room. The joists and other members of these open roofs are decorated in different ways, although many of them employ 45-degree chamfering.

Most importantly – and this marks a significant break with Tudor-gothic – he abandoned the irritating 'shoulder' at the bottom of a gable. In a Tudor-gothic house, the junction between the top of the wall at the eave and the gable was masked by a parapet which rose above the eave, which gave the shouldered effect; at best, this parapet was a kind of raised haunch. The gable then appeared detached from the structure of the wall in an odd way, and it was a problematic detail because rainwater tends to sit at the junction of the gable and the parapet. In Pugin's houses, the gable descends *below* the eaves, and the wall below is built out sideways to cover the end of the gutter; he generally added an ornamental termination to the bottom of the eave itself. The rainwater problem was logically solved. This simple distinction, which alone easily distinguishes gothic revival proper from Tudor gothic, is itself a clear demonstration of the structural form of the roof.

3.55 (opposite)
The porch at Rampisham.
The small triangular chamfered projections either side of the base of the opening are a typical Pugin detail.

3.56
Part of the cloister route at St John's Hospital, Alton, leading between the principal door and the chapel.
These cloister routes often had a variety of different roofs, giving them a narrative quality. The pair of arches at the junction with the next arm of the cloister was a characteristic Pugin feature, and provided logical variety with minimal cost.

Having chamfered wall surfaces and constructional timber members on the outside of his buildings he did it within, too. By the early 1840s he had devised a consistent language for panel members and architraves which appears in all his houses, large or small, and, furthermore, it was consistent across all the rooms of a house so that a servant's bedroom in the attic would have the same doorcase as the reception rooms on the ground floor. His architraves were a simple 1.25" timber beading, a device he invented; possibly he was inspired here by the half-round stone beading around openings in the hall of Kenilworth castle (fig. 3.57; see fig. 3.50). It is a way of saying that the consistency of the architecture of the house is more important than the conventional hierarchies of the social life within, a remarkable statement and a clear indication of a scientific and tectonic mind at work. In the case of decorative plasterwork, he simply avoided it: his rooms never have plaster cornices; there is no ornament such as those thin imitation tracery patterns one occasionally sees on the ceiling of the grander Tudor-gothic houses; and instead of the deep hard plaster skirting familiar in a classical-Georgian house, Pugin used narrow timber strips, four inches high, and cut at an angle along the top. The one mediaeval prototype for Pugin's most simple style of interior design is the early fifteenth-century parlour of the abbot's lodgings at Muchelney abbey, a tall, spare whitewashed room with moulded ceiling joists on stone corbels, a richly carved fireplace, and a pair of ornate straight-headed traceried windows (see fig. 2.22). This if anything was Pugin's House One interior – and yet, and yet: there is no evidence that he ever saw it.

When one thinks how an architect like Carter, at that monstrous Tudor-gothic parsonage in Louth, was obliged to devise all manner of curious and illogical details, such as crazy tracery and ungravitational overhangs, one realises that what Pugin was doing was an illustration that one need not invent, or stick things on: the basic requirements of the constructional envelope of a building provide all one needs to express any particular emotion one may feel. The buildings are entering into the lives of their residents; they seem to expand and

3.57
Pugin generally used the same type of architrave for all his rooms, major or minor. It took the form of a 1.25" beading, a form possibly derived from the stone beading he had seen at the hall of at Kenilworth Castle (see fig. 3.50).

contract through the raising and lowering of ceilings, through the prominence or modesty of the constructional materials, through the variation of the sizes of rooms, the variations of ceiling type, and of window jambs along a route, in response to the activities of people within. This is the birth of a new type of architecture: it is hard to quantify the immediate effect it had on the average parsonage builder, but it must at least have begun to suggest whole new possibilities for design. Until Pugin there had been no distinct house type for the parson, firstly because a building had not in the past been expected to join in the daily life of its inhabitants, and secondly because the parson's social ritual was not really distinct from that of the minor gentry or middle class amongst his neighbours. In his brief discussion of residential architecture in his book *An apology*, published in 1843, Pugin wrote that that 'Our domestic architecture should have a peculiar expression illustrative of our manners and habits...the smaller detached houses which the present state of society has generated, should possess a peculiar character'.[100] His ecclesiastical residences have exactly that.

There is a further aspect of Pugin's houses which is important in the contrast it makes to the work of his contemporaries: he was entirely uninterested in landscape design. We have heard how at least until the mid 1830s, the design of a house was considered as being to some extent the response to its location; this central theme in picturesque design had been a familiar one since the days of Sanderson Miller, and Loudon had often repeated it. There is not so much as a hint of it in Pugin's work: in many of his drawings the landscape was shown to be flat. In his plans, he always showed the quadrangles of his courtyard buildings as blank rectangles. His perspective drawings for the Grange show a plain lawn to the south of the house; beyond this, immediately above the chalk cliffs facing the English Channel, he designed a garden which was memorably described by John Hardman Powell: 'The Garden was masculine in design, "no arbour for catterpillars to drop on you" but beds well dug out of the chalk, the best of Kent soil carted there, reservoir in centre, and various novel fences to break great gales' (fig. 3.58).[101] The 'catterpillars', I am sure, are derived from the comic routine of Nicholas Nickleby's mother, who reminisces about 'an exquisite little porch with twining honey-suckles and all sorts of things, where the earwigs used to fall into one's tea on a summer evening'.[102]

Pugin did not care for garden things. The lack of a garden door at the rectories, as at his own house, has been mentioned above.

On the other hand, the siting of some of his small presbyteries does show a certain willingness to engage with the surrounding built landscape. At Warwick Bridge he could have sited the presbytery on the generous plot wherever he wanted to in relation to the church. He chose to angle it slightly so that the front door of it was inclined so that those going in through the west door of the church would be aware of it; in so doing he echoed some of his earliest sketches of imaginary scenes where he seemed to have a liking for this type of setting (see fig. 3.23).[103] He very probably added the porch wing to the crude Tudor-gothic presbytery by Derick and Hickman at Banbury in Oxfordshire so that the entrance to the house would similarly be visible from the street side of the church (fig. 3.59). At Marlow Pugin located the west door of his Roman Catholic church so that it would have been directly visible from the front door of the neighbouring *Anglican* rectory (but for the garden wall). All this contrasts with the practice of conventional Tudor-gothic architects: in nearly every case we have seen, the front door of a parsonage would be located away from the church; indeed, at Walkeringham, our first example, the front door faces in the other direction, at the end of a lengthy drive.

There could be no clearer evidence than this that Pugin's houses were intended to link their priests visibly, as well as architecturally, to the church that represented their community. So although his structural and constructional message arrived precisely as the architectural profession was becoming more complex and more demanding technically – indeed, Thomas Leverton Donaldson, first professor of architecture at University College London, wrote in 1842 of the present day that 'Perhaps there was never a period in this Country when construction was generally better understood' – it also became known exactly as the early success of the Oxford Movement resulted in a whole army of young clergymen taking up incumbencies across England who were both morally committed and financially able to build a house that would be a lasting testimony to their dedication to their churches, and that would unmistakably speak of truth and consistency.[104] It was because of this that the new parsonage of the 1840s and 1850s came to exemplify a fundamental and lasting change in English domestic architecture.

3.59
It seems likely that Pugin interfered with the design of the presbytery alongside Derick and Hickman's church of St John, Banbury, Oxfordshire, as it was going up in the late 1830s. The addition of a cross-corridor section with its entrance facing the street, seen here at the left of the house, aligned the front door with the church porch in a typically Puginesque manner whilst extending the amount of circulation space within.

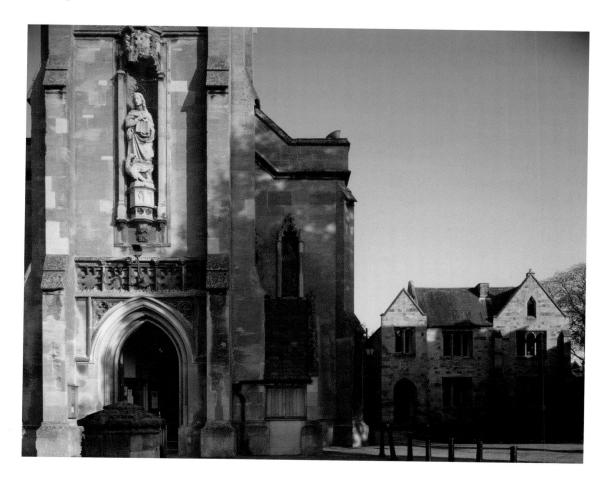

Chapter Four

The 1840s: In a state of transition

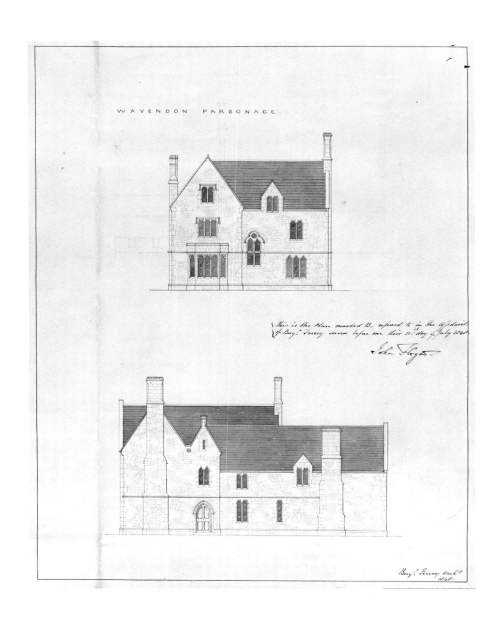

As the first years of the reign of Queen Victoria got under way, architects across England continued, of course, to do the best they could, using the methods and ideas they were used to and changing their working methods only when professional and technological innovations made it inescapable. They did however have plenty of scope for experiment, for the decade saw a considerable increase in the number of new parsonages: both the Oxford and Norwich diocesan collections have more applications for new houses in the 1840s than in the earlier three decades put together.[1] A number of architects were already established as specialists in parsonage design, and their work across a lengthy period of time gives us an insight into how their minds were working. A good example is that of George Wightwick (1802–72). Wightwick is probably best known to us as the young man who acted for a short period in 1826–7 as pupil, amanuensis and reader of evening stories to the aging John Soane, and, consequently, as the purveyor of some of the best stories about him; he was also a competent draughtsman, having worked on John Britton and A. C. Pugin's *Public buildings of London* and published his own views of Roman antiquities.[2] As an architect he was less memorable, but not unimportant because of the many surviving works and drawings that he left behind him from a long and critical period of work between establishing his practice in Plymouth in 1829 up to about 1851, when his work was considered not to be authentically mediaeval enough for modern church builders.[3] His houses illustrate what happens when a talented and engaging character is doing his best in an age of architectural hiatus, between one established style and the next.

Wightwick's work varied between Tudor-gothic and classical-Georgian without any apparent chronological sequence; unfortunately there is little record of mortgage application drawings for his parsonages, so we do not have the full picture that we do for other architects; and dating some of his work is difficult. The houses themselves, and his drawings at the Royal Institute of British Architects Library Drawings Collection, are often the best we have to go on.[4] In common with other architects, he drew working drawings without any graphic indication of the proposed materials; in his case, his gothic detailing took the form of applied surface relief and was not a part of any structural organisation. Much ornament was executed in uniform grey cement, and did not vary from place to place. The choice of

4.1
The rectory at Wavendon, Buckinghamshire, designed by Benjamin Ferrey in 1848. Ferrey was one of the most prominent architects to be directly influenced by A.W.N. Pugin, his work achieving increasing competence and subtlety during the 1840s. See also fig 4.21.

detailing at St Dominick's (1843) (fig. 4.2) near the River Tamar in Cornwall, for example, adjacent to a remarkable parish church that has a delicate jettied and pinnacled spire, and close to the mediaeval Cotehele House, is little different from that at Probus (1839), a characterless settlement just east of Truro.[5] Wightwick designed pointed front doors, but other openings were square-headed and invariably with cement hood moulds. His gables were set at 45 degrees, with the gable set over raised haunches presumably intending to disguise the gutter ends and creating that shouldered effect so typical of Tudor-gothic design. These gables sat low over the upper floor, so that upper floor windows projected up into them, and Wightwick very

4.2
The entrance (north-west) elevation of the rectory at St Dominick, west of Cotehele, Cornwall, designed by George Wightwick in 1843.
The architect did not appear to have been inspired by the delightful, and delicate, mediaeval church next door. The castellated upper storey of the porch was added later and the architect's Tudor-gothic 'shoulders' at the base of the gable have been removed.

often decorated them with blind lancets or trefoiled insets. At Liskeard and Pelynt (1843) he devised a chimney gable where a central chimney disappears into the gable parapet mouldings from below, and then emerges from them above; the mouldings themselves resemble barge-boards cast in cement (fig. 4.3).[6] At Pelynt he also experimented with a type of dormer window which appears more than anything classical, and he provided each of the external doors with its own shouldered gable porch. The plans were generally central-corridor types.

In general, Wightwick used classical-Georgian architecture for his more substantial or public buildings, although there were exceptions.

4.3
Wightwick's vicarage at Pelynt, west of Looe, Cornwall (1843). Although slightly altered the house retains some of its architect's eccentricities, including chimneys that merge at the gable with cement-covered pseudo-bargeboards and unusual dormers.

He designed some small parsonages in the classical-Georgian style, for example at Wedron in 1838 and at St Ives.[7] Decorative detailing in these two houses was reduced to the minimum – consoles supporting flat projections above windows, and in the case of Wedron, a pediment over a projecting porch.

Wightwick is typical of architects of his period who when attempting a Tudor-gothic building essentially attached pattern-book detailing onto a neutral background: before the early 1840s, there is no expression of constructional logic in the exterior of a building in anything but a clumsy way, such as those haunches which look as if they are moulded from a single material. And so one has decorative features all over the place, a leading characteristic of the Tudor-gothic style, and almost no variations in plan from convention. An architect like Wightwick might be followed by that of William Donthorn (1799–1859), whose drawings are also in the RIBA collection. He too was a prolific architect of parsonages from the 1820s to 1852, although in a sense he represents a later stage of their development, one which shows the increasing use of Puginian devices without them being allied to any overall new approach: one might bluntly say that he was the same type of architect as Wightwick, but that he had the fortune to be more in touch with the latest fashions. His parsonages, like Wightwick's, were generally but not invariably Tudor-gothic, although he used less render and considerably more carved stone; and his detailing, whilst not authentically historical, became increasingly more severe and more consistent than Wightwick's ever was. Although he did use the standard plan types – for example, the back-corridor plan that we have already seen at the executed version of the Italianate parsonage at Moulton St Michael in Norfolk of 1831, and the L-corridor plan, at Oundle in Northamptonshire – his particular contribution to the plan type was to help establish in his many buildings the conventional use of the staircase hall that Pugin had introduced in his parsonages.[8] A curious early plan for the parsonage at Thrapston in 1837, which incorporates parts of an older building, has a minimal staircase hall reached by a corridor.[9] At Fontmell in Dorset (1844) and at Weybridge in Surrey (1848) however, this stair hall is large enough to be used as a room and placed at the front centre of a symmetrical elevation, but the plan is in other respects unremarkable (fig. 4.4).[10] Then, at Dummer in Hampshire, of 1850, a large and impressive house, a central front door

4.4
Fontmell rectory by William
Donthorn (1844): the entrance
elevation. Note the very
typically Tudor-gothic
shouldered gable above the
porch [RIBA Library Drawings
Collection, Donthorn
[Fontmell] 1].

leads into the left-hand corner of a stair hall which is as large as at least
two of the principal rooms, and which seems to contradict Donthorn's
characteristically strictly symmetrical facade.[11] At a late project,
a remodelling of an existing building at Rushbury in Shropshire in
1852, another large new central staircase hall was created out of the
old fabric.[12] This rectory also abandons the last traces of the old Tudor-
gothic shouldered gables which had persisted in Donthorn's work as
far as the Dummer house, and the top of the wall is at long last built
out Pugin-fashion – sideways under the gable as it descends below
the eave, and not upwards to create a parapet. Principally, however,
the development in Donthorn's plans seems to reflect the increasing
importance of the hall in the planning of the house; it may also be a
conscious imitation of those plans, such as Pugin's pinwheel houses,
where the staircase hall also acts as the hub of a relatively small house.
With prominent designs such as these appearing all over the country,
it was hardly surprising that new fashions eventually filtered down to
provincial builders.

Technical precision

But there were factors other than stylistic ones that soon influenced
the way architects in general worked and designed. The first is a
greater theoretical awareness, appropriate for an era of rationalisation

and classification. By the late 1830s architectural writers no longer recommend choosing a different style for a house on the basis of its size or status; it is as if by emphasising the idea of 'principles' in architecture, designers began to realise that future decisions would come about from the form and construction of the building itself, rather than being attributed by metaphor from philosophy or literature. Over the ten years that follow Loudon's *Encyclopaedia* one notices a change of tone in architectural writing as architects settle down to attend to the technical issues facing them and to start to see how they might be expressed in a building. An illustration of the extent to which practical necessities were making inroads into traditional commentaries is provided by Joseph Gwilt, whose *Encyclopædia* of 1842 was published soon after Pugin's *The true principles*, although the author took pains to point out that his own work had been in preparation for some nine years.[13] His conclusion on the subject of use and beauty lies in a quotation from Archibald Alison's *Essay on the nature and principles of taste* of 1790:

> I apprehend that the beauty of proportion in forms is to be ascribed to [fitness] and that certain proportions affect us with the emotion of beauty, not from any original capacity in such qualities to excite this motion, but from their being expressive to us of the fitness of the parts to the end designed.[14]

There had always been 'principles', but now it was their increasing specificity and application to architecture which characterised the period. By the end of the 1830s the exact character of these new technical 'principles' was beginning to concern academics. In 1842 T. L. Donaldson's *Preliminary discourse* – in effect, a precis of his forthcoming first lecture series at University College, London – summarised that 'A recurrence to first principles was never more essential than at this moment. For not only our own school, but those of our continental neighbours have reached a most critical period. We are all in fact in a state of transition'.[15] He would have known of Pugin's arguments – he could hardly have failed to have done – and because of the frequency of cases where architects, builders and their clients conflicted over building standards, costs and failures, he would have known too that the architectural profession was under pressure to achieve higher standards of construction. But of course he had no way of knowing where this 'transition' was leading.

At this period a large number of technical architectural publications make their appearance; they include books such as S. H. Brooks' *Designs for cottage and villa architecture*, of 1839, which was predominantly a detailed construction manual, and distinctly non-judgmental about style (fig. 4.5). But one single recent publication for architects would have given Donaldson an insight into a world of professional competence which is not that dissimilar to that of the

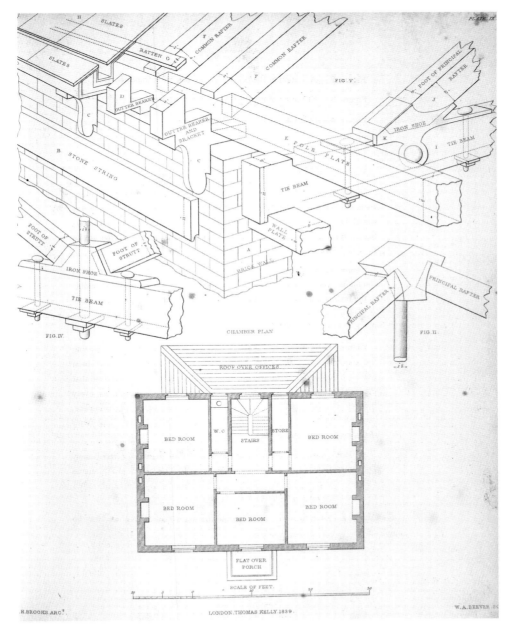

4.5
S. H. Brooks' *Designs*, probably published in 1839, concentrated on the technical solutions, rather than the stylistic language, of new buildings: books like these were already a long way removed from the pattern books of the previous decade. Brooks wrote that 'every building ought to exhibit that peculiar style which is indicative of the particular uses for which it is erected' (page 30).

early twenty-first century. We have already come across extracts from the lengthy introductory essay to Alfred Bartholomew's *Specifications*, first published in 1840 and then again in 1846; but the bulk of the book is given over to providing technical advice, and gives us a clear picture of the rapidly increasing awareness amongst architects both to the technical and constructional innovations, but also to the legal and professional ones which were beginning to govern their profession. Bartholomew, whose brief editorship of the *Builder* was cut short by his premature death in January 1845, began his career as a writer on the fireproofing of dwellings. The *Specifications* was primarily intended for architects now required to provide detailed drawings and specifications when signing a contract at the outset of a building project, a subject we will return to shortly.[16] The introduction is valuable here too, for it projects over the whole book a philosophical as well as a practical justification. Bartholomew was aware that technical literature 20 years beforehand had been in 'a coarse state of vagueness' and his approach to his subject was that of technical suitability based on his practical experience since that time:

> It is the architect's business, to produce the greatest convenience strength duration and beauty, out of the funds which are entrusted to his care.[17]

From this premise, the book proceeds to its second part: lists of extensive building specification clauses for all aspects of construction, including sample detailed specifications for various building types.[18] One of these is for 'a small rectory' (in Essex, with a living valued at £400 per annum), and another for a large one (£800 p.a.).[19] The smaller rectory specification begins with a list of 11 drawings – plans, sections, elevations, and interior and exterior details – that the architect must provide. Well over a hundred clauses specify the works required, from the demolition of the old house to the hanging of the bells. The 21 sections on bricklaying include not only the method and extent of the masonry, but also the requirement for the contractor to dispose of excavations and waste.[20] Bartholomew has not forgotten that the architect may have been required by Queen Anne's Bounty to reuse old bricks in his new building, and there is a clause allowing this. Another one requires the bricklayer to provide half a rod of best stock brickwork as a basis for extras; and another specifies the proper method of forming brick funnels at the feet of soil pipes. The house will have two marble chimney pieces with slabs, valued in whole at ten guineas.[21] A comparison with a typical architect's specification of the time will give some indication of the radical scope of Bartholomew's recommendations. The carpentry and joinery clauses of any typical specification of the time were generally amongst the longest items in it, but any reference to the auxiliary elements, rather than merely to primary ones such as sashes, architraves, doors and so on was very limited. James Pritchett, writing his specification in 1841 for the parsonage at Bossall in Yorkshire referred, for example, to the provision of 'grounds' for the door architraves, and 'proper bearers' for the deal staircase treads.[22] Bartholomew, no doubt with the experience of 101 on-site squabbles, left nothing to chance: the contractor was 'to provide and fix all requisite shores, struts, stints, puncheons, oak-wedges, ties, cletes, beads, stops, fillets, tilting-fillets, backings, blocks, linings, casings, furrings, and rolls'.[23] Further sections give sizes for wallplates, joists and sleepers; and the £400 p.a. rectory has 'countess' slates throughout, whereas the £800 one employs the larger 'duchess' size over its south attic windows.[24] The latter also had artificial stone ornament outside, and five ceiling roses, called 'enriched flowers with frames...each value 5s' within.[25] The provision of the up-to-date building technology of the time can, of course, be precisely ascertained here too. There are to be cast-iron air gratings around the base of the exterior walls for damp proofing; elsewhere, Bartholomew provided instructions for isolating brick piers from ground-floor sleepers by lead; for internal wall battening; and for waterproofing stucco ('of best new quick pure Parker's cement').[26] The smaller house is to have 'the very best pan water-closet apparatus' – he recommended Findon's patent – and the larger house is to have two, with wash hand basins, all fitted up 'with inch fine Spanish mahogany'.[27]

Until recently, specifications submitted with applications to the Bounty might well have consisted of a single sheet of instructions. At the time of writing, Bartholomew would have seen examples similar to that made by Peter Thompson in the same year of 1840 for his proposed parsonage in Sutton, Norfolk, of which the principal drawing was a sheet of paper less than 17" wide by 12" high, onto which were squeezed a pair of simple outline plans at an eighth of an inch to the foot, a single sketchy elevation enlivened by some scrawled greenery, and a list of rooms with their overall dimensions (see fig. 2.47).[28] It is rare at this time to find a detailed, priced specification as part of a Gilbert's Acts application; W. Hambley of Holloway provided one to accompany his otherwise unexceptional application for his curate's house at Theydon Bois as early as 1839; and during the same period Richard Carver in Taunton, of whom more later, usually did this.[29] The fact that most architects, surveyors or builders did not at once adopt Bartholomew's methodical and thorough clauses in their entirety – indeed, when I was being trained in the 1980s it was still something of a struggle to ensure that everything was properly written down – is a fine testament to the irrationality of the architectural profession. As late as 1871 it was left to the Bishop of Winchester himself to add a water closet to a plan drawn by the great George Edmund Street to a plan for a parsonage at Purbrook in Hampshire.[30]

From the 1820s up to the 1840s architects were faced not only with increased expectations of technical proficiency, but also with demands for more consistent administrative procedures. The methods of approving applications to build new parsonages provide plenty of examples of how this developed into a further wing of the general movement of the period towards increased centralisation, and indeed to what is sometimes called governmentalisation – that is, the expansion of a public bureaucracy which increasingly imposes itself on the transactions of daily life. A note found with a file of 1816 for a new house at Merton, south of London, reveals that the Bounty was already issuing applicants with printed instructions drawing their attention to the basic requirements of Gilbert's Acts, in particular the need to have their estimate verified by a surveyor, and to provide an 'undertaking on the part of a Surveyor or other respectable Workman, to do the Work in a good substantial and Workmanlike manner, according to the Plan and Estimate, for the sum stipulated'.[31] Christopher Hodgson, the secretary to the governors of the Bounty from 1822, published in 1826 a useful guide for incumbents and their agents who wanted to rebuild. *An account of the augmentation of small livings by the governors of the Bounty of Queen Anne*, to give it only part of its long title, began with a description of the Bounty itself, providing a history of the first fruits and the tenths drawn from earlier sources. Hodgson demonstrated the will of the governors to meet their obligations by explaining that they were prepared to increase vastly the sums they had originally put aside for providing mortgages, hinting at the very good business it had already become. He provided the texts of the original and currently relevant legislation; and he also gave a detailed description of the required procedure for obtaining a grant for house-building under the augmentations legislation of 1803. Unlike Gilbert's Acts, this later act placed the procedure clearly under the jurisdiction of the Bounty, rather than of the local bishop, thus allowing Hodgson to define what the governors expected. He wrote sharply that

> As the Governors of Queen Anne's Bounty are very particular and strict with regard to the plan, specification, estimate, undertaking, affidavits, and other documents mentioned in these instructions, it will save trouble to all parties, and be creditable to the Surveyor, if pains be taken by him in preparing the same in a correct and proper manner; and the Incumbent is particularly requested to examine the same minutely, and to satisfy himself before he transmits the same to the Bounty Office, that they are drawn out nearly as circumstances may admit, and duly authenticated, according to these directions, and afterwards to see that the works are performed according to the specification and undertaking; and to give notice to the Secretary of the Governors if the same shall not be so performed.[32]

In any case, it was evidently possible by 1840 for the Bounty to approve an augmentation for the building of a new house, but demand that this new house be then mortgaged under the Gilbert's Acts to pay for the services of a curate, so the building would in practice have to be approved under the requirements of those acts in the first place.[33] There are examples of letters amongst the various parsonage files in the record offices of correspondents apologising for having earlier omitted required documents or otherwise not complied with the regulations.[34] Various applicants across the country were late with their paperwork, started without permission, requested variations mid-way, or otherwise set the cat amongst the well-ordered pigeons at Dean's Yard. Hodgson reminded his readers that the Bounty would not allow for 'grates, stoves, coppers, or other articles usually accounted fixtures', which explains why some estimates price these separately, together with other minor items such as bells, and some pieces of ironmongery.[35] This demand for precision seems to have aroused some panic amongst applicants – for example, the vicar of South Newington in Oxfordshire took the trouble to ensure that the Bounty would not object to his last-minute substitution of wallpaper for paint.[36] Hodgson's book of 1826 was completed by a list of benefices, indicating which had received augmentations, by how much, and in what year, thus making it the first comprehensive work of reference on the subject. From this date onwards a process at work in other areas of society – the preparation and publication of properly compiled information as a first step towards implementing reform – arrives in the field of the provision of new parsonages. Editions of Crockford's *Clerical directory*, which was first published in 1842 and henceforth appeared annually, indicated by an asterisk which of the listed benefices had a parsonage house 'fit for habitation'. Although the list does not appear to be entirely accurate – occasionally one finds an example of a parish where the parsonage is marked as being unfit, whilst other evidence suggests that a house had been recently built – the decision to include this information is a reminder that the Bounty, and the church authorities in general, intended the directory to remind parsons that a fit residence was not only desirable, it was also possible if the rules were correctly followed.

Alongside the condition that applications be made in a consistent and thorough way came the introduction of standard forms to be completed. When the Gilbert's Acts' legislation was first deployed in the 1810s the bishop appointed his commission and received his reply on a plain sheet of paper, often the same one. From 1840 there were printed forms available, and the bishop's clerk had only to fill in the names and the places as necessary, although it clearly took time for these to reach all regions: in Norwich the first recorded form appears in 1844, but in Bath and Wells not until 1846.[37] The increase in the amount of form-filling required continued throughout the nineteenth century: comparisons can easily be drawn between changing standards where a parsonage is built with a mortgage, and then rebuilt or remodelled sometime later. The very early application for the substantial sum of £200 to extend Rustington vicarage in Sussex by a stair hall and three new rooms on each floor, for example, of 1804, consists of a handful of papers; when the Reverend John Cheale's early twentieth-century successor, J. Louis Crosland, wanted a grant of £25 to add a bathroom and a few other very minor changes in 1915, he was required to submit a large stack of documents.[38] This process is one that begins with Hodgson's idea of order, and with Hodgson's book. And the grasp that Hodgson had over his office was remarkable. He was appointed secretary in 1822 and combined this office with that of treasurer in 1831; he then proceeded to rule over the proceedings of the Bounty for another 40 years, living beside the shop in an arrangement that blurred the distinction between his private and personal life.[39] A 'congratulatory certificate' attached to the index of volume 24 of the minutes of the board of governors on the occasion of Hodgson's laying the first brick of what in effect became his private apartments at 3A Dean's Yard in August 1846 gives something of the flavour of the regard in which he was held by the six assistants who signed it: it testifies to their 'high regard for your person and appreciation of the great kindness which induced the exertion recently made to secure the useful and comfortable additions to the office'. The following year a further office extension was built not only beside but also above Hodgson's new residence, so the two were certainly architecturally intertwined (see fig. 1.1).[40]

The business going on within was by now considerable. Towards the end of the decade, in April 1849, Hodgson recorded that the Bounty had granted 1,498 mortgages, worth a total of £733,760.5.11; the sum of £60,000 was being made available for new mortgages each year.[41] It was in that meeting that he noted that the low price of corn was badly affecting the ability of parsons to pay their instalments; by way of avoiding any future threat to the stability of the fund he proposed that the governors continued to lend the same amount – for 'the object of providing fit houses for the Residence of Incumbents of Benefices is universally acknowledged to be the most important' of its uses – but that it should be spread over a greater number of applicants.

Hodgson's demand for standards that were higher than had been traditional in the historical way of commissioning and building houses was not an artificial imposition: by reading the technical sections of, for example, Loudon's *Encyclopaedia*, one can easily discover that the incumbents themselves, and their families, would have reasonably expected new plumbing and kitchen arrangements including various manufactured and patent devices to be incorporated into their new houses (fig. 4.6). A small early nineteenth-century house might typically include a scullery and a pantry in addition to its kitchen; towards mid-century an outside court with a range of different uses was common. Even Thompson's modest house at Sutton, mentioned above, had a glass room, a store, a scullery and piggery, a knife room and a coal house in addition to a pair of what he called 'vespasians' (privies), and a stable block with separate fodder and chaise stores.[42] Architects could have some fun with these requirements: we have already seen Arthur Browne's application for Hepworth with its assortment of stylish and rustic buildings (see fig. 1.25); and in 1846 Samuel Sanders Teulon was able to exploit a minor extension project at Potton in Bedfordshire to design a stable block with a most curious and decidedly un-gothic round window.[43] A remodelling of a larger house in 1837 by Carver of Taunton included a complex and comprehensive range of kitchen offices, including a coal house, shed, scullery wash and bakehouse, dairy, larder, butler's room, servants' hall, wine cellar, a china and store pantry, a beer cellar, and a shoe and knife house, in addition to further storage provided by the basement of the house.[44] Each of these areas required equipment or fitting out of some different

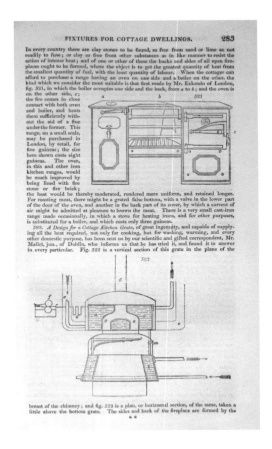

4.6
The latest kitchen equipment, illustrated in Loudon's *Encyclopaedia* (book 1, chapter 3, page 283). In book 3 Loudon presented a highly sophisticated plan by a Mr Mallet for a large new kitchen.

kind; again, the parsonage files unfailingly provide useful detailed examples of the growth of the Victorian back-stairs.

Everything that was to be provided had to be drawn; and to some extent the drawings themselves provide a commentary on changing attitudes. One interesting fact is that the room titles labelled on drawings show that it was not unusual to have the drawing room on the upper floor of a house even in an isolated country location, perhaps where the lower rooms might have been susceptible to damp; another is that during the first half of the nineteenth century, a dining room seems often to have been called an 'eating room' in East Anglia. The drawings provide a commentary of their own in other ways, too. The earliest submissions are only very rarely attractive as drawings; and the less 'architectural' elements of the scheme, the kitchen yard or offices, are often left out of the elevations or obscured by planting.[45] Joseph Stannard's imposing classical–Georgian elevation for the new vicarage at Sutton in Cambridgeshire ignored the large office and stable blocks flanking it.[46] Not for nothing had Pugin often ridiculed modern architecture by showing a variety of round-the-back boiler sheds and functional additions which had somehow escaped the attention of the architect when viewing the house from the front. Mark Thompson, he of the splendid Boxford rectory in Suffolk, had sometimes submitted his applications in the form of one tidy page, including a minute watercolour illustration (see figs 1.23, 2.5).[47] Rather more professional and neat drawings in coloured ink, with watercolour, became more common in the mid 1830s. Occasionally these have perspectives attached, such as on the application for the new rectory at Badlesmere in Kent, by George Russell French of Chancery Lane, London, in 1836 (fig. 4.7).[48] Another attractive drawing in the

4.7
Part of the application drawing for Badlesmere rectory, between Faversham and Ashford, Kent. The house was designed by George Russell French in 1836, during the Tudor-gothic era of William IV [*Canterbury Cathedral Archives, DCb/DC/B1/1*].

Canterbury collection for that period is the small and careful design for a strange, asymmetrical plain classical-Georgian house for Stockbury by R. C. Hussey, in 1834, before the architect had been redeemed by the gothic revival (fig. 4.8).[49]

The standard of draughtsmanship in the country generally improved during the 1840s, and even dull drawings are increasingly neatly and finely prepared. Mid-century applications can have fine drawings: the set prepared by Teulon in 1849 for Tathwell in Lincolnshire is particularly attractive, and furthermore the architect drew the house in both his submitted perspectives with the kitchen offices highlighted in the foreground, showing the effect of first Loudon's and then Pugin's teachings. There is amongst them a dairy with a charming spirelet, a far cry from the hidden or invisible kitchen blocks of earlier decades (fig. 4.9).[50] William Bennett, 'builder of Portishead', submitted in 1851 a fine and complex drawing for his alterations to the parsonage in the town: it is a great deal more sophisticated than any 'builder' would have presented 20 years beforehand.[51]

One interesting example of the value of drawings is the way in which architects or surveyors drew the remains of the houses that they

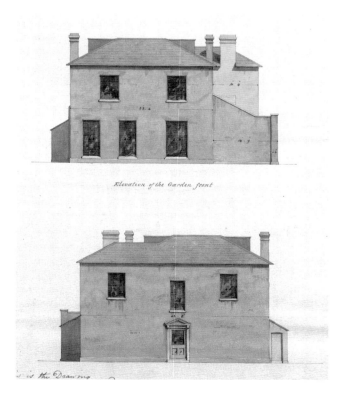

4.8
The rather haunting asymmetrical elevations for Stockbury, between Sittingbourne and Gillingham, Kent, by the future goth R. C. Hussey in 1834 – already working for Thomas Rickman and two years before taking over the partnership.
The gothic revival evidently offered a solution to curious arrangements like these [*Canterbury Cathedral Archives, DCb/DC/S35/1*].

4.14
William Railton's competition design for the Houses of Parliament, 1835, showing his proposed Old Palace Yard with entrances for the King, Lords and Commons. He won fourth prize, and was complemented by the judges on his layout [*The National Archives, ref. WORK 29/64*].

apologetic gables on prominent shoulders and little ornamentation (fig. 4.15). In January 1838 he heard that the Bishop of Ripon was intending to build himself a new residence and wrote to the Ecclesiastical Commissioners asking permission to submit proposals for it; thereafter his name crops up in connection with that house – for which he was selected following a competition in which Salvin and James Clephan also participated – and with the palaces at Stapleton (for the Bishop of Gloucester and Bristol) and of Riseholme (for the Bishop of Lincoln).[75] He does not appear to have held an official position as the architect to the Commissioners at this time and indeed the Ripon job got off to an inauspicious start when he had to ask his own bank to hand over the first instalment to the building contractor after being unable to convene the Commissioners in time to issue the payment. So in fact it was as a veteran of the various scandalous manoeuverings between the prelates as they struggled to outdo each other in the provision of grand new residences at public expense that he was commissioned to design a series of parsonages based on model types.[76]

The Ecclesiastical Commissioners, who were composed of both senior churchmen and politicians, took the matter of parsonage design very seriously; there is considerable record of it in their minutes, although in fact they were responsible for the design of very few of them: a schedule published in mid-1845 shows that they had so far approved a mere 57. In Dean's Yard Hodgson and his small staff were dealing with many more and with the minimum of a bureaucratic apparatus;

4.15
Grace Dieu Manor, between Loughborough and Ashby-de-la-Zouch, Leicestershire, seen from the south-east. The main house is by Railton and was built in 1833-4; Pugin extended the chapel porch upwards to form a tower in 1837; a few years later he added the service wing seen here on the right.

the Commissioners on the other hand passed lengthy resolutions on the matter, and in 1845 handed the matter down for further discussion by a select committee of five; other committees, such as those dealing with finances, and the appointment of surveyors and architects, were also involved. This was in part because the Commissioners had demanded from the first complete control over the design of the houses. In 1842, in their first recorded discussion of the subject, they resolved that 'in every case in which the Commissioners make a grant towards the building of a House of Residence for the incumbent of any living, such house be erected and completed entirely under their direction and control, and to this end all benefactions to meet such grants be paid over to the Commissioners before any contract is entered into for the building'. This resolution came following a discussion on some suggestions of Railton's: that he should prepare a standard parsonage house type from which only minor deviations would be allowed; that a standard building contract would be 'kept ready printed' for the execution of all the works 'by one contractor and for one sum'; and that he, Railton, would handle these houses for a fixed charge rather than for his usual charge of £5 per cent.[77] A few months later, the Board accepted that 'Every house proposed to be purchased must be surveyed by the architect of the Commissioners, and every new house must be built according to his designs and under his exclusive superintendence; the Commissioners entering into the necessary contracts'; they also made various decisions regarding policy when meeting benefactions intending for the provision of new parsonages.[78] The next decision on the subject was even more restrictive. The Commissioners appear to have been annoyed that they had agreed to the building of larger houses than Railton had originally designed, but that incumbents had then been unable to pay for them; and then they had had to ask for the plans to be reduced again, causing 'confusion and unnecessary expense'. The Board decided to fix the number of reception rooms at three – 'two sitting rooms, 16×14, a study about 12 or 13 feet square, kitchen, scullery, and usual offices of corresponding dimensions, and six bed Rooms' – and the costs of any alterations, including the addition of stabling, would have to be met directly by the incumbent himself.[79] The extent of the Commissioners' interference is the more remarkable bearing in mind the fact that 'as a general rule' they paid for no more than half the cost of a new house in the case of a parish in public patronage, and only two-fifths where there was a private patron.[80]

The designs that Railton came up with were dull in the extreme. For two parsonages in or close to London, at Muswell Hill and Rotherhithe, he designed plain central-corridor plans with conventional gable-and-bay front elevations.[81] Another four houses have almost identical back-corridor plans, the only variation amongst them being the study by the front door, which had either an internal or external chimney.[82] The unusual care with which Railton presented his constructional cross-section drawings, and the special attention given to the design of the front door and porch, contrast markedly with his characterless elevations of notionally classical-Georgian houses decorated with minimally Italianate chimneys, flat string courses formed from bands of raised stucco, shallow gables with projecting rafters, and a modest pediment above the front doors. This stylelessness was not Railton's own invention – a contemporary application for a curate's house at Derry Hill near Calne in Wiltshire submitted in 1843 by a pair called John Guthrie and B.B. Jones suffers from just the same artless dreariness.[83] There are others, too. In an Italian landscape, with Italian sun, houses like these might have just worked; in gloomy England they were depressing (fig.4.16).[84]

Amongst the critics of Railton's work were the writers of the *Ecclesiologist*, the journal of the Cambridge Camden Society – an organisation that had been established at the end of the 1830s by a group of undergraduates to appreciate and promote mediaeval gothic architecture and to revive it for modern church-building. In their June 1843 article on parsonages they issued the following condemnation:

> We have now two [parsonage designs] before us, which we regret to see approved by the Ecclesiastical Commissioners, one of them in the ordinary nondescript style of the day, the other professedly Gothick; but it will sufficiently shew how entirely the architect has mistaken the very principles of his art, to state that the ground plan, and in fact the whole design in the two, is identical. A square dripstone over each of the windows and the door, the insertion of a few mullions, a trifling additional elevation given to the roof, and a high roof placed over the porch, is apparently in the opinion of this artist all that is necessary to convert an Italian (if we may so call it) into a Gothick edifice.
>
> Now it is clear that the very first principles of good architecture are here violated.[85]

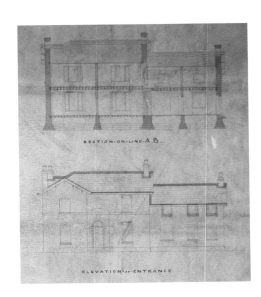

4.16
St Barnabas' parsonage, Bristol: details of the nominally classical-Georgian elevation from Railton's contract drawing in the RIBA collection. All his parsonages were very similar to each other [*RIBA Library Drawings Collection, Railton [1]*].

The Ecclesiologists might have suspected what Railton admitted during the course of an interview two years later: that he designed in this way because he believed the results to be cheaper than a true gothic building.[86] Agreeably for the gothic party, his attempts at resisting the new style coincided with his protracted and painful downfall as architect to the Commissioners. A number of his parsonage houses began to have problems even whilst they were under construction, and as a consequence the process by which these were investigated and discussed by his employers – interviews, committee and sub-committee meetings, and proposals, motions and decisions – provides a wonderful example of the value of early Victorian parsonage records in depicting the professional life of the architect of the period. The first sign in the Commissioners' files that things were going wrong was in the case of the house for Mr Smelgar, incumbent at St James' church, Mathon, in Herefordshire (fig. 4.17). Not only were applicants for grants towards houses required to pay their part of the costs up front to the Commissioners; they also had to pay an inspection fee of five pounds in advance of the architect's first visit to the site.[87] Since the Commissioners' secretary insisted that Railton minimise his travelling expenses by combining visits to sites in the same region there was often a delay at the outset at the project, and Smelgar was clearly annoyed by it.[88] He had also wanted a gothic house, and Railton had ignored this because of his belief that gothic was more expensive.[89] When Railton's plan finally arrived, at the end of July 1844, Smelgar wanted changes, but Railton encouraged him to sign his approval of them to save time, and said he would make the alterations later.[90] Smelgar was greatly disappointed that his architect was to provide him with a wine cellar but not a beer or cider one – space for the latter two was 'one of the most necessary and ordinary comforts' of a modern home, he thought – and he now personally faced the extra cost of adding these subsequent to the signing of the contract.[91] Smelgar thought the bricks of bad quality too, and, he seems to have added for good measure his belief and that of people in his locality that the Commissioners were shielding Railton from criticism by people such as himself because Railton had in some way a personal connection to the Commissioners' staff.[92] It appears also that Smelgar or his builder, McCain, complained that McCain had had to pay Railton personally a fee on being awarded the contract, which must

Mathon vicarage,
Herefordshire, designed in
1844 by Railton for Mr
Smelgar – the first of several
unsatisfied clerical clients.
This house was designed in
Railton's economic version
of gothic that violated 'the
very first principles of good
architecture'. Few of his
parsonages seem to have
survived in their original form.

have implied to Smelgar that Railton was in everybody's pay but his.[93]
Railton's replies to these charges, in an interview in July 1845 with
members of a select committee established by the Commissioners, give
an interesting picture of the changing state of professional methods.
He explained that he had not taken any improper fee – rather, that
consistent with correct contemporary practice, tendering contractors
would agree to paying a surveyor a fee of 20 guineas to take out
quantities from their plans and specifications and thus provide a secure

basis for submitting their prices; and that the successful contractor eventually pays the bill.[94] He described the old system of tendering without quantities as 'very dangerous'.[95] Smelgar's suspicions had no doubt been aroused because the surveyor here was Railton's own employee Thomas Morris, whom Railton trusted to do the job well; and Morris had received his cash from the builder whilst actually present in Railton's Regent Street office.[96] His questioners sought reassurance: 'But is it the universal custom of the trade that a respectable Architect has his own Surveyor who takes out the quantities and who must be paid by the successful competitor?' 'Yes', Railton replied, later adding 'Every respectable builder knows it'.[97] The committee members acquitted Railton of improper soliciting of fees when they finalised their report later the same day, although they now wanted the fee to be paid through their offices rather than Railton's; they also found nothing to criticise in the actions of their assistant secretary James Jell Chalk, who, as it happens, had indeed been responsible for introducing Railton to the Commissioners in the first place.[98] They did however criticise the rigidity of Railton's plans, and offered to pay for Smelgar's beer and cider cellars.[99] However Smelgar's was only one of a series of 'remonstrances or complaints' that had arrived at Whitehall Place.[100] Railton was summoned for a further interview on 26 June 1846 and faced no fewer than 144 questions from three angry Commissioners, the bishops of Oxford, Worcester, and Gloucester and Bristol, who represented some of the most aggrieved incumbents and questioned him most aggressively.

At Upleadon near Bristol there was 'no Cesspool or drain'; nor was there 'a Coalhouse, or Place for a Gig'. At Saul in Gloucestershire the architect had over-certified, allowing the builder to be paid for work he had not carried out. At Bridlington Quay the wrong timber had been used; at Mathon the offices were too small. In one case a Captain Duncombe had offered to raise the quality of building work by making a personal donation, and Railton had profited by this by taking a percentage on the extra costs. At the end of this painful interrogation, a Commissioner – most probably Samuel Wilberforce, Bishop of Oxford – rose up at the end to give the architect a lecture on the prestige he obtained by working for the board, and why this should compensate for the lack of greater financial gain from it:

the Payment of the Architect employed by this Commission is, first, the Number of the Houses which ultimately may come to him; Secondly, the Distinction he acquires on being Connected with our Board; it is the very Thing for a young Man starting in business, we all of us by Experience in our own Dioceses [know] that Architects of a very high Character are ready to give gratuitous Services to our Diocesan Societies merely for the sake of such a Connexion; therefore we cannot shut our Eyes to the Fact that Connexion with us at Head Quarters would be the making of any young Man of Character, Skill, and Talent in your Profession; it is not fair to strike that out in estimating how much the architect is to be paid. The Architect of a public Building who gets a great deal of public Work takes that Office for lower than he would if his whole Living was paid for from that Building, therefore there is a great deal in the Argument.[101]

The committee members consequently reported back to the next full board meeting that they 'cannot but express their strong Opinion, drawn from their careful examination of Mr Railton, that the existing arrangements of the Commissioners as to the erection of Parsonage Houses need immediate alteration'.[102]

Of all the disasters to date, that at Upleadon was much the worst, and considerably exaggerated by the fact that the vicar, Andrew Sayers, seems to have been both aggressive and paranoid. His contractor, W. Robertson, was an experienced parsonage builder for Railton, having worked on five other similar houses in the region: those at St Barnabas in Bristol, Cherhill, Knowle Hill, and St Paul's Newport in Monmouthshire, but also that at Saul where Railton had been accused of over-certifying.[103] Sayers in fact fell out with Robertson as his house was going up when Robertson allegedly overcharged Sayers for some work he was doing elsewhere.[104] Sayers then started finding fault with the new house. He asked Robertson for a copy of Railton's specification so that he could check that the house was being constructed as the architect had agreed, but got a 'saucy' refusal from Robertson, who walked off the site leaving the house unfinished in the autumn of 1845 but claiming the balance of the contract sum, just over £60.[105] Sayers wrote complaining letters to the Commissioners, and they promised that a surveyor would be sent down to investigate.[106]

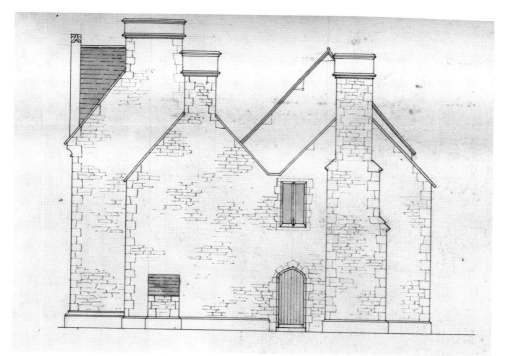

major rooms; study, drawing room and dining room, are arranged in an approximation of a pinwheel, the change in axis between them signalled on the outside, from the front, by the projection of the drawing room wall beyond that of the study.[129] The gesture is a modest one, however; up to mid-century at least, Ferrey is primarily an example of an architect who imitated Pugin's style in his parsonages, but without any radical change to their layout; and it seems to be inevitable that it is experiments in plan, rather than in elevation, which above all else have determined an architect's place in history.

Nevertheless, Ferrey is important here because of the nature of his professional career. There had been diocesan surveyors throughout the centuries, but never before had there been one able to impose a certain order into the design and building of parsonages across the diocese, in accordance with an unprecedented rate of technological and administrative change. Ferrey, too, was an Institute man: he became a fellow of what was now the Royal Institute of British Architects in January 1839, proposed by P. F. Robinson, one of its original vice-presidents; by Charles Barry; and by Thomas Cundy junior.

And Ferrey, in turn, proposed for fellowship in 1850 an architect who more than any other individual turned the design of parsonages into a lifetime's industry: Ewan Christian (fig. 4.22). According to a

4.21
The garden elevation of
Ferrey's rectory at Wavendon,
Buckinghamshire, now on the
edges of Milton Keynes (1848).
The pointed window lights the
staircase, which is thus in the
conventional position for a pre-
Pugin L-plan house. See also
fig. 4.1.

lengthy appreciation published some years after his death in the *Journal of the Royal Institute of British Architects*, Christian designed some 380 parsonages (and 40 further episcopal and other clerical residences) during his long career, which stretched from 1841 to the week of his death, aged 80, in 1895.[130] As a teenager he had been articled to Matthew Habershon for whom he drew examples of Tudor timberwork; and in the early months of 1836 he worked, ironically as it turned out, for Railton.[131] His first parsonage was at Preston in Lancashire, in 1845, so the great majority of his work lies outside the scope of this book. He is however an enormously significant figure in marking the change that had come over the architectural profession in respect of parsonage design from the early years of the century. Christian makes his first appearance in the minutes of the meetings of the board of the Commissioners in relation to a very minor matter where he was asked to survey on their behalf at Wolverhampton at the end of 1850, and it appears that his formal appointment the following year was not recorded there at all – perhaps the last echoes of the Railton dispute were still being felt.[132] In 1853, his report on the Beresfords' Kilndown house put Ferrey's judgment in a very unflattering light, and perhaps the incident confirmed the Commissioners' high opinion of him, rather as earlier incidents had adversely affected Railton to the benefit of Ferrey.[133] Christian moved his own practice to the offices of his employers, at 10 Whitehall Place in London; when the Commissioners later needed more space he moved to 8a, at the rear of Clutton's office, and remained at hand, and in the same post, for the rest of his life.

Christian is well known today mainly as the architect of the National Portrait Gallery, behind Trafalgar Square, a late building not at all characteristic of his work. His architectural style is not greatly remarkable nor easily definable but for a certain preoccupation with Puginian themes which he retained for much of his career. In 1848 he designed for the Reverend D. Barclay Bevan a house (not in fact a parsonage) called Casterton Grange in Westmorland that is designed around a top-lit central staircase hall, with radiating rooms on the ground floor, and which has an entrance front remarkably similar to the garden elevation of Pugin's Grange in Ramsgate; it has a four-storey square-plan tower to the right of

4.22
Ewan Christian. From the memoir published in the *RIBA journal*, 30 September 1911.

a bargeboarded, gable-and-bay elevation (fig. 4.23).[134] It must surely be a conscious reference to the Ramsgate house. As befits a busy and productive man, Christian relied on conventional layouts, although occasionally he often added to these a Puginian staircase hall type without any apparent chronological development: he designed a vicarage with one of these early in his career, at Acton in Suffolk, where the hall takes up the full width of the house and the two principal reception rooms are simply arranged in a row on one side of it; and he used a similar plan in conjunction with a Queen Anne elevation at a late house of 1880 for St Edmund's, Salisbury.[135] The Acton house, like the Casterton one, has decorative bargeboards, a favourite characteristic of his. Interestingly, he reverted to Tudor-gothic for his large private house at Woodbastwick, Norfolk, in 1886 – perhaps a search for an English way of building related to the contemporary enthusiasm for Queen Anne. As with many other unfashionable High Victorian architects it is salutary to be reminded that his houses were not seen at the time to be as plain as they seem to us now: an admiring client wrote tellingly that 'my own house...is as pretty as if it were not comfortable, and as comfortable as if it were not pretty; and the two together is all one wants – except an occasional visit from the architect'.[136] But it is as an administrator and setter of standards that Christian is important to us here. By the 1850s his drawings and presentations were meticulously prepared and his specifications resembled those prescribed by Bartholomew himself. Like Bartholomew, in fact, he had a 'terse and abrupt manner'.[137] From his desk in the stable yard at Whitehall he could preside over the administrative machine, but he also applied his standards to the variety of other activities within and without his profession that mark him out to us as a representative of his period. His daily working schedule was carefully planned to allow him to visit a great number of projects within a very short period of time, and, like Pugin, he used the railway journeys themselves as opportunities to work. He was also a member of the committee of honorary consulting architects to the Incorporated Church Building Society; in 1880 he became a member of the RIBA's first board of examiners in architecture; and he served as president of the institute from 1884–6; he was the Royal Gold Medallist for 1887; and he also contrived to teach at Sunday school for 35 years. Ewan Christian clearly showed that it was possible to build a successful and prestigious career in which the design of parsonages was perhaps as important for him and his clients as the design of churches.

Bath and Wells

A study of the records in any of the diocesan archives provides an opportunity to see how national developments affected the architecture of the provinces: in particular, one sees how Puginesque ideas – including higher and more consistent standards of detailing, staircase halls at the centres of houses, and the separate expression of rooms externally through distinct ridges – very soon spread about the country.

No doubt the particular character and experience of the various bishops that approved or rejected local applications for mortgages played some part in the process. At Bath and Wells there were three bishops during the period of this study and each must have brought with him a distinct approach even if all of them eventually suffered from considerable infirmity in their old age, for the bishops of this prestigious diocese held the position until their death. Richard Beadon, appointed in 1802, had himself considerable first-hand experience of pluralism and knew exactly what it was like for a parson to be residing away from his parish. A fellow of St John's College, Cambridge, and a former public orator of the university, he had held on to the incumbency of two parishes in Essex as well as the positions of archdeacon of London and prebend of Mapesbury even after being appointed Bishop of Gloucester; only when the transfer to Bath and Wells came 13 years later did he give them all up. Evidently a modest man of kindly and liberal disposition, he eventually became infirm, dying in Bath at the age of 87 in 1824.[138] His successor, although also a sometime fellow of a Cambridge college, could not have been more different. George Henry Law was a high Tory who as Bishop of Chester from 1812 countered the social threat brought about by the industrial change that was transforming his region by establishing schools and supporting changes in factory and educational reform; later, and after some personal intimidation at his palace in Wells, he vigorously opposed the Poor Law amendment measures of 1834, and he was the only bishop to support Peel's attempts at limiting factory working hours for children. Before arriving at Wells he had experience of the workings of the Bounty, because he served for two years, from 1822–4, on a committee that advised its governors on augmentations.

And finally with Richard Bagot, who succeeded Law in 1845, one sees the early impact of the theological and artistic reform that was to sweep the Church of England. Bagot was transferred to Wells after getting into hot water as Bishop of Oxford. He had been sympathetic towards Tractarians in the early days – J. H. Newman apparently referred to him as 'my pope' – but as for many others Tract 90 of 1841 turned out to be more than he, or his official position, could allow, and his attempts at negotiating between conservatives and radicals resulted in his being shunned on both sides. With the conversion to Roman Catholicism of Newman and others in 1843 his judgment would have appeared more than usually suspect. He successfully pleaded with Peel to inherit Law's post, but on arriving at Wells seems to have had a nervous breakdown that effectively incapacitated him. When one considers the political overtones of the stylistic debate of the 1840s and 1850s – culminating, of course, in the famous Government Offices *débâcle* of Palmerston and Scott, and of which more in the chapter that follows – it is not difficult to see how incumbents and their architects might have geared their applications to suit their bishops to some extent. And indeed here at Wells the neat division of the era into three – one aging Regency gentleman, one vigorous Tory reformer, and one weak Oxford sympathiser – provides what is almost a caricature of the process that England's ecclesiastical life was undergoing.

The Gilbert's Acts' collection from the Bath and Wells diocese, now at the Somerset Record Office, includes 91 files for the years between 1800 and 1850 inclusive, and in only a few cases, principally the early ones, are the plans missing. The diocese covered the tenth largest area (out of 22) in England in the mid 1830s, placing it somewhere towards the middle.[139] It had 441 benefices, the eighth largest; and it also had the eighth largest net income amongst the sees.[140] Its centre was in Wells itself, the town which Pugin had himself so often enthused over, and which contained, with Glastonbury, some of the finest surviving mediaeval domestic architecture that he and his father's men had recorded.[141]

The first outstanding characteristic of the diocesan collection is that architects were encouraged to reuse existing buildings in their entirety; and, unlike in other areas, the architects were not embarrassed about the reuse, giving it some prominence both in plan and elevation.

4.23 (opposite) Casterton Grange, near Kirkby Lonsdale, Westmorland: Ewan Christian's house of 1848 was not a parsonage but was built for a clergyman with a parish elsewhere. The architect borrowed directly from the garden elevation of the Grange (see fig. 3.31). The tower was originally topped with a pyramidal slate roof.

4.24 (below)
Abbas Combe, between
Shaftesbury and Yeovil,
Somerset. The ground floor of
the old house runs along the
top, converted into a servants'
hall, larders, kitchen and
brewhouse (with a new oven
and copper); the new house
below, to the front, provides
three modern, regular
reception rooms [*Somerset
Record Office, D/D/Bbm/62*].

4.25 (below, right)
The ambitious Richard Carver
at the start of his career: an
unremarkable design for the
rectory at West Quantoxhead,
north-west Somerset, 1815
[*Somerset Record Office,
D/D/Bbm/40*].

There is an interesting example of 1833 at Abbas Combe where the designer, a carpenter and builder called Richard Read of Salisbury, simply attached a new L-corridor house to the old block, which was, like many others, long and low; a passage running along what had been the outside wall of the old house, and the back wall of the new house, separated the two, a surprisingly modern solution (fig. 4.24).[142] The old house was to become the brewhouse, kitchen and servants' hall; possibly the incumbent, Thomas Fox, had a strong personal attachment to it, because, as he pointed out in a letter to the bishop, it had been his own family home; he had himself succeeded to the advowson on the death of his father in 1820. In other examples, retained old houses are made into the back parts of a new back-corridor plan.[143] At Charlecombe, for example, the old house has a new Tudor-gothic gable-and-bay type elevation grafted onto it; in others, reception rooms, or minor additions or alterations sufficed to bring them up to date.[144]

A further characteristic at Wells is the dominance of a comparatively small number of architects over many of the applications, and the near absence of London designers. The most prolific of the former was Richard Carver, an architect from Taunton, who designed or re-

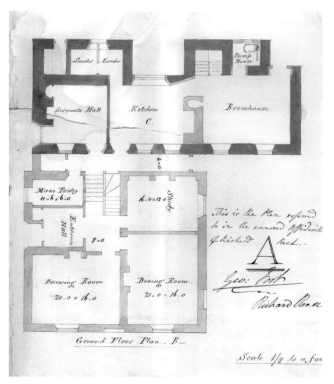

modelled at least seven houses between 1815 and 1846. Carver, a former
pupil of Sir Jeffrey Wyatville, was county surveyor between 1832–46,
in some ways therefore the lay equivalent of Ferrey. The rising
standard of Carver's work provides a mirror for developments
nationally. At West Quantoxhead in 1815 he produced a simple design
for the alteration of an old house, adding a kitchen and kitchen court
to the back of a simple classical-Georgian house, to which he added a
pretty trellis around the front door (fig. 4.25).[145] 17 years passed before
Carver's name again appears on a mortgage application, this time for
Cutcombe in 1832. This house marks the first appearance of one of his
planning idiosyncrasies: an L-corridor plan where the staircase part of
the L is widened, so that it becomes a kind of staircase hall deep within
the house: in this case he provided there a broad spiral staircase (fig.
4.26).[146] The vicarage at East Brent was a large, symmetrical Tudor-
gothic house; it had the full complement of kitchen offices referred to
above (fig. 4.27).[147] Carver had by now become county surveyor and he
used the title in his affidavits; he was also the architect of Chard town
hall, and various other large buildings, and perhaps his self-
importance is reflected in this stylish set of drawings. By 1839, the date
of his house at Westonzoyland, his only classical-Georgian parsonage,

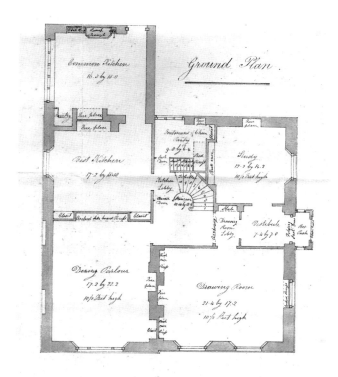

4.26
A broad spiral staircase –
an unusual feature in
contemporary parsonages –
in the centre of the L-plan
vicarage at Cutcombe,
south of Minehead. By Richard
Carver in 1832 [*Somerset
Record Office, D/D/Bbm/60*].

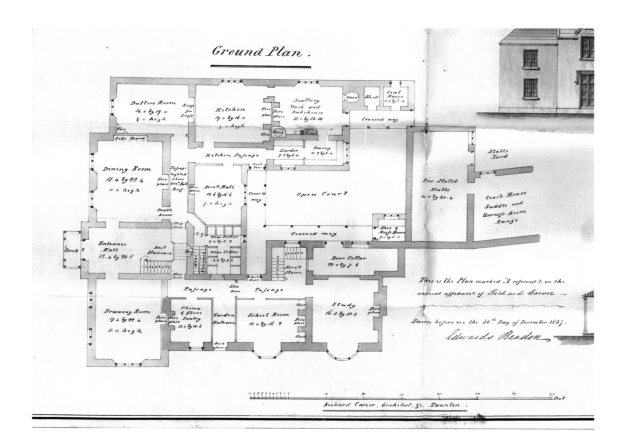

Ground Plan.

4.27
East Brent vicarage, south of Weston-super-Mare: the proposed remodelling by Carver in 1837. The greater part of the ground floor of the house is taken up by kitchen offices. The entrance hall to the left is flanked by the dining and drawing rooms (above and below, respectively); there are a study and school room to the lower right-hand side of the main block. All the rest is service area [Somerset Record Office, D/D/Bbm/71].

his applications are accompanied by well-organised and detailed estimates with a price for each clause, suggesting that he was acting as contractor as well as designer.[148] Only five years earlier a house that had cost half as much, designed by a surveyor called Churchhouse, had been accompanied by Somerset's last single-sheet specification.[149]

Two other architects submitted more than a couple of applications: Maurice Davis junior, of Langport, and Jesse Gane, a builder from Evercreech. Davis' work is often colourful and stylish: his first application, for the rectory at Sparkford, is accompanied by a pretty watercolour that shows the curtains through the glass of the front room windows (fig. 4.28).[150] One has a feeling here and elsewhere that Davis was perhaps wasted in Langport. The house he designed two years later at Hinton St George was basically a back-corridor type, but he divided the passage into a series of vestibules of different shapes for variety, an engaging device and something that few others seem to have thought of (fig. 4.29).[151] His three remaining projects are largely unexceptional, but his addition to the vicarage at Merriott is interesting because it consists of a substantial stair hall as well as a

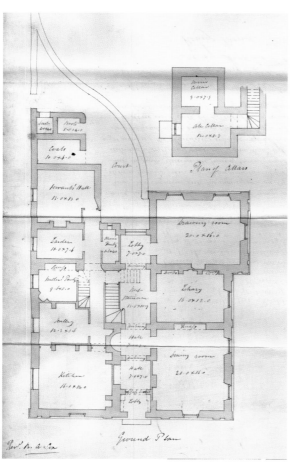

4.28 (above)
Maurice Davis junior's elevations – with curtains – at Sparkford rectory, between Shaftesbury and Bridgwater (1837) [*Somerset Record Office, D/D/Bbm/69*].

4.29 (below)
Further evidence of Davis' theatrical style: the corridor of the curate's house at Hinton St George, near Crewkerne (1839), is divided up into a series of vestibules en filade. The major rooms run, in back-corridor-plan fashion, along the right-hand side of the house: drawing room, library, and dining room (from top to bottom) [*Somerset Record Office, D/D/Bbm/76*].

dining room, and as such it is representative of a phenomenon that was appearing all over the country (fig. 4.30).[152] Wherever one looks one sees them, and they were inserted even where the original plan made it difficult, for example at the plain central-corridor house designed by Mark Thompson in 1821 at Hartest in Suffolk, which we encountered long ago, and where a new stair hall was carved out of the centre, creating an L-corridor plan but with a generous open space at its centre in 1854.[153] At Butleigh, back in Somerset, Francis Penrose cut a substantial chunk out of the centre of an old house in 1846 to provide a large stair hall, signifying it with a window on the entrance front.[154] New houses of the period, such as that at Compton Dando, have these large stair halls in them too, clearly demonstrating the new fashion (figs 4.31, 4.32).[155] And another new stair hall was designed by Jesse Gane when he enlarged the early Tudor-gothic parsonage at Dinder, in so doing turning the charming small thatched house by Charles Wainwright into a building that was a great deal drearier.[156] Gane also

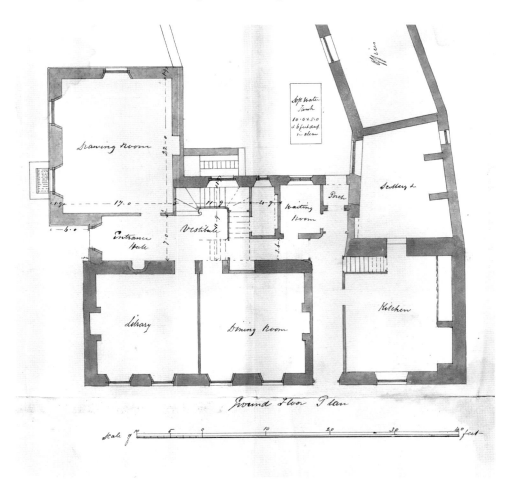

4.30
Merriot, between Yeovil and Chard, extended by Davis in 1851. The old house ran in an irregular L shape around the bottom and right-hand side of the plan, and Davis added a large drawing room but also an imposing Puginian stair hall. Stair halls like these were now being implanted into old houses across the country [*Somerset Record Office, D/D/Bbm/109*].

designed one other extension to an old house, and a new parsonage of his own, neither particularly distinguished.[157]

London architects made few inroads into the design of parsonages here, but the few that did so may have made some impact. Sampson Kempthorne, practising from 36 Clarges Street, Piccadilly, is best known for having been the architect to the Poor Law Commissioners in the mid-1830s, and for employing George Gilbert Scott as his assistant. The vicarage he remodelled at Cheddar in 1839 had a very irregular plan, and he added a few gothic touches to what was largely an old house.[158] Francis Penrose – he that inserted the large new stair hall and dining room at Butleigh – worked from 4, Trafalgar Square, and one imagines Railton's Nelson's Column slowly going up before his eyes as he drew. Two years after Butleigh he designed an interesting rectory, a variation on the L-corridor type, with convincingly gothic detailing outside, in an imposing setting at an isolated site for the parish of Alford with Hornblotton.[159] The third interloper is perhaps the most intriguing: Edward J. Andrews, of 47 Upper Bedford Place. This address is just the other side of High Holborn from Ferrey's offices in Bedford Street, and perhaps Ferrey knew him and recommended him for the job. His rectory at Compton Martin of 1841 is in a strange Tudor-gothic style, with an irregular and pretentious version of a back-corridor plan but with a large entrance hall, and turrets and buttresses at the corners (fig. 4.33).[160] The imposing entrance front is symmetrical, with back stairs and a store hiding behind the grand windows to the left of the front door; the main garden front is picturesque and irregular. It is perhaps an attempt at copying and downscaling a much larger Tudor-gothic country house, and it is hard to believe that even by then Ferrey thought much of it.

The Whichcords at Canterbury

The seat of the primate provides another window into the way in which architectural changes spread across the country. The extent to which the archbishop himself was involved in approving schemes is unknown, although of course his own signature like that of his junior colleagues appears on commissions and other documents. It is perhaps worth reminding ourselves who the archbishops were during our period. The first was Charles Manners Sutton, a former dean of Windsor, who had been appointed thanks to royal support over the

4.31 (above)
The parsonage of 1848 at
Compton Dando, south of
Bristol, by Samuel Tripp.
A prominent two-light gothic
window indicates that there
is a newly fashionable stair
hall within.

4.32 (right)
The interior of the stair hall at
Compton Dando.

4.33 (opposite)
The rectory at Compton Martin
between Bristol and Wells by
the London architect Edward J.
Andrews, 1841. The style,
although sophisticated, is
most unusual and perhaps
represents an effort to take
the Tudor-gothic in a new
direction.

preferred candidate of William Pitt, the prime minister (fig. 4.34). A grandson of the third Duke of Rutland, one of his earliest appointments had been to the family living at Averham cum Kelham, well before it had had the generous but stylistically confused additions designed by William Patterson in 1838 that we have seen in Chapter Two. Politically, he opposed Roman Catholic emancipation but supported relief for Protestant dissenters. He was in his fiftieth year when he was appointed to the post in 1805, and he stayed there until his death in 1828, a long tenure.

His successor was William Howley, a 'high and dry', distant, cold man who had supported George IV against Queen Caroline on the former's accession, a fact which no doubt contributed to his promotion to Canterbury on Manners Sutton's death; he was opposed to both Roman Catholic emancipation and to political rights for dissenters (fig. 4.35). He was an academic and had been Regius Professor of Divinity in Oxford from 1809. He seems to have brought something of the starchy flavour of a distant lecture hall to his ministry: a former curate from his diocese looked back nearly 60 years later on his own ordination ceremony at Howley's hands at Lambeth Palace in December 1833 and remembered that 'there was nothing solemnizing or impressive in his mode of conducting the ordination': there is probably no other bishop that so well personified the desiccated character of the church and its ceremonies immediately before the Oxford Movement began to make its impact.[161] Appropriately, too, for the era, he spent much of his time around the board tables of Dean's Yard and Whitehall Place, often chairing a meeting a week at both, and sometimes a very long and wearisome one. It was he that came with the lord chamberlain to Kensington Palace at 5 a.m. on the morning of 20 June 1837 to wake the young Queen Victoria on her accession: no wonder she preferred to place her confidences in Lord Melbourne. Howley was at last succeeded after his death in February 1848 by an altogether more sympathetic character, John Bird Sumner, who had been born in Kenilworth in 1780 (fig. 4.36). He studied at Eton College and King's College, Cambridge, and was sent by the latter to the valuable living of Mapledurham in Oxfordshire.[162] His first preferment came in 1828, when the Duke of Wellington appointed him Bishop of Chester, and his early ministry was marked by a distinctly pragmatic touch, which he first demonstrated when he unexpectedly voted for Roman Catholic emancipation, and which was to stand him in good stead during the various internal squabbles of the church in the late 1840s. He was also industrious, unlike many of his fellow bishops, and arrived at Canterbury with the reputation of having built 200 new churches and many schools in his former see. Following that first appointment by a Tory prime minister, he was elevated to Canterbury by a Whig, Lord John Russell. Described by his colleague Wilberforce as 'good, gentle, loving, and weak', he remained at Canterbury until his death in 1862.[163]

The Canterbury diocesan collection contains many unusual buildings, and we have already seen quite a number of them. In total, there are records of far fewer applications than at Bath and Wells, and for comparatively few entirely new ones: only five new houses from the 1820s; ten from the 1830s, and 12 from the 1840s.[164] One imagines that Howley, in particular, had little interest in it. One of the earliest documents there is a design by Thomas Dearn, the author of the two books called *Sketches in architecture* of 1806 and 1807, and much else, for the vicarage at Cranbrook in west Kent, the town where he himself lived. The original elevations have disappeared, and the plan is in very bad condition, but from it we can see that the house had an unusual symmetrical design, basically a central-corridor type but with a stair hall in place of the corridor, and a cross-passage running along the centre of the house which divided the two reception rooms from the kitchen and offices.[165] It does not however exist in exactly that form any longer, because like many other parsonages in the county it was partially rebuilt by the Maidstone architect John Whichcord, who with his son, also John, dominated the applications to build or rebuild in the diocese, making at least 13 applications between the mid 1830s and 1852 for new houses and other alterations.

The work of the Whichcords (the son joined the father from the mid 1840s) varied tremendously in quality and originality, never really seeming to develop in any particular direction. John Whichcord senior (1790–1860) was born in Devon but settled in Kent in the early 1820s as a result of working in the office of Daniel Asher Alexander on the design of Maidstone gaol. His earliest buildings were largely in a stripped classical style derived from his prison work. The Oakwood hospital of 1830 to the west of Maidstone sports a continental air: a five-sectioned symmetrical facade has a pedimented five-bay centre

with a projecting loggia; the rest of the building is almost completely unornamented, with the exception of a cornice and horizontal string courses.[166] The style is consistent with his other works of this period, which included churches and workhouses. Some of Whichcord's designs were then gothic, but his classical architecture was designed with considerably more conviction; either way, most of his early parsonage work is dry and uninteresting, and only the occasional detail stands out, such as a row of pretty rustic columns at an extension at Smarden in 1835.[167] At Cranbrook, Whichcord merely rebuilt Dearn's kitchen offices. At Harrietsham in 1838 he attempted a staircase hall, replacing the 'ancient timber structure'.[168] At Warehorne in 1839, he designed a crude Tudor-gothic rectory (fig. 4.37); the following year, at Newchurch, he designed a crude classical-Georgian one, and one that with a great deal of blind windows signally fails, as we heard in Chapter One, to exploit the potential of the entrance elevation of its back-corridor plan.[169] A house of 1843 at Sissinghurst, for which there are unfortunately no records of a mortgage application, suggested that he too might have been familiar with Parker's *Villa rustica* of 1833: although there are here no blatant Italian mannerisms, the front, east elevation of the house, is elegantly composed of three bays on two storeys, the central bay recessed slightly; there is a verandah unifying the ground-floor openings, and also obscuring the perennial problem of the conflict between the need for an imposing central bay on the one hand, and the common arrangement of a narrow corridor central between two principal reception rooms on the other.[170] It can at any rate be said that there is a suggestion here that Whichcord was watching contemporary fashion carefully, even if he was not very good at imitating it.

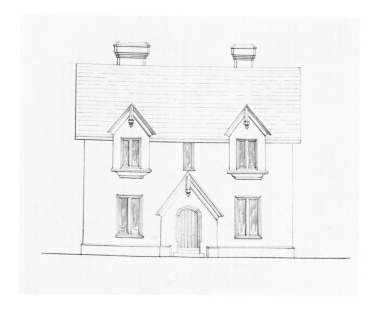

1843 was the year in which Pugin embarked upon the design of the Grange at Ramsgate, and the house was externally complete by the end of the following summer. It seems very possible that Whichcord saw it, because a parsonage design of 1847 at Barham, about 15 miles south-west of Ramsgate in east Kent, reflects some aspects of its design.[171] The house was built on a secluded site well to the north of the church; and its combination of plan and elevation indicates the extent to which Whichcord was experimenting with recent ideas, for he has merged here a conventional central-corridor plan with a Puginesque elevation in a not entirely resolved way.

At Barham, the principal elevation is to the south, and the entrance elevation to the east. It has a cross between a central-corridor and an L-corridor plan, arranged so that part of the corridor with the stairs in is at the centre of the garden front (fig. 4.39). Whichcord tried to imitate Pugin's Ramsgate house by putting an elevation with a gable and a bay on this garden side rather than (as was more common) on the entrance front (fig. 4.38).[172] Indeed the fact that the central bay of this garden front leads into the central corridor has been obscured in two respects. Firstly, the French window into the corridor is matched by further, larger, French windows either side; secondly, the corridor French window is in fact partly false, being taken up on the right-hand side by

4.37 (opposite, bottom) Crude Tudor gothic, by John Whichcord for Warehorne on Romney Marsh, Kent, in 1839 [*Canterbury Cathedral Archives, DCb/DC/W24/1*].

4.38 (left) Barham rectory, Kent, designed by the Whichcords in 1847. The architects have used a gable-and-bay elevation for the garden, as opposed to the entrance front, which was unusual before the construction of Pugin's Grange in nearby Ramsgate.

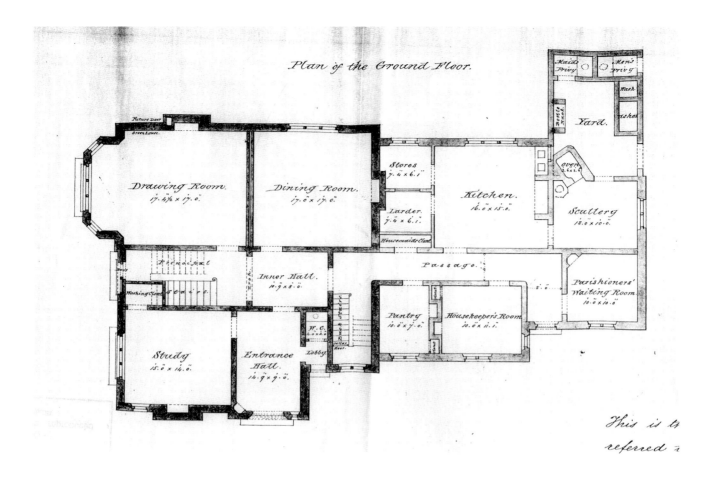

Plan of the Ground Floor.

Drawing Room.
17. 4½ x 17. 0.

Dining Room.
17. 0 x 17. 0.

Kitchen.
16. 0 x 15. 0.

Scullery
12. 0 x 10. 0.

Stores
7. 4 x 6. 1.

Larder.
7. 4 x 6. 1.

Yard.

Maids Privy   Men's Privy

Oven.

Principal

Inner Hall.
10. 9 x 8. 0.

Passage.

Parishioners'
Waiting Room.
10. 0 x 10. 0.

Washing Closet

Study.
15. 0 x 14. 0.

Entrance
Hall.
14. 9 x 9. 0.

W. C.

Lobby

Pantry
10. 0 x 7. 0.

Housekeeper's Room.
10. 0 x 11. 1.

*This is t...
referred a...*

4.39
Barham rectory. The Whichcords' plan is an unusual hybrid between the L-corridor and central-corridor types, and the elevations are an anglicised, uncontroversial adaptation of Pugin's Grange in Ramsgate. Ground-floor plan. Main block, clockwise from bottom right: entrance hall, study, stairs, drawing room and dining room [*Canterbury Cathedral Archives, Dcb/DC/B13/1*].

a 'washing closet' under the stairs, reached from the adjacent study. The entrance elevation is also to some extent a conventionalisation of Pugin's design, for the porch lobby is turned into a major, full-height bay (fig. 4.40). The chimney alongside however still provides the dominant vertical, as it did at for example the Rampisham rectory. The design of this house strongly suggests Whichcord had seen the outside of the Ramsgate house but not managed to get inside it and to see how its exterior related to its plan. The detailing of the Barham house also indicates to what limited extent the architect was prepared to or could adopt those of Pugin's ideas he could easily see. The house is built of knapped flint but has regular cemented quoins. He has preferred to use a more familiar 45-degree gable to Pugin's characteristic 60 degrees, but like Pugin he has used bargeboards, exposed and moulded eaves sprockets, and, mainly, casement windows. The entrance-door bay is composed of picturesque features derived from English vernacular architecture, most notably a projecting flat-roofed timber window bay at first floor, with a half-timbered gable above, an example of the way in which conventional architects were inclined to anglicise Pugin's French-looking designs.[173] Whichcord's windows have flush frames with few mouldings, and the four-pointed front door with a hood mould, moulded spandrels and a ribbed embrasure is the only truly 'gothic' part of the house. This at least implies the learning of a Puginian lesson, for generally Tudor-gothic houses applied gothic ornament anywhere for picturesque effect. Amongst those architects who abandoned the Tudor-gothic for the gothic during the period in which Pugin established his reputation, it seems possible that there were some who had learnt that gothic ornament was superfluous if it did not '*have a meaning or serve a purpose*', or who had themselves come to that conclusion in any case.[174] But neither Whichcord, senior nor junior, seems to have continued to learn from that or any other lesson. The later houses are as uninspired as the earlier ones. The next three parsonages they designed, at Nonington, Postling and Newenham, are in dull classical-Georgian styles, with conventional plans.[175] Or did this signify a conscious attempt to get away from the dangerous implications of an architecture associated with a famous Roman Catholic propagandist? Pugin was a notorious character in Kent, even amongst people with no connection to architecture.

The Barham house has a further interest for us because of its connection with the Ovenden family who lived at Broome Park, the splendid seventeenth-century mansion nearby (fig. 4.41). John Whichcord's client was Charles Ovenden, but Charles' older brother Ashton had previously served at the parish as curate, and, following a successful career as a devotional writer, which led to his becoming (to his own considerable surprise) Bishop of Montreal, he wrote a book of copious reminiscences, describing there the situation at Barham as he remembered it in his youth.[176] Writing at the end of the nineteenth century, it is clear that Ashton Ovenden was appalled at the condition of the church as it had been, and proud of the changes that had come over it in his own lifetime: a telling example that he gives is that when he had attended a school in Ramsgate in his youth there had been in the town but a single church, the mediaeval St Lawrence's; 70 years later, there were seven.[177] Later, he had been a pupil at Harrow School with the future Cardinal Manning.[178] Soon after completing his studies at University College, Oxford, in 1827 he

4.40 (right)
The Whichcords anglicised an otherwise Puginesque design at Barham by adding half timbering and a projecting gable onto the entrance front.

4.41 (below)
Broome Park, near Barham, from an undated postcard that shows the front of the house before its remodelling for Lord Kitchener [*National Monuments Record, BB84/ 2777*].

Fields in London; sadly, it fronts only a conventional central-corridor plan.[191] By contrast, the church which Roberts designed at much the same time there was Romanesque.[192] However in 1846 he reutilised the Southborough layout, with refinements, in his Tudor-gothic parsonage at Norbiton in Surrey (fig. 4.44).[193] A library and drawing room, planned cross-axially to one another, which formed one bar of the L, and the third room, the dining room, completed the layout in pinwheel fashion; part of the volume of the stair hall, however, was given over to a waiting room, and there was still no expression of it on the outside. The kitchen here was above ground and reached through the stair hall; externally, it was expressed as a separate volume. The detailing was conventional Tudor-gothic, with gables over parapet shoulders and a strongly dominant horizontal emphasis. Looking at all this it seems that although Roberts was prepared to investigate new plans and was using a pinwheel plan simultaneously with Pugin, he did not share Pugin's ability to see the impact of the plan on the appearance, or the concept, of the building as a whole; nor did he apparently show any reaction to Pugin's published writings on style or materials.

4.42 (opposite)
The rectory of St James the Less, in Bethnal Green, London, by Lewis Vulliamy (1840). The design is oddly atavistic, suggesting the remains of a Romanesque structure that has been built over.

4.43 (above)
The entrance elevation of Vulliamy's rectory at Balsham, south-east of Cambridge (1839). The layout is of the standard central-corridor type – a fact which is concealed by its exterior appearance [*Cambridge University Library, Ely Diocesan Records G3/39 MGA/40*].

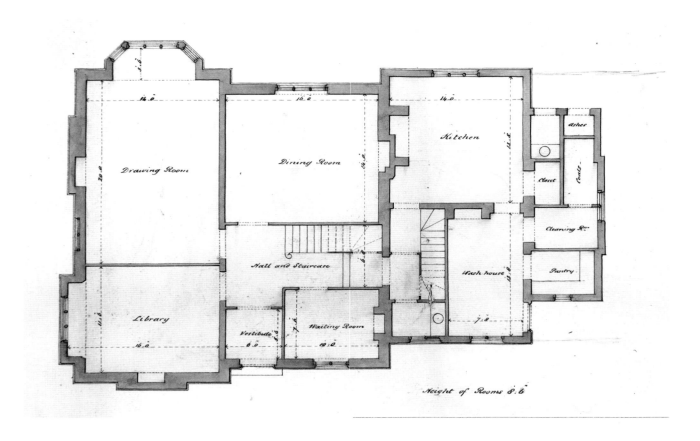

4.44
Norbiton parsonage, Surrey, by Henry Roberts (1846): this is almost a pinwheel plan, with reception rooms rotating around a central staircase, but Roberts has shrunk from the full implications of the design by casting the overall house in the form of largely unrelieved box. Clockwise from bottom left: library, drawing room, dining room. The detailing – Tudor-gothic – was old-fashioned, too. The house has been demolished [*Surrey History Centre, 472/23/2/2-4*].

The reaction

There is some evidence that architects working on Anglican parsonages in Staffordshire and Leicestershire, where Pugin's rural building most probably had its greatest impact, actively avoided the gothic style with which he and the Roman Catholic church were now clearly associated. There was, for example, an angry Anglican reaction to missionary activities being carried out in and around the Charnwood Forest in Leicestershire, by Pugin's friend and patron Ambrose Phillipps, who built his monastery there; and, in Staffordshire, where the Roman Catholic revival sponsored by the Earl of Shrewsbury was much in evidence, one finds examples such as the parsonage at Lapley in Staffordshire which was designed in a plain Georgian style by an architect who both before and afterwards practised elsewhere in variations of the Tudor style.[194]

We first met William Parsons (1783–1855) in Chapter One when he had a run-in with the Bishop of Lincoln over the cost of the new house at Thurmaston.[195] Parsons was a major practitioner in Leicester, and designed public buildings of all kinds as well as many parsonages almost exclusively in the county and the adjoining areas. An early vicarage of 1825 at Diseworth in Leicestershire shares the split-personality of Thompson's earlier Boxford: it is Tudor-gothic at the front, and classical-Georgian at the rear.[196] The style of the additions Parsons made in 1829 to the rectory at Galby, which we have already seen in the opening chapters above, was a fancy Regency gothick.[197] At the Aylestone and Thurmaston parsonages, both approximately ten years on from Galby, his style was still Tudor-gothic – as befits the reign of William IV – but it had also become both more substantial, and also more reserved.[198] Yet when the bishop had objected to the cost of the Thurmaston house, Parsons evidently rejected the possibility of building in a cheaper, unornamented, Georgian style. In 1847 he designed a series of almshouses at Bitteswell in Leicestershire in the form of semi-detached cottages with a central gable above the two front doors (fig. 4.45). Built close to the area Phillipps was studding with Pugin buildings, Parsons chose a very minimal and sober form of Tudor-gothic, a far cry both from his flamboyant Galby style, and from the stucco and bargeboarding of Thurmaston of 1838. No villager would be likely to confuse these plain buildings with Pugin's version of gothic: they were clearly 'Old English', the protestant style associated with Henry VIII and Elizabeth. The same changes occur in areas beyond the immediate influence of the Roman Catholic revival. Edward Blakeway Smith (1804–75) of Stanton Lacy in Shropshire built parsonages both before and during Pugin's ascendancy.[199]

We have already heard about his simple Georgian cottage of 1832 at Brampton Bryan, the one that had some gentle Tudor touches added, perhaps to indicate an awareness of current fashion.[200] At Stokesay in 1839, however, he designed a conventional classical-Georgian house, of urban plan and pattern in spite of its rural site, with no Tudor touches, and resorted to a blind window on the entrance front to avoid asymmetry; then at Wheathill as late as 1852, he designed another conventional classical-Georgian rectory with a central corridor plan (fig. 4.46).[201] It seems that Smith no longer considered Tudor, or Tudor-gothic, as being a merely fashionable way of building, either because it had now to be done in a more thorough fashion; or, conceivably, because it carried high church or Roman Catholic connotations. It is noticeable that there was considerable Tudor or Tudor-gothic parsonage building in the area going on in the mid 1830s, but by the

4.45 (above)
William Parsons' almshouses at Bitteswell, near Lutterworth, Leicestershire. The architect has made these buildings of 1847 robustly Tudor in contrast to the gothic structures designed by Pugin for Roman Catholics nearby.

4.46 (right)
Stokesay, Shropshire, by Edward Blakeway Smith of 1839. His houses increasingly moved away from the playful Tudor he had experimented with earlier in the decade [*Herefordshire Record Office, HD/44 1839*].

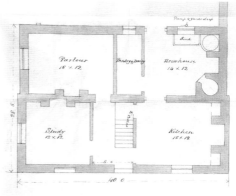

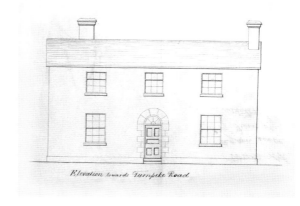

1840s classical buildings had the upper hand. Thomas Nicholson of Hereford, for example, designed at New Radnor just outside the county a conventional central-corridor house which was essentially Tudor-gothic in composition, but the external detailing is carefully, and safely, classical-Georgian.[202]

More ambitious architects might have wanted not only to appear to disassociate themselves with Pugin's architecture but more intelligently also to prove that classical architecture could be both flexible and imaginative in response to the principal challenges of the new young goths. The career of Ignatius Bonomi (1787–1870) seems to suggest that. In his early days in practice, which began in the first decade of the nineteenth century, Bonomi at first accommodated both the classical and the Tudor-gothic. His lodges at Lambton Castle, of c1815, were Greek, but his work of the mid-late 1820s at the Castle itself was gothic.[203] The Hermitage, in Chester-le-Street, was 'faintly Tudor'.[204] However the house he built for himself and his sisters in 1828–9, Elvet Hill just outside Durham, was originally a remarkable gothic house.[205]

The house was designed as a castle-like residence, not exactly gothic but certainly not Tudor. It was two floors high with a flat roof; there were angled buttresses at the corners, and the windows were traceried – in most cases, simple depressed-arched tracery of the kind seen in mediaeval collegiate architecture, but in the drawing room it was more complex and cusped. One bay of the eastern elevation had a further central buttress. There was originally a two-storey oriel on the north side, triangular in plan and perhaps an attempt at recalling the complex windows at Thornbury Castle in Gloucestershire illustrated in the third volume of the *Architecture antiquities*.[206] The plan was essentially designed in the form of two adjacent squares, one slid forward from the other. The western square contained Bonomi's offices, and the principal entrance to both house and offices. The main staircase was located in an approximately square room in the centre of this block. Above there was a servant's bedroom, and one other staircase. The second, eastern, square contained the lower and upper principal rooms, one at each corner. In the lower floor, access to the principal rooms was via a 'hall waiting room' in the south-west corner; above, a central corridor led to the centre of the block from the landing on the west side. It is an original plan, and not a very convenient one in that it required a large amount of circulation space to reach all the rooms; its eccentricity is perhaps characteristic again of an architect's first house for himself. At all events, Bonomi did not remain there very long. The house was locally nicknamed 'The Rising Sun'.[207]

Bonomi's parsonage architecture of the 1840s – as Pugin's chapel and other work was rising at Ushaw nearby – was however classical, and sophisticatedly so. The almost contemporary parsonages at Loftus in Cleveland (1843) and Wilton (1844) are both three-bayed, two-storeyed classical houses with low roofs, sash windows, a columned porch, an ornate cornice, and quoins: they are elegant, accomplished Italianate houses quite removed from the classical-Georgian prototypes of earlier decades (fig. 4.47).[208] Nor do they as much as hint at the English picturesque version of the rural Italianate of houses like Nash's Cronkhill. They are urbane and disciplined. At Loftus the three bays at the front have regular windows, with a porch at the centre bottom; however, at Wilton, the asymmetrical plan is marked externally by a blind window above the front door, and by an altogether irregular side elevation. Bonomi was trying to show here that classical architecture is in fact capable of making the external expression that the plan demands without having in any sense a naive character to it. He had evidently rejected the claim that only gothic architecture could do that.[209] In that respect he provides a contrast to his local colleague, John Dobson in Newcastle, who had designed one of the first real Tudor-gothic revival parsonages when he had added to the pele tower at Embleton in 1828. Dobson's early gothic, at for example St Mary's Place in Newcastle, had often been very superficial and unsatisfactory; but as time went by he designed imaginative and authentic Tudor houses, such as Sandhoe House of 1846–7, and the tiny and charming keeper's cottage for the Whittle Dene Water Company of 1849.

The clearest way of summarising the transformation in the English domestic architecture of the 1840s as it is exemplified by the new parsonages is this: only the very laziest designers ignored the changes that were coming across the profession. Plans, styles, and professional conduct were now developing with tremendous speed. There has been no other single decade in English architectural history when the design of something so small as a house with two or three reception rooms changed so much.

4.47
Wilton parsonage, 1844.
The entrance front has a neat
dolls'-house appearance,
but on the sides Bonomi chose
an unusual irregular pattern
of fenestration as if to
demonstrate that neo-
classical architecture could
also be functional.

Chapter Five
The 1850s: A kind of pattern house

In many ways it is not only the parsonage houses themselves that change so radically during the 1840s but also the significance of them to architectural history in general and the way in which we record and remember them. These little houses start to play an important role in the broader history of the gothic revival, becoming part of one of the most popular episodes in English architecture. Once William Butterfield's house at Coalpit Heath comes along in 1844 one has the sense of rejoining the familiar narrative of the nineteenth century. The curious hiatus encountered in conventional histories of the third and fourth decades, almost devoid of the great names of the profession, is over. Suddenly, it seems, there is at least one distinguished small building in every village. The ambitious architects of the revival used their parsonage designs to experiment with the ideas that Pugin had raised in different ways, and the story of the houses becomes to a great extent the story of those individuals and their search for architectural expression. These men designed a very large number of parsonages between them, and henceforth the most logical way to discuss the houses is as part of the history of each architect's work, rather than as subject in their own right. The revolution had happened.

The Bounty continued to approve parsonage designs for mortgages until the early years of the twentieth century; usually about half of the parsonage files in diocesan records refer to approvals given after 1850. It would be possible to continue to ramble through the rest of the century, and perhaps one day it will be done. Many of these documents are fascinating in their own right: one goes on seeing here the work of unsung architects who specialised in the field; the youthful efforts of the famous of the future; and the most minor of the projects of the great London-based designers which their biographers and critics have had little time for. Every record office contains surprises. There is a set of drawings in the Wiltshire and Swindon Record Office from 1877 of a small extension by John Pollard Seddon, for Chirton, near Devizes, a mere addition of a rear wing for a kitchen, dining room and offices, but one which transforms a plain central-corridor house of an earlier period into a tiny, effortless free-style villa, too humble and too vernacular to be 'Queen Anne' but of course actually styled with enormous care by a leading designer (fig. 5.2).[1] Here and there a provincial builder can be found running up the same type of house that he, or his father, had been building since the beginning of the century;

5.1
An early parsonage by George Gilbert Scott: Weston Turville, near Aylesbury, Buckinghamshire, of 1838. His first attempt at designing a parsonage had been for his father at Wappenham in Northamptonshire; he later described the rectory there as 'very ugly'. He no doubt would have said the same about this one.

5.2
Chirton parsonage, near
Devizes, Wiltshire (1877)
by John Pollard Seddon.
A charming vernacular design
from an accomplished gothic
church architect [*Wiltshire &
Swindon Record Office,
D1/11/250*].

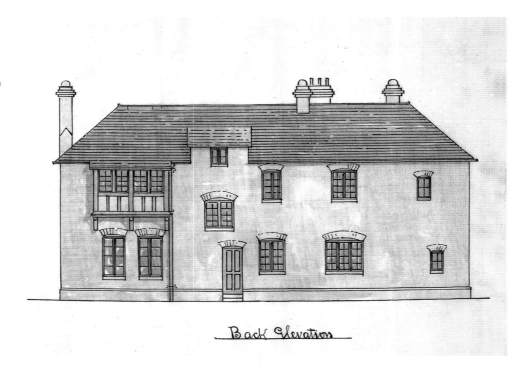

Back Elevation

and there are plenty of designers that never wanted to go gothic, or like
Bonomi at Loftus and Wilton picked up the gauntlet that Pugin had
thrown down by designing classical houses in a much more sensitive
and original type of way; but the emphasis of the story is already
elsewhere. The inescapable fact is that at mid-century, the generic
types of plans and elevations that characterised the opening decades of
this story all but vanish. The hybrids disappear too. A house designed
by the young Raphael Brandon in the middle of 1850, for Leighton
Buzzard, tells us everything we need to know about what has replaced
the old conventions: it has a large central staircase hall, with three
reception rooms radiating around it; it has a bold three-dimensional
form rather than a front and back with sides; and the style is
competently and consistently gothic.[2] So the best way to conclude the
chapters that have been written is to take a general view of what was
done with the ideas that had already been raised, to note the
experiments that were being made, and to watch the alliance that is
very soon formed between the designers and the internal reformers
of the Church of England. The adoption of a particular set of
architectural ideas by those with the money, the energy, and the
patronage to implement them on the one hand marks the posthumous
success of Pugin's architectural experiment; but on the other, it is a

reminder that architects alone will never have the power or the influence to change ingrained patterns of building.

It is possible to show that designers all over England started to incorporate elements of Pugin's buildings in their own work, and yet it is extremely difficult to show that the new leaders of the gothic revival were directly aware of what he was doing. Pugin published no plans of his presbyteries and parsonages. In 1842 he did in fact illustrate the principal floor plan of his Bishop's House in Birmingham in an influential Roman Catholic journal called the *Dublin review*, in the second part of a pair of articles that he subsequently published in 1843 as a book called *The present state of ecclesiastical architecture in England*; but it is difficult to believe that this alone would have attracted a great deal of response: at any rate, the complex circulation system, the most remarkable characteristic of the plan, is scarcely discernable from it (fig. 5.3).[3] He was prevailed upon to make what was for him a very unusual finished colour perspective of his house in Ramsgate for display at the Royal Academy in 1849, but there is no sign of the house's unusual plan there (see fig. 3.58).[4] We do know of a few isolated occasions on which his work was seen (or to be more accurate, was probably seen) by influential designers. When, for example, George Gilbert Scott was working on the restoration of St Mary's, Stafford, in the early 1840s, he 'came to Cheadle … & admired every thing *exceedingly*', according to a letter to Pugin from Lord Shrewsbury.[5] At the time, Pugin's remodelled presbytery in the town was probably under construction.[6] A few years later, in 1846-7, Scott designed Christ Church, a small church in Vale Square, Ramsgate, and only a few hundred yards from the Grange, and it is inconceivable that he did not walk over and see the house at least from the outside.

But avowed acceptance of Pugin's work by his contemporary professionals was never likely to be comfortable. In a period when an ambitious and newly-qualified young high churchman could be stoned by his parishioners for wearing a mediaevalising surplice – as happened to the unfortunate new incumbent at St Columb Major in Cornwall in the mid 1840s – it is clear that openly associating with the work of a prominent Roman Catholic was problematic.[7] The fact that references to Pugin's work are so rare during and immediately after his working period could mean either that he was ignored, or, just as probably, that architects with healthy Anglican connections did not

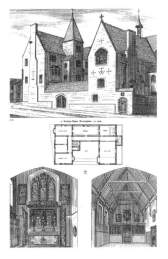

5.3
Pugin's own plan and views of the Bishop's House, Birmingham, from *The present state of ecclesiastical architecture in England* (1841 -2), plate 11. He evidently did not advertise the unusual nature of his plans.

want to mention him. William White, the architect of a number of distinguished gothic parsonages in the decades ahead, including as it happens the new one at St Columb Major, gave in 1851 and 1853 talks to fellow ecclesiologists about the design of small and medium-sized houses and illustrated his talks with drawings of what were very clearly Puginian principles without mentioning the name 'Pugin' as much as once.[8] His own architecture was pointedly drawn from the relaxed vernacular of authentic mediaeval buildings – his delightful scheme soon after for remodelling the vicarage at Milton in Kent has a long, low front that owes a great deal to the early fourteenth-century vicarage at Muchelney in Somerset (see fig. 4.11).[9] And yet the staggering amount of Puginesque work that suddenly went up from the late 1840s onwards suggests that architects had seen what Pugin was doing. Provincial or minor architects were now trying out isolated mannerisms that somehow they must have seen or heard of, and a look into the parsonage records of any diocesan collection will confirm that these tendencies were beginning to form an irregular pattern nationally. Furthermore, in London the prominent architects of the period were now using Pugin's principles as the basis for the design of their smaller houses, and the work that emerged forms part of the definitive canon of the English architecture of the high and late Victorian eras, at least as much as the churches and the country houses which now for the first time in generations shared the same consistent architectural language.

Imitation

Some architects simply copied Pugin's work: of these, the two Hansom brothers from Leicestershire were so successful that in many cases their buildings are mistaken for that of their mentor. Neither Joseph Aloysius, famously also the inventor of the Hansom cab, nor his brother Charles designed Anglican parsonages, for they were Roman Catholics. They worked both separately and in partnership with each other (from 1854-9), and Joseph Hansom was for a short time the partner of Pugin's quarrelsome son Edward.[10] The brothers' many institutional buildings are similar to Pugin's; at Ratcliffe College in Leicestershire Charles Hansom continued in 1849 to build Pugin's quadrangle of 1843 onwards in an almost seamless way, in the days before an architect could claim copyright on his design. They were thought to be cheaper as architects than Pugin was, and possibly also less trouble;[11] the latter was probably referring to them when he said that certain rivals '*steal* their brooms *ready made*'.[12] When Charles Hansom received a compliment for his 'understanding of detail' and 'harmony of composition', Pugin wrote angrily 'By george it is too Bad. a man who entices the men away to work what is done, I should like to see him locked up till he drew out a niche'.[13]

There is one case where we know that Joseph Hansom stole a job from under Pugin's nose, and since it is a Roman Catholic church with a presbytery attached it is of some interest to us. Pugin told John Hardman in June 1848 that 'Hansom, the *other Hansom* [*i.e.*, Joseph] has written to me to resign the *york church* in his favour!!! I do not even know if there is a site to build it on'.[14] This is St George's in York (fig.5.4). The plan is unremarkable, for the site is very small, but the simple exterior and the internal detailing have been largely composed from elements drawn directly from Pugin's own work. With its 60-degree gable to the west side, a homogenous brick wall surface, plain square-headed windows with irregular stone quoins, very limited decoration and an irregular fenestration on the staircase side, the house is

5.4
The presbytery of St George's Roman Catholic church, York, designed by Joseph Hansom in 1848 and subsequently altered. The houses of Pugin's imitators were generally flatter in appearance and more horizontal in their proportions than the real thing.

distinguished from one of Pugin's mainly by its horizontalising string-course between the ground and first floors; for Pugin, ever inspired by the vertical proportions of Nodier's romantic prints, did not like horizontal string courses.[15] It is fascinating to see that although Hansom copied Pugin's simple skirtings throughout the house, he thought that the half-round timber architraves, one of Pugin's inventions, were fit only for the servants' rooms at the top of the house; the principal room doors have bolder composite mouldings not dissimilar from conventional ones.

The Hansoms' work is usually somewhat lifeless compared to Pugin's, mainly because one looks in vain there for the oddities and exceptions that characterise the latter's work. Other Catholic architects copied more imaginatively. William Wardell is mainly well known for his career in Australia, but before he left England in 1858 he designed a small number of presbyteries with some distinctly Puginesque elements. Wardell described Pugin as 'our own great master'.[16] The presbytery at the church of the Holy Trinity, Brook Green, in Hammersmith includes a truly Puginian device and one that was rarely imitated by other parsonage builders. He linked the house to the back of the church by a long corridor that wraps around the edge of the site boundary, emerging to form the spine of a back-corridor type of plan (fig. 5.5). The drawings for this are with Wardell's other papers in New South Wales, an example of how far from home one can find parsonage or presbytery drawings. For many years local

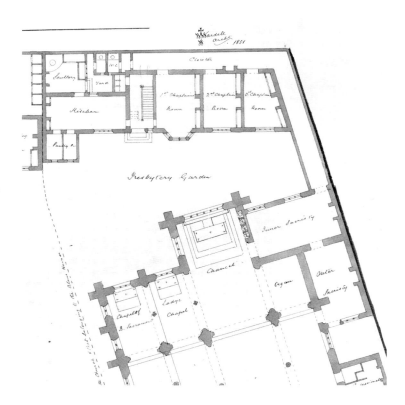

5.5
The presbytery of Holy Trinity, Brook Green, Hammersmith, Middlesex, is linked to the outer sacristy of the church by a lengthy cloister: a Puginian gesture from his admirer William Wardell. A detail from an original plan held in the Mitchell Library, State Library of New South Wales, Australia [*ML ref. PXD 380 f. 14a*].

anecdote attributed the church and the other Puginesque buildings of Hammersmith's 'Pope's Corner' to Pugin himself.[17] It would be interesting to see whether Wardell took with him to Australia Pugin's influence in the realm of domestic architecture as well as that of the ecclesiastical.[18]

There are others, not Roman Catholics, who clearly imitated Pugin's work and in doing so were transformed from very ordinary architects into competent and stylish ones; and there were some who cannot be said to have at first copied directly, but who were evidently rooting in his direction, and who later both borrowed blatantly and were the better for it. Samuel Daukes designed in 1840, early in his career, two absolutely conventional Tudor-gothic parsonages for the Hereford diocese: at Brinsop, on an L-corridor plan, in 1840; and at Colwall, where the house was the symmetrical, back-corridor type (figs 5.6, 5.7; see also fig. 2.55).[19] In May 1844 (when the plan of the Grange was still unlikely to be common knowledge amongst professionals) he designed a rectory for Toft cum Caldecote, Cambridgeshire, which has three major rooms in pinwheel fashion, although without a central staircase hall (fig. 5.8).[20] Some years later he designed a house called Horsted Place in Sussex in imitation of Pugin's Bilton Grange as it had been eventually built, around a long and broad central gallery; he used Pugin-esque detailing, incorporated fitments designed by Pugin himself, and Pugin's builder Myers executed it. It is certainly often thought to be the most impressive building Daukes ever produced (fig. 5.9).[21]

5.6 (below, left) West elevation, Brinsop vicarage, near Hereford: a pre-Puginian Samuel Daukes design of 1840 [*Herefordshire Record Office, HD8/15 1840*].

5.7 (below) A typical back-corridor type ground-floor plan: Colwall rectory, near Great Malvern, Herefordshire (Daukes, 1840): see also fig. 2.55 [*Herefordshire Record Office, HD8/15 1840*].

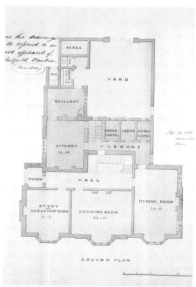

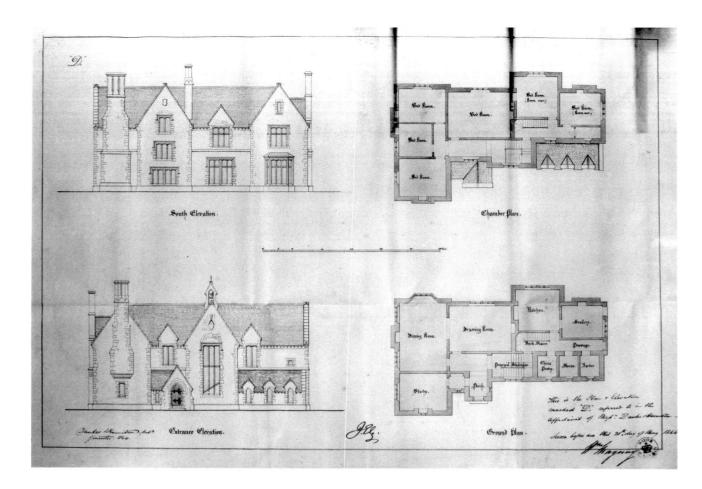

South Elevation.

Chamber Plan.

Entrance Elevation.

Ground Plan.

5.8 (above)
Daukes' proposed ground-floor plan for Toft cum Caldecote rectory west of Cambridge, designed in May 1844 when Pugin's Ramsgate house was almost complete. This is quite a different type of house both organisationally and stylistically from his pre-Puginian Brinsop and Colwall of only four years beforehand. Although there is no central staircase hall, the principal axis of each of the three wings revolves in pinwheel fashion [*Cambridge University Library, Ely Diocesan Records G3/39 MGA/50*].

5.9 (right)
Horsted Place, near Uckfield, Sussex, designed by Daukes in the early 1850s and built by Pugin's builder George Myers. By this stage Daukes had evidently become a competent Puginesque architect.

Inspiration

Much more interesting is the extent to which established architects in England took hold of Pugin's ideas almost immediately for Anglican parsonages of their own, and experimented with his ideas to produce houses with plans and exterior forms which were unprecedented in their own work. Anthony Salvin, born in 1799, had been in practice since the mid-1820s and had already acquired a reputation as an architect of competent, if dull, country houses in Elizabethan styles, including the eccentric parsonage of 1827 at Northallerton which has already been mentioned.[22] In 1848 he designed a gothic parsonage for his church of the Holy Trinity in Finchley, which unmistakably adapted Pugin's rectory designs (figs 5.10, 5.11).[23] Around an

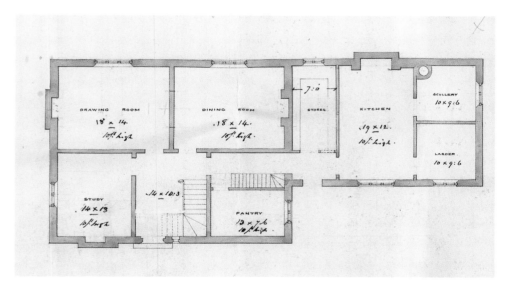

5.10 (left, above)
Anthony Salvin's design for the parsonage at Holy Trinity, Finchley, Middlesex. Although this is more of an already popular L-plan, rather than a pinwheel, Salvin has turned the entrance lobby into a substantial stair hall in imitation of a Pugin arrangement [*London Metropolitan Archives, ACC 1083/3*].

5.11 (left)
The entrance elevation at Finchley. This is again 'modified Pugin' on a small scale, with more English-looking lower gables and brickwork patterns. The window positioned at the bottom right of a gable seems to imitate a similar one at Ramsgate (see fig. 3.31) [*London Metropolitan Archives, ACC 1083/3*].

approximately square staircase entrance hall he placed a study,
a drawing room and a dining room in the same order as they had been
at Lanteglos. The house is not exactly a pinwheel, because the drawing
room and dining room share the same long axis; but although he
likewise did not imitate Pugin's pair of stair windows on the entrance
front, he applied at least two of his mannerisms: he took the decorative
dropped hood-mould for the front door from that at Rampisham,
and above it he located a small window between the bottom of the
adjoining gable and its adjacent wall, a strange detail that Pugin had
used at Ramsgate for the short passage between the two principal
upper-floor bedrooms (see fig. 3.31). Soon after, T. H. Wyatt (1807–80)
provided two wonderful examples of the rapid incorporation of
Pugin's work into that of respectable London architects. A member
of the architecturally prodigious Wyatt family – he was the brother
of the better-known Matthew Digby Wyatt, and the second cousin
once removed of Sir Jeffry Wyatville – he had practised as an
undistinguished designer of neo-Elizabethan buildings for some 15
years before receiving the commission in 1852 (the year of Pugin's
decline and death) to design a vicarage at Alderbury near Salisbury,
the very village where Pugin had built his first home. The results, dated
13 April 1852, are fascinating. Wyatt took Pugin's parsonage model
and converted it into a much more English-looking house (fig. 5.12).[24]
The plan is reversed from that of Rampisham and Lanteglos (fig. 5.13;
see also fig. 3.40); and like Hansom at York he did not have the nerve to
explore the full implications of Pugin's work; indeed, like Hansom he
copied Pugin's architrave detail for backstairs areas only. The three

5.12
A blatant example of a Pugin
pinwheel house imitated and
anglicised, this time by T. H.
Wyatt at Alderbury, close to
Pugin's own first house St
Marie's Grange. The horizontal
string course and the
ornamental brickwork turn a
pinwheel-type elevation into a
structure more recognisable
as an English house [*Wiltshire
& Swindon Record Office*,
D1/11/112].

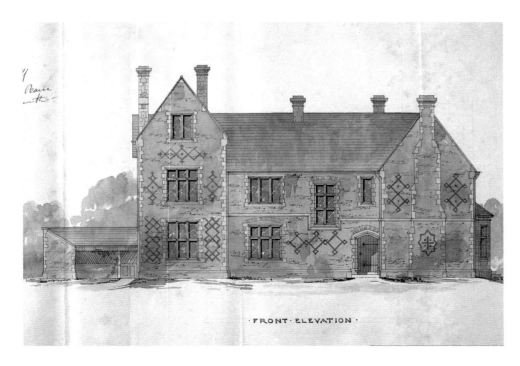

· FRONT · ELEVATION ·

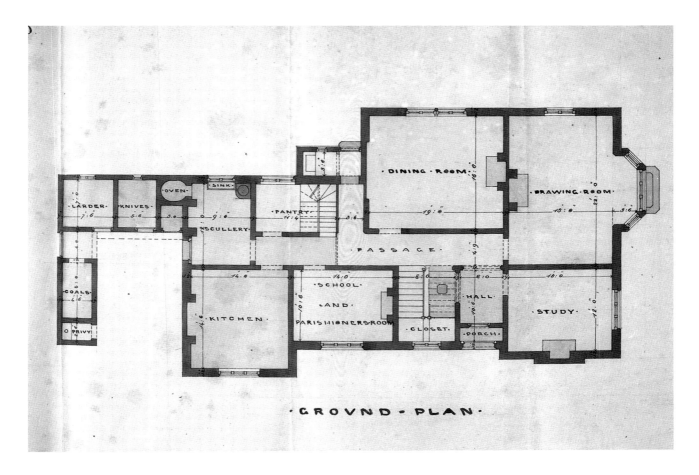

reception rooms were arranged in the form of an L around his hall and
stairs, but these, whilst taking up the same space as one of Pugin's stair
halls would have done, were more compartmentalised; possibly Wyatt
wanted the upper floor to be more cut off from the front door. For the
entrance elevation he took a series of Puginian motifs such as the
chimney-gable end of the study wall to the right of the front door and
the great staircase window to the left of it. From this point on, however,
he conventionalised, or perhaps simply anglicised, Pugin's designs.
His back stairs were hidden around the other side of the house, so that
their window did not appear on the front elevation: this was similar
to the Grange, but unlike the other pinwheel houses where they were
visible on the front; and by adding a string course and various brick
diaper patterns to the front of the house he gave it a much more
horizontal emphasis than Pugin liked to do. On the other hand, some
of the brick patterning seems reminiscent of that at St Marie's Grange.

Exactly six weeks later, Wyatt submitted a design for another
Puginesque parsonage, for the Wiltshire village of Upton Scudamore,

5.13
Wyatt's plan at Alderbury:
this is an L-plan rather than a
pinwheel layout, as the rooms
lack the dynamic rotating
quality of one of Pugin's own
designs; the stairs, likewise,
are at the centre of the house
but are compartmentalised
and thus less prominent
[Wiltshire & Swindon Record
Office, D1/11/112].

between Trowbridge and Warminster. He was a little braver this time (figs 5.14, 5.15).[25] The decorative brick patterning had disappeared, and the stair window had grown to be a more striking part of the composition. A tall gothic porch signals the front door and a Puginesque bay window is visible around the corner, marking the drawing room. Inside, the area given to the stairs is a great deal more spacious than in the Alderbury design, and a pair of parallel corridors linking the front door with the garden porch (and the water closet) establish a richer, more layered space than previously. It does not seem to me to be plausible that Wyatt could have designed these houses without seeing at least the Rampisham house, not far away to the south-west. He had at first copied Pugin's ideas; then, having first put them into practice, he began to adapt them and play with them. It seems likely that the situation with Salvin had been similar. In Wyatt's later projects these Puginian experiments come and go. He remodelled Vulliamy's clumsy house at Burston in 1862 by inserting a large central staircase hall into the middle of it, which required rebuilding a great deal of the rest; but ten years later he produced a gothic house with an old-fashioned central-corridor plan at Horringer with Ickworth, further testimony to the contemporary fashion amongst artistic people for simplification.[26]

The deanery at Lincoln was designed by the country-house architect William Burn when he was almost 60, perhaps at the peak of his

5.14
Another Puginesque elevation by Wyatt of 1852, this time six weeks later at Upton Scudamore near Warminster, Wiltshire [*Wiltshire & Swindon Record Office, D1/11/113*].

ELEVATION OF ENTRANCE FRONT.

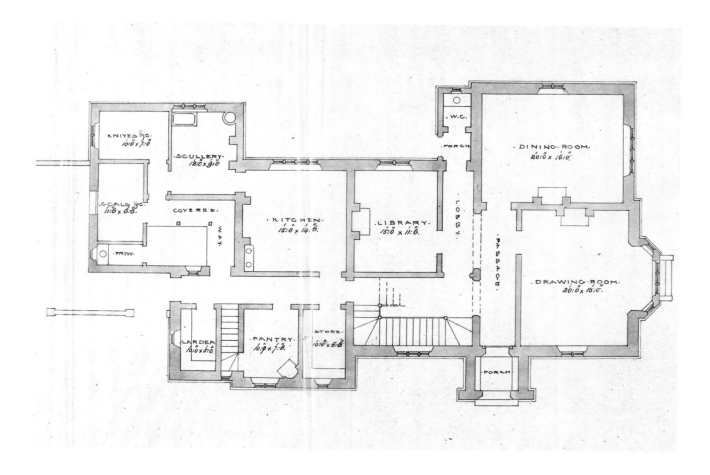

reputation if not any longer of his powers.[27] It was an expensive building: the Bounty awarded a mortgage of £2,500 in March 1846, and a few months later agreed to raise the sum to £3,000 'should the Dean require it'. He did.[28] The house went up in 1847 to the north-east of the cathedral, and its entrance facade faced north (figs 5.16, 5.17). It is a dour building with very little ornament; it survives today with the loss only of its kitchen-office wing.[29] A pair of gables large and small mark the entrance, in the Pugin fashion derived from Great Chalfield Manor; and, as at Rampisham, the larger of the two is relieved only by a chimney; at this house, however, the entrance door gable steps forward slightly from the principal mass of the block. This porch leads into an entrance hall: to the right is the dean's study, and to the left, a service corridor runs behind the entrance front to serve a water closet, a butler's pantry and the housekeeper's room, leading to the back stairs (fig. 5.18). Continuing straight ahead from the entrance, one reaches a central, top-lit stair hall. Immediately ahead there is a dining room, its long axis perpendicular to that of the entrance route. To the right there

5.15
The plan at Upton Scudamore. With the liberation of the main staircase into the volume of the hall, and the appearance of a back-stairs window on the front elevation, it appears that Wyatt is becoming bolder in his application of Puginian ideas. Perhaps the rapidly declining architect was on his mind [*Wiltshire & Swindon Record Office, D1/11/113*].

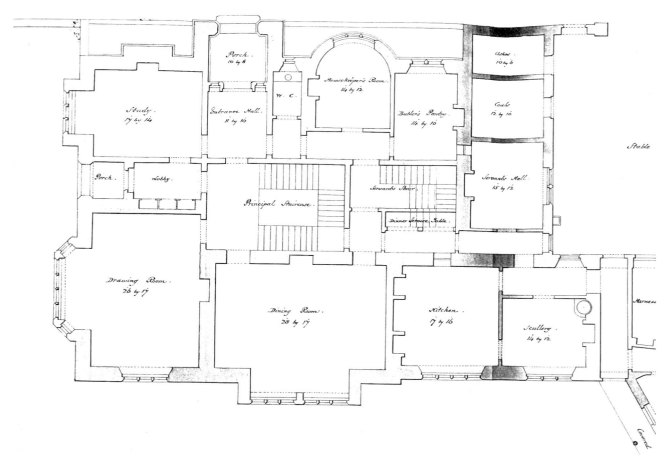

is a drawing room. The substantial office wing to the east was reached though a door under the stairs. The house layout exhibits all the sophistication for which Burn became recognised in the planning of a complex modern house, but it also carries echoes of Pugin's pinwheel type houses, and in particular the best known of them, the Grange. Looking at the house from the eastern end one can see that Burn chose to emphasise the blocks in front of and behind the staircase by giving each its own gable, a true gothic-revival trait that distinguishes houses of this type from the persistent Tudor-gothic of an architect of the same generation such as Edward Blore, who liked to cap his houses with a single roof.[30]

Elsewhere one can see similar examples of a Puginesque house by other established architects at a late stage in their career. Charles Fowler (1792-1867), a largely classical architect, provides one excellent example. At the parsonage of Bovey Tracey in Devon of 1850 the west, garden, elevation is of a gable-and-wall type in the Tudor-gothic style that was by now familiar (fig. 5.19). The house has a narrow, central staircase hall, but the principal rooms on the ground floor do radiate around it in imitation of Pugin's pinwheel houses that were by now all complete (fig. 5.20). Some of the detailing is clearly derived from Pugin's work: windows have substantial but plain stone mullions, and depressed lancets on the principal floor; and backstairs joinery has Puginesque detailing, with timber beads for architraves to office rooms, and a chamfered newel.[31]

For some years now, architects would copy very closely certain aspects of Pugin's designs whilst ignoring others: there is a fine example of this at Southwater in Sussex, where the London architect Joseph Clarke, well known for church restorations, designed a house that copies the double-gabled entry to the Rampisham house, although he married this to a conventional central-corridor plan (fig. 5.21).[32] Another design from the 1850s that takes one characteristic at the expense of others, and of logic, is a bizarre plan submitted for Highcliffe, Hampshire, in 1859 by Henry Parsons, district surveyor for South Lambeth, in which the front elevation is taken up by a winding cloister-like corridor which makes its way along from the front door to a staircase in a projecting bay.[33]

5.16, 5.17 (above)
The deanery at Lincoln by William Burn (1847), immediately north of the cathedral cloister. The building was designed a short time before Richard Norman Shaw and William Eden Nesfield became Burn's articled clerks.

5.18 (below)
The ground floor of the deanery at Lincoln. Pugin's influence is clear from the disposition of the rooms around a central stair hall [*Lincolnshire Archives, MGA 315 1847*].

5.19 (top)
Bovey Tracey vicarage, Devon, by Charles Fowler (1850): Fowler's gothic designs had become considerably more sophisticated since his archdeaconry at Exeter (see fig. 2.36).

5.20 (right)
Bovey Tracey, Devon. The rooms in Fowler's design of 1850 imitate Pugin's pinwheel plans, although the staircase hall creates less of an impressive space. Clockwise from top right: study; drawing room; dining room [*Devon Record Office: Exeter Diocese, Faculty Petitions*].

5.21 (opposite)
Joseph Clarke designed the parsonage at Southwater, near Horsham, Sussex in 1853 incorporating Puginian devices such as the double-gable bay at the porch. Clarke was a prolific and competent restorer of churches.

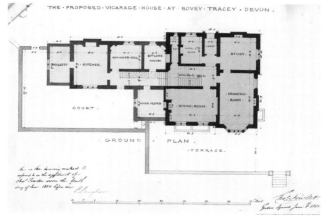

Politics and architecture

The real impact of Pugin's changes could only come once high-profile and ambitious architects began to use them as a basis for experimentation over a period of time long enough to create a strong new architectural image that could be readily identified and adopted; and since the most dramatic and pervasive architectural influence in the mid-nineteenth century was in the field of church design, lasting change was also dependent upon the adoption of Pugin's ideas by leading church architects. The critical moment was the patronage (to varying extents) of a set of approved church architects and their ideas by the *Ecclesiologist*, the publication of the Cambridge Camden Society that was read by supporters of the Oxford Movement in the Church of England. The *Ecclesiologist* promoted the building of new churches according to authentic mediaeval models, and it is very probably because of an old problem – that there were so few known mediaeval parsonages – that the journal, often so thundering and opinionated, had for some time nothing to say about their design. The first real appearance of the parsonage came in the second volume of the journal, in June 1843, accompanied by the apologetic comment that the subject would have been raised earlier but 'there were other matters of still greater importance which called for our more immediate and undivided attention'.[34] There followed a rather predictable castigation of contemporary parsonages for their similarity to vulgar modern villas, and then, after a quotation from Wordsworth ('A reverend pile/ With bold projections and recesses deep')[35], a short paean to the humble solidity of ancient houses, which exemplified the 'hospitality, humility, contentment, and devotion characteristick of the pastoral office'.[36] It is an old-fashioned comment, not only because it ignores the constructional, technological way in which new houses were beginning to be designed and discussed by professionals, but also because it is reminiscent of the language of the despised villa designers of the early nineteenth century who had presented buildings in terms of the sentiments and 'principles' appropriate for different types of residence. One realises with passages like this how vast the gulf is between architecture and the use of words: the goths of the Cambridge Camden Society hated the architecture that their parents' generation had favoured, and yet they used the same type of language in order to describe the houses they wanted as their predecessors had done.

The writer of the article had grasped at least part of the message of Pugin's *The true principles* because he says of one design he dislikes that 'it is clear that the exterior ought to be adapted to the requirements of the internal arrangements, instead of the latter being made to accommodate, and in a manner *pack into*, a preconceived uniform shell'.[37] And yet in 1843, with Pugin's first pinwheel house not yet designed and his reputation as an architect resting on a handful of small, cheap buildings mostly in the Midlands, it is obvious that there is no new strong stylistic image to hand. And so we hear of the parsonage that 'it ought to be distinctly religious in character, and to stand in protest against the luxury and worldliness of modern domestick buildings', and nothing of what it ought to look like instead.[38] The writer pointed to various surviving mediaeval parsonages that met with his approval: since they were mostly located within a few miles of each other between Stamford and Peterborough, at Barnack, Uffington, and Market Deeping, it appears that little progress had been made since the days of John Britton, whose historic buildings are often located in groups in a single area, implying that the finding of them was more a matter of serendipity than of anything else. The *Ecclesiologist*'s choice of examples on this occasion probably reflects day trips for Cambridge undergraduates.

There were, in fact, no references to new gothic parsonages in its pages until Pugin had completed at least seven Roman Catholic presbyteries; they finally came in the form of a notice without architectural description in July 1845 of the completion of new houses at Coalpit Heath, Brasted and Toft;[39] the following year there was a single reference, to Marchwood parsonage by Henry Woodyer: this had 'that peculiar character which ought to distinguish a parsonage', without illustration of what this might mean.[40] Interestingly, the editors of the journal may not have been fully aware of what their own subscribers were up to. A list of members elected in May 1843 appeared in the same issue as the lengthy article quoted above: it included Thomas Hellyer, an architect at Ryde in the Isle of Wight.[41] In 1847 Hellyer submitted a design for a delightful small house for the parish of Kingsclere Woodlands near Newbury in Berkshire that was modelled on Pugin's pinwheel houses: it had a comparatively large stair hall with a prominent window at the front of the house, and its two reception rooms were set at right angles to each other on one side of it (figs 5.22, 5.23).[42]

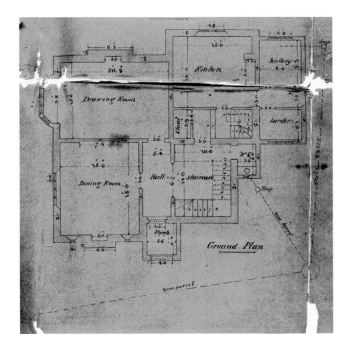

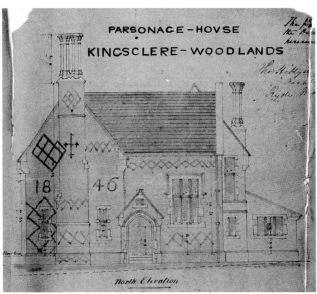

One entered through a porch alongside a tall gable wall, and the brick surfaces were decorated with a great deal of fancy diaper work. Very short notices, however, followed in February 1848 of three parsonages by the partnership of Mallinson and Healey (whom we have seen doing late Tudor-gothic, at Shinfield the year before; see fig. 2.65) at Low Moor and Wyke in the West Riding of Yorkshire, and at Swinfield near Newark.[43] Each was in a different style, and the reviewer noted that he preferred the middle-pointed style of Wyke, but considered the 'Debased' third-pointed style of Swinfield unsuccessful.[44] Four months later, there is another short but this time favourable notice of 'two Pointed parsonages', Monkton Wyld in Dorset and an unexecuted scheme for Buxted in Sussex, by R. C. Carpenter.[45] When covering a subject, even an important one, that was beyond the realms of historical authenticity, the journal had little to offer its readers.

Late in the 1840s the subject was pursued in earnest by the Architectural and Archæological Society for the County of Buckinghamshire, which was founded in January 1848. The Society's inaugural meeting was not only reported in the *Bucks herald* for 3 February of that year, but in the august pages of the *Ecclesiologist* itself; in time, it could count William Butterfield, E. B. Lamb, George Gilbert Scott, and John Britton's sometime collaborator Charles Boutell amongst its members.[46] A particularly active member of the society, the Reverend A. Baker, gave a paper entitled 'Hints for Improvement in the architectural character and arrangements of Parsonage Houses' in April 1849.[47] The *Ecclesiologist* did not give the text of Baker's remarks, subsequently pronouncing them 'exaggerated'.[48] It did, however, later report in some detail on comments Baker had received about them from 'an eminent church architect' which were read out at a subsequent meeting of the society: these dealt with entry and dining arrangements, the necessity for the parson to be close to his flock, and the superfluity of Baker's blatantly Puginising proposals for an oratory and a cloister; but in general, the anonymous but eminent architect was approving. The parsonage was to be '*real*, *simple*, and religious, as you have well said'.[49] We can only speculate whether the words '*real*' and 'religious' in this context would have meant the same thing for all of the society's members. Inspiration for genuine change was not going to come from the pens of the propagandists of the ecclesiological movement: it could only come from the drawing boards of the architects whom they trusted.

Scott

Could George Gilbert Scott have been that eminent church architect?[50] It is a not insignificant fact that parsonages were amongst the very few small houses of any kind that the greatest and the busiest of the architects of the gothic revival were ever able to turn their attention to: in fact, of the architects mentioned in detail here, the only one who did design a comparatively large number of small houses that were not parsonages was William Butterfield, who for example built several cottages in the village of Baldersby in North Yorkshire. Scott came from a clerical family – at his birth, his father was vicar of Gawcott near Buckingham – and according to his obituary in the *Builder* he designed 23 English parsonages, some for members of his family.[51] He was also a friend of Benjamin Ferrey, designer of so many parsonages himself, and with whom he went on a memorable tour of Italy in 1851.[52] How much time did they spend speaking of Pugin? Scott's *Recollections* leave one in no doubt of his debt to him and to his architectural ideas. He further professed his debt to 'the great reformer of architecture', in his *Remarks on secular and domestic architecture*, and it seems improbable in the light of his comments there that he had not by now made himself familiar with Pugin's unconventional small and

5.24
Scott's parsonage at Weston
Turville (1838): five years later
he had become a committed
goth. See fig. 5.1.

medium-sized house plans.[53] We have already seen that he troubled in early years to make the cross-country journey from Stafford up into what is now often called 'Pugin-land', Lord Shrewsbury's estate in the north-east of the county.[54]

Scott is distinguished from the new gothic architects of his generation, such as the younger of those who subscribed to the Buckinghamshire society, by his having been in practice as an architect well before his 'conversion'. In 1838 he had designed a simple central corridor-plan type parsonage in classical Georgian style at Weston Turville (figs 5.1, 5.24).[55] Later work emerging from the office of Moffatt and Scott was Tudor gothic, and the planning sometimes original: the parsonage at West Knoyle, designed in 1842, is an asymmetrical variation on the central corridor plan; although still Tudor gothic, it has only the narrowest of shoulders at the base of its

gables (fig. 5.25).[56] Unfortunately I have found no plan for the parsonage at St Giles, Camberwell, designed in 1843 soon after Scott enlisted to the new gothic cause and now demolished; such few photographs as exist show that with its flush-framed, square-headed traceried windows it is in stylistic terms at least a candidate to be the first Puginesque building of the Church of England.[57]

Scott's gothic detailing was usually confident but it was often also unexciting where he was working on a small scale. He undoubtedly contributed a great deal to the *Ecclesiologist's* search for authenticity, and his interest in English historic detailing can be deduced from his sketchbooks in the Royal Institute of British Architects collection. He drew for example both the surviving mediaeval house at Lanercost Abbey in Cumberland and the former prior's lodging at Wenlock Priory in Shropshire, which Pugin apparently had not (see fig. 2.23).

5.25
The parsonage at West Knoyle, north of Shaftesbury, Wiltshire, was designed during the period of the Scott and Moffatt partnership, but here it was the latter who signed the plans in 1842. By looking at the bases of the gables it is clear that Tudor-gothic has almost turned into gothic here.

It is, however, his continuing interest in Puginesque planning that makes him so interesting. A parsonage at Great Haseley, of 1847, illustrates an early stage in this development (fig. 5.26). The house's principal front, to the garden, places the dining room, the drawing room and study in a row, rather as one would expect from a typical Tudor-gothic, back-corridor parsonage of the period or immediately before: the obvious difference is that the detailing is a great deal more authentic, and consistent with the materials used.[58] The rooms are distinguished by different windows but otherwise create a formal elevation which is almost symmetrical in its massing. Within, however, there is a different type of house altogether. The porch leads into a central, double-height staircase hall, and the doors to the three principal rooms lead off much as they do in one of Pugin's pinwheel houses. In a slightly later project, the house for St Mary, Stoke Newington, of 1856, Scott managed to leave a trace of this arrangement in a very small and simple plan.[59]

Remarkably, Scott's later plans adopt Pugin's pinwheel planning almost in its entirety. By 1863, at Tydd St Giles in Cambridgeshire and for his brother John, he was still experimenting with large staircase halls whilst attempting an original plan: in this case, three corridors

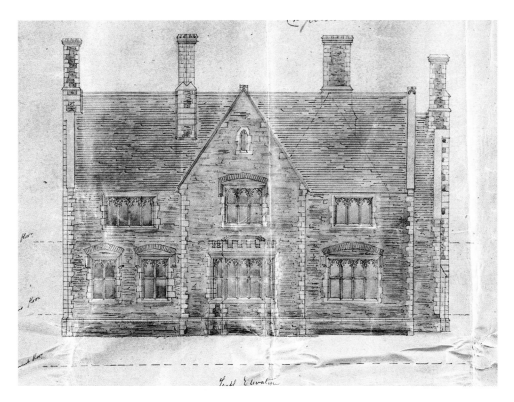

5.26
Scott's parsonage houses are unfailingly interesting. This one at Great Haseley, south-east of Oxford, of 1847 combines the type of elevation that is associated with a back-corridor plan with a pinwheel and a double-height hall [*Oxfordshire Record Office, MS. Oxf. dioc. papers b.103/7*].

lead into the central hall at different angles, one to the front door, one from the dining room, and a third from the kitchen offices (fig. 5.27). In a sense he was developing Pugin's original idea a stage further, by emphasising the dynamic quality of the routes through the building. As in the earlier houses, none of this is evident from the almost symmetrical entrance elevation, which, like the other drawings in the set, seems to have been rapidly and crudely executed. It was here that Scott provides us with a drawing for a two-inch cavity wall, with 'the ends of all bonding bricks tarred or vitrified, and intermittent hoop iron bonds'.[60] At Christ Church, Ealing, in 1866, a porch leads directly into a large, square hall which has a staircase running up two sides of it – very similar to one of Pugin's; the drawing and dining rooms are axially aligned to the left, but the library is located opposite, to the right of the hall, in a way which would have highlighted the domestic processional route between the two sides of the hall (fig. 5.28).[61] Assuming the library was used for parish business, one can easily see

5.27
Tydd St Giles rectory, near Wisbech, Cambridgeshire, by Scott for his brother John (1863). A variant on the pinwheel-plan type that emphasises its inherent dynamism by multiplying routes through the house [*Cambridge University Library, Ely Diocesan Records G/39 MGA/91*].

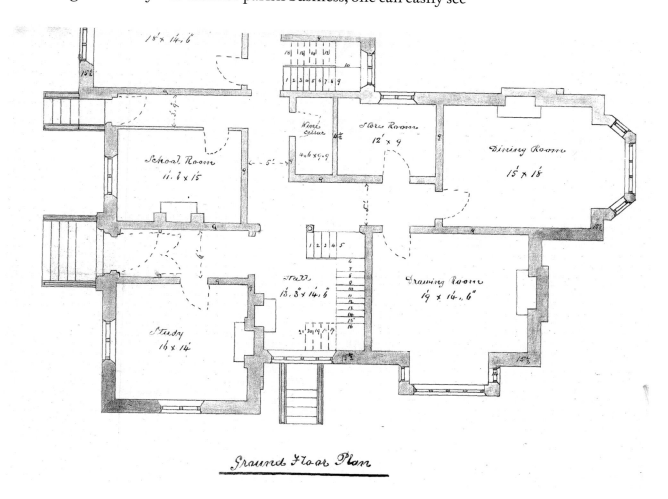

Ground Floor Plan

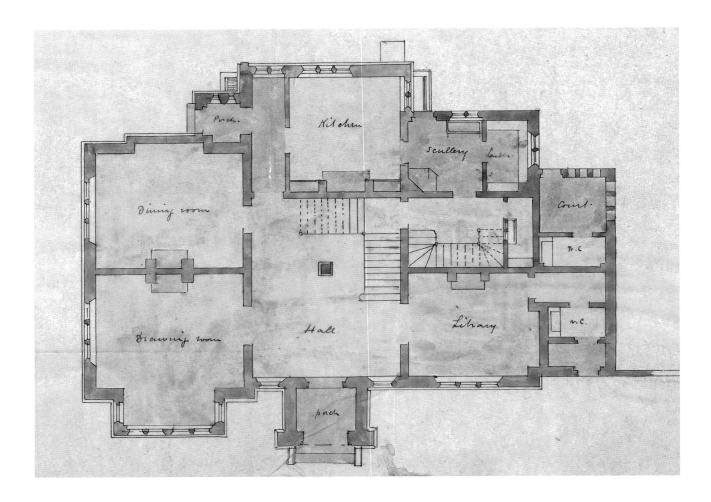

that there has been something of a revolution since the days when
the parishioner was required, as he or she had been long ago at
Walkeringham, to slip in through the back door. Now they would
see the parson's domestic arrangements in their full intimidating
splendour whatever door they came in.[62] Finally, four years later,
when building for a further member of his family at Hillesden,
Buckinghamshire, his office finally produced a plan that closely
resembles that of Rampisham (fig. 5.29). The axes of all three rooms
leading off from the stair hall are in fact parallel, but the similarity is
unmistakable.[63] The elevations here are in a vernacular, half-timbered
style with clusters of brick chimneys, almost presaging the Queen Anne
revival, but a bold Puginesque stair window dominates the entrance
front (fig. 5.30). This series of designs indicates a number of interesting
points: in particular, it shows that Scott was turning Pugin's plans over
in his head for about 25 years; and it also shows that as time went by,
and the architects he employed in his office managed to sway their

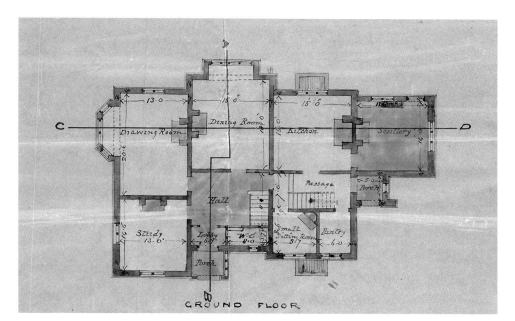

5.29
Scott's office at its most
Puginesque in 1870: a central
hub-type hall at Hillesden,
near Buckingham [*Oxfordshire
Record Office, MS. Oxf. dioc.
papers c.1479*].

master towards a more vernacular and more mixed way of styling
buildings, his enthusiasm for the original purity of the staircase hall
type simply grew. The Hillesden design was almost certainly mainly
the work of one of Scott's assistants, for example George Gilbert Scott
junior or John Oldrid Scott, then established in their father's office.
Scott junior, and his immediate circle, were enthusiastic admirers of
Pugin's.[64]

Bright young men

One of the intriguing aspects of Pugin's work is that architects who
admired it found different ways of expressing their interest; in a sense,
it is that variety of responses that establishes the importance of what he
had done over a comparatively short period. In the case of the work of
the young architects associated with the ecclesiological movement it
appears that at first, at any rate, it was Pugin's insistence that authentic
historical architecture had been both varied and expressive of use that
captured their imagination. In *The true principles* he had written that
'Each part of these [mediaeval domestic] buildings indicated its
particular destination'; and 'the architects of the middle ages were the
first who *turned the natural properties of the various materials to their
full account*, and made *their mechanism a vehicle for their art*'.[65]
The colourful variety of shapes and forms that suddenly emerged from
the mid 1840s illustrates both of these axioms to the full.

5.30
Hillesden parsonage.
The house is scarcely gothic at all: an intriguing contrast to the Puginesque plan within.

R. C. Carpenter was Pugin's contemporary – he too was born in 1812 – and Pugin knew him: he was one of the few architects of the period of whom there is at least some evidence that he may have seen Pugin's Ramsgate house.[66] His first authentically gothic parsonage came in 1843, at Brasted in Kent (fig. 5.31).[67] This house bears more of a superficial similarity to genuine mediaeval domestic architecture than the work of his contemporaries: its long low ranges and something of its stylistic detailing appear to have been derived from the rear elevation of the former prior's lodging at Wenlock Priory, or possibly again that mediaeval vicarage at Muchelney. In general, Carpenter employed a style which combined a flat, plain wall face with rich decorative detailing.[68] His most distinct planning device was a return to the back-corridor plan, and he did this by arranging the house in the form of two distinct parallel ranges: one faced the garden and contained the principal rooms, and the other contained the corridor, the stairs and the offices. He expressed this division very prominently on the narrow elevation: each of the two ranges has its own tall gable. This was not completely unprecedented – there are, after all, plenty of classical-Georgian houses composed of two parallel blocks with separate roofs – but to make a feature of this on an entrance or major front is unusual. There is a rare example in the new rectory at Holford in Somerset, designed in 1832 by Richard Down & Son, but it was certainly contrary to the practice of the great majority of classical-Georgian and Tudor-gothic architects.[69] In contrast to Scott, Carpenter seemed uninterested in Pugin's own planning devices, preferring instead to express the layout of the house with this pair of parallel ranges. The advantage this arrangement gave him was that he could line up the three principal rooms along the garden front so as to show

5.31
Richard Cromwell Carpenter's first authentically gothic parsonage, at Brasted near Sevenoaks, Kent (1843). Here he established his characteristic planning principle of two parallel ranges.

off the difference between them by the use of differing fenestration, thus demonstrating Pugin's requirement that the building should use natural means to express the differences between the rooms' functions. At Brasted he actually brought the front door out onto one of the principal long sides, but at Monkton Wyld in Dorset, built to accompany his church of 1849, he placed it where logic determined – below the gable of the service range to the left-hand side of its tall, narrow, and somewhat intimidating entrance front (fig. 5.32).

For this house he derived the required 'Englishness' by again borrowing from Great Chalfield Manor in neighbouring Wiltshire:

5.32
The entrance front of the parsonage at Monkton Wyld, west Dorset, by Carpenter (1849). The left-hand range contains the hall, stairs, and rear areas; the principal rooms facing the garden front are in the right-hand part.

his father appears to have been, as we have seen above, a subscriber to the third volume of Pugin's *Examples* which illustrated it. This time he took something of its general form rather than its popular double-gabled porch, for his house is arranged on the garden front between two stone gables, both of which are decorated with ornate traceried bays; and the major chimney of the house is placed on this elevation (fig. 5.33; see fig. 3.48).[70] In trying to reconcile the principal front of a modern house with this mediaeval precedent, Carpenter faced a difficult problem. The Manor is a hall house, with a single large room at its centre; Monkton Wyld parsonage on the other hand has the entirely different and modern back-corridor plan that required the garden elevation to be divided into three. Inside, Carpenter experimented with Puginesque minimal joinery, even developing for his ground-floor corridor a skirting that, like some of the architraves, was a composite made from Pugin-like beading. In spite of the grandness of its rooms, and the richness of the detailing, the house is an unresolved one in that one feels that the individual elements of the facade do not combine coherently; but it is a useful experiment in combining the new and the old to produce a fresh and distinctly Victorian type of architecture. As such it attracted the attention of the *Ecclesiologist*, which looked both at it and the architect's unexecuted scheme for Braxted in Suffolk, before concluding that historical English architecture had little or nothing to offer the modern designer: 'Most of the specimens we have seen, which aim at anything better than late Third-Pointed, seem rather timidly to avoid glaring faults, than boldly to seize the spirit of the earlier style. Nuremberg should be more studied by our architects'.[71] Pugin, we know, would have agreed.[72]

Carpenter made a further attempt at a large modern parsonage, and this time in a more relaxed way, at Kilndown in west Kent (fig. 5.34). This parsonage, which was completed in 1855 and which replaced the recent structure by Roos which had proved so unsatisfactory for its incumbent, is likewise a back-corridor type of house and is essentially the mirror image of Monkton Wyld, on a more modest scale. It is again divided into two parallel ranges, and again presents the visitor with a pair of gables, major and minor, about the entranceway, but this time the front door below the service wing gable is obscured by a short external cloister, imitating another Puginian trait (fig. 5.35).[73]

Ewan Christian had criticised the entry arrangements in Roos' house as 'mean and dark', and it perhaps it was as a result that a Puginian 'cloister' was added to the entrance side of the new house; its function is in fact to provide an entrance hall, because otherwise the front door would have led straight into the end of a long and comparatively narrow corridor.[74] At any rate, this cloister softens the entrance front in a way which, whilst it may not please purists, certainly provides a friendlier first impression than Monkton Wyld. Financed by the Beresfords and managed by A. J. Beresford-Hope, the chief benefactor of the ecclesiologists, this was an expensive building designed to advertise the prestige of the gothic revival as much as was their own church nearby; and although Carpenter limited himself to his usual flat wall planes with repetitive tracery, he provided a highlight in the form of a deep and more ornamental bay on the garden side.[75] This was his last parsonage; in addition to these three buildings he had designed a further seven.[76] At Cotes Heath in Staffordshire, and at Little Cornard in Suffolk, in 1846 and 1847 respectively, he attempted open staircase halls, and indeed the latter house has something of a pinwheel-like arrangement of rooms with a study, dining room and drawing room rotating around a comparatively small entrance stairway, a surprise within a house that externally is styled in an almost Tudor style.[77]

Carpenter died young in 1855; William Butterfield on the other hand lived to the age of 86, and worked at least until the age of 80, his last known designs being made in 1895. He therefore provides an almost exact chronological parallel to Ewan Christian. Pugin knew him well – he was 'one of our best customers', he told Hardman – and later correspondence reveals that Butterfield relied directly on Pugin for decorative work at least until 1851.[78] It appears that in his architectural work he was, similarly, attracted by the sculptural and formal potential of materials rather than by any imitation of Pugin's plans and layouts. In common with well-known architects such as T. H. Wyatt, and established provincials like John Whichcord, Butterfield's first approach to Pugin's architecture seems to have been the desire to anglicise it. Like Wyatt, he at first applied more horizontal proportions to his designs than Pugin had done; and like Whichcord, he eventually added what must have been seen as traditionally English details: timber bays, sash windows and even the half-timbering which appears in his work from the Alvechurch parsonage of 1855 onwards,

5.33 (above, left)
The garden front at Monkton Wyld. Carpenter borrowed from mediaeval houses, such as the well known fourteenth-century manor at Great Chalfield, Wiltshire (see fig. 3.48), but adopted its basic elements to suit a back-corridor plan. The timber struts on the left have been inserted recently to support the bay window.

5.34 (above, right)
Another fine Carpenter parsonage, this time at Kilndown in west Kent (1855), seen here from the garden (north) front. The house replaced the disastrous one by Alexander Roos described in Chapter One.

5.35 (below)
A view of the entrance cloister at Kilndown. The pointed window indicates the position of the staircase. The plan of the house is similar to that at Monkton Wyld but on a smaller scale.

The vicarage by William Butterfield in the village of Baldersby St James, near Thirsk in Yorkshire, where his patron was Viscount Downe of Baldersby Park. In this case Pugin's ideas were adopted and anglicised with English-looking half-timbering. A photograph of 1966 in the National Monuments Record [*AA80/1035*].

and in the various village houses at Baldersby towards the end of the decade (fig. 5.36).[79]

In common with Carpenter, Butterfield did not develop any new distinctive plan types and he too preferred houses which placed the three reception rooms in a row, allowing him to vary the external appearance of each and thus easily distinguish it from its neighbour. This was already the case at his first, at Coalpit Heath in Gloucestershire, in 1844, the year in which the Grange was largely completed (fig. 5.37). This house is often thought of as the first domestic building by an architect who designed right from the beginning of his career in a way that reflects Pugin's influence.[80] In one of many variations of the back-corridor type of plan, he placed the three major rooms along the length of the entrance elevation, but, like Carpenter at Brasted, he brought the corridor through to the front of the house between two of the three rooms.[81] The staircase was hidden towards the back of

the house. The major decorative architectural elements of the exterior of the house – the external chimney, the buttresses, the tall gables and the flush stone window surrounds – were characteristic of Pugin's style, regardless of the fact that they were not local to the area.[82] Butterfield also experimented with internal detailing and internal joinery, no doubt inspired by the many of Pugin's geometrical patterns that he was so familiar with. Like Carpenter, he preferred in the 1840s to use comparatively flat patterns for stone window surrounds, tracery, and joinery, and the use of bold geometrical patterns such as mouchettes and ogees, but he varied this with a great deal of chamfering inside and out; the metalwork he himself designed is usually simpler and flatter than Pugin's work. He also reintroduced the Georgian use of brick for window and door quoins, lintels and cills, where Pugin had nearly always used stone.[83] Although in his long career he does not seem to have aimed for a standard set of details, as Pugin did, he certainly designed every detail for each house just as he did for a church.

The basic planning arrangements of the Coalpit Heath house were redeployed henceforth throughout Butterfield's career. The differing functions of the main rooms in this layout were expressed by varying

5.37
Coalpit Heath parsonage of 1844, now on the northern outskirts of Bristol and photographed in 1987. Butterfield seems to have been the first of Pugin's significant admirers who was a gothic architect right from the start [*National Monuments Record, A45/6076*].

Butterfield was not greatly influenced by Pugin's plan types, but he did adopt his predecessor's use of different types of window to indicate different rooms – here (left to right) library, drawing room and dining room. This is Alvechurch, near Bromsgrove, Worcestershire, of 1855. Photographed in April 2004.

the design of the vertical bays on the exterior beneath a continuous ridge: at Alvechurch in 1855, for example, the bays increase in size, and massiveness, from west to east, from library via drawing room to dining room – in other words, the definition of the uses within is more blatant than was Pugin's standard practice (fig. 5.38). Butterfield did use a stair hall, pinwheel-type plan at least once, at Bamford (1862), but this was an isolated occurrence rather than a progression. The parsonage of 1871 at Landford (figs 5.39, 5.40) was essentially a reversion to a conventional back-corridor type.[84] Designed in the year after Scott's remarkable Pugin-revival plan at Hillesden, however, Butterfield's design also shows a remarkable nostalgia for the simplicity of Pugin's own designs. There are comparatively few window openings; the entrance elevation, on the opposite side now from the main rooms, is dominated by a great stair window, a gothic door, a water-closet window and little else; and the simple pairs of gables on the east and west sides, and even the pattern of a cross worked into the brickwork, are all reminiscent of the freshness of the 1840s. Isolated specifically Puginesque details occur, such as the square bay window of the Great Woolstone parsonage of 1851 which, although largely of timber, echoes that of the Bishop's House in Birmingham or

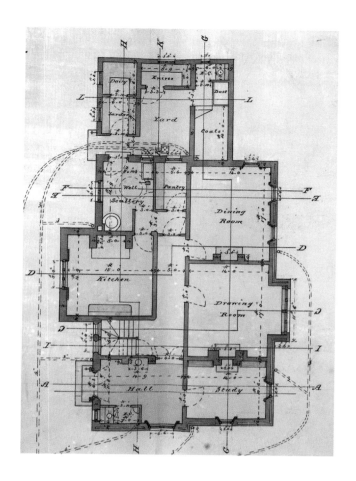

5.39 (left); 5.40 (below); Butterfield's rectory at Landford, Wiltshire (1871): a powerful design that scarcely depends on gothic imagery beyond the imposing front door. The planning, however, was conventional: a back-corridor plan allowed him to place his three major rooms in a row, with the drawing room at the centre, and thus express their different characters along the outside [*Wiltshire & Swindon Record Office, D1/11/206*].

The 1850s: A kind of pattern house

at Warwick Bridge (fig. 5.41).[85] In general, as Paul Thompson has observed in his monograph, Butterfield appears to have been inspired by Pugin's use of brick as a comprehensive building material; and he concentrated his attention to the exploitation of this building material through the use of subtly differing planes, such as at Avington in 1847, and eventually through colour.[86] Unsurprisingly therefore it is in his creation of three-dimensional forms through the paring of a material by complex patterns of chamfering, for example in his fonts and other smaller-scale ornamental designs, that he comes closest to Pugin; the clergy house at All Saint's church, Margaret Street in London, designed in the late 1840s, owes its Puginesque vertical proportions only to its tiny site (fig. 5.42). But then Pugin's influence can be found now wherever nineteenth-century architecture was evolving.

George Edmund Street, born in 1824 and thus a younger architect than Butterfield and Carpenter, likewise began to design parsonages during the period when Pugin's professional career was at its zenith; and he enjoyed, according to his son, 'intimate relations' with Benjamin Webb, founding secretary of the Cambridge Camden Society.[87] The design for his parsonage at Wantage was completed in November 1849, soon after he had left the office of George Gilbert Scott and following the display of the perspective of St Augustine's church and the Grange at the Royal Academy; its plan was based around a large and almost square staircase hall.[88] The house replaced one which had horrified W. J. Butler, its incoming parson, in 1846: his predecessor had been simultaneously dean of Windsor, and had preferred to live there, leaving behind in Wantage a house that was ancient, thatched, and dilapidated, and was also 'the coldest [Butler] had ever lived in'.[89] Street's gothic house was, by contrast, a comfortable modern residence (fig. 5.43). The principal rooms were not however arranged around the hall in pinwheel fashion: the drawing and dining rooms were located to one side of the hall, and the study at the other; and the staircase window on the front elevation was at ground floor, rather than intermediate, level. Street gave written instructions in his accompanying specification that 'particular attention [was] to be given to making the Bond of the Masons on the exterior naturally irregular', and he used flush stone window surrounds, rustic buttresses, a stone bay window, and other Puginian devices (see fig. 1.4). The house was Puginian too in its 'convenience': the original incumbent, writing later to Street's son, described it as 'one of the most convenient and pleasant of dwellings, and it has been a subject of never failing surprise to all who have seen it and inhabited it, that a house so bright and attractive could have been built for so small a sum of money as it actually cost'.[90] Given the derision often heaped on the little houses of the formative stages of the gothic revival, it is important to remember that they gave a great deal of pleasure.[91] There is a free, and rather camp design of 1852 for a parsonage at Cuddesdon in Oxfordshire in which the three major rooms and the large kitchen are arranged irregularly three sides around a stairhall; it is noteworthy that the oratory is not only prominent on both front and back elevations but it also clearly labelled as such on the plans – a sign of the impact of the Oxford Movement since Pugin had had to be so discreet with his at Rampisham six years earlier (fig. 5.44).[92] It is a long narrow house that gave Street an opportunity that could illustrate Pugin's remark in *An apology* that 'If our present domestic buildings were only designed in accordance with their actual purposes, they would appear equally picturesque with the old ones!'[93] Similarly, when Street remodelled a small thatched cottage parsonage at Barford St Michael three years later, he left the long straggling house much as it was, adding a fashionable large staircase hall at the centre of it.[94] The design of his small houses subsequently however showed little developing interest in the genre: the plan of the Denstone parsonage of 1862 is complex and unresolved, arranged about a central corridor which winds around the three principal rooms to reach a rear stair hall. The thinking is Puginesque, but the execution strangely restless. In common with Butterfield, Street's interest in Pugin's work appears to have been largely limited to exploiting the planar qualities of building materials; of arranging principal rooms in a row so that they could be easily read from the front; and of trying to break away from conventional planning. He certainly did this at Melksham in Wiltshire in 1877, where he converted what appears to have been a fairly ramshackle collection of rooms into an expensive picturesque house of great charm (see fig. 4.12).[95] Behind the austere facades is an organic plan centred on a new staircase hall in the heart of the house, which leads on to a drawing and dining room either side of an indirect corridor out into the garden. Street separated the flight of stairs from the rest of the hall by a row of columns, and provided the remaining part of the room with a great fireplace, embedded into the

5.41 (above)
Butterfield's parsonage at Great Woolstone, Buckinghamshire, now within Milton Keynes (1851). The strongly orthogonal bay window is reminiscent of several by Pugin, including those at Warwick Bridge (fig. 3.24) and the Bishop's House, Birmingham.

5.42 (right)
The clergy house at All Saints' church, Margaret Street, London, by Butterfield, photographed in May 1990.

5.43 (opposite, above)
The vicarage designed by George Edmund Street in 1846 for the leading Tractarian, the Reverend W. J. Butler, later dean of Lincoln, at Wantage, Berkshire (now Oxfordshire).

5.44 (opposite, below)
Street's architecture was rarely camp, but this is an exception: Cuddesdon vicarage, near Oxford, 1852. The oratory is top left in the elevation. The house was built close to the palace of Samuel Wilberforce, bishop of Oxford, for Alfred Pott who established the Anglo-Catholic Cuddesdon College on the bishop's behalf two years later. Street also reordered the church [*Oxfordshire Record Office, MS. Oxf. dioc. papers c.1789*].

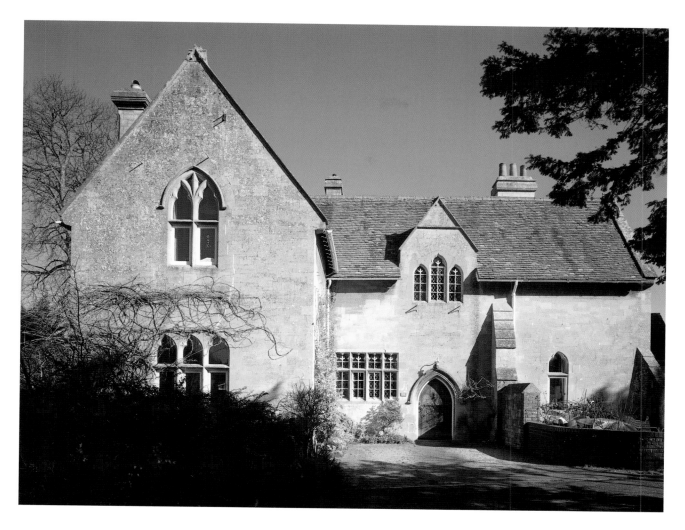

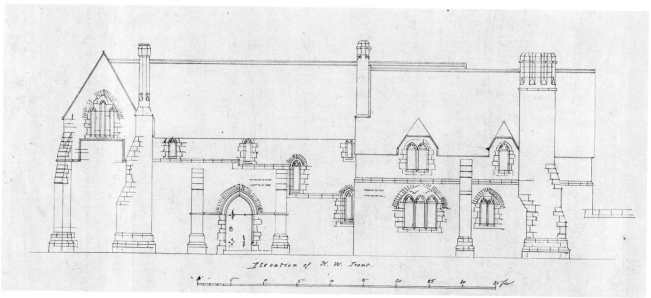

Elevation of N. W. Front.

pre-existing fabric: it appears that he was trying to do what Pugin never did, to make the staircase hall into some kind of furnishable, useable room. He also exploited the picturesque potential of the remains of the old parts of the house, retaining some parts of exterior walls, and furnishing them with new uses and new windows. In both these respects he was clearly foreshadowing later events: this is a romantic building that already has the flavour of the late century about it. It is an interesting project, furthermore, because it indicates something of a shift in Street's attitude to existing buildings. In a recent remodelling project, at Purbrook in Hampshire (1871), he had demolished the old part of the house altogether and retained only the office wing at the back.[96]

In mentioning Street, it is impossible to avoid a medium-sized family house that was neither designed by him, nor a parsonage, and yet because of its great fame it is unavoidable. Philip Webb had worked in Street's office, and his Red House in Bexleyheath of 1859 for William Morris provides an example of the direction in which the Puginian ideas adopted by both Street and Butterfield were leading: it employs Pugin characteristics such as a homogenous walling material and the use of brick modelling instead of applied ornament or carving; internally it has a broad hall, and a staircase that acts as a hub, linking two major passages on both floors. On the other hand, it employs Butterfieldian sash windows, brick pattern-making, and curious forms such as round windows and pointed doors (figs 5.45, 5.46).[97] Sheila Kirk's recent study of Webb's work has drawn attention to the conscious debt that Webb owed Pugin, in particular in respect of the latter's aim of creating an architectural language from the physical properties of materials, and from constructional method.[98] Photographs of the house typically show the decorative, free-style, south and east elevations, rather than the bleaker north, or more severe west. In fact this last front is in several respects similar to many others of the 1850s, and it is a harbinger of much work of the coming decades at least as much as the more famous parts of the building; that small extension at Chirton, by Seddon, referred to above owes a great deal to it (see fig. 5.2).

The work of eccentric and flamboyant gothic architects such as Samuel Sanders Teulon provides a useful conclusion to this description of what happened next. In Teulon's case, not only did he design a number of parsonages, he also provides something of a bridge between the work of the Tudor-gothic and gothic-revival architects because at the start of his career he had worked for the Tudor-gothic architect George Porter (c1796–1856). Porter had employed a vigorous symmetrical Tudor-gothic style, at for example the Watermen's Company's Almshouses at Penge in 1840-1, enlivening a dull plan with bold verticals (fig. 5.47). This style appears to have influenced Teulon's early parsonages, which share the latter characteristic. He designed quite a few schemes in the mid 1840s of varying quality but invariably beautifully drawn and often with one or two stylish idiosyncrasies. At Winston vicarage in Suffolk he produced an already old-fashioned combination of a central-corridor plan with a gable-and-bay elevation, but it did have crowsteps.[99] A year later, in 1845, he designed a back-corridor plan for a large rectory at Hollesley, also predominantly Tudor-gothic in manner (although it had haunches rather than shoulders at the bottom of the gables); he included windows that poked through the chimney stacks, providing a detail of this in his application drawings.[100] He settled on this style for a while, often providing perspectives to judge the effect; there are several more examples in the RIBA collection.[101] The first buildings that follow on from the zenith of Pugin's career indicate however an idiosyncratic attempt to remodel a Tudor-gothic composition in such a way as to express the internal functions. At the parsonage of 1849 at Tathwell in Lincolnshire, the seven-bedroom house with the substantial kitchen court and stable yard that we have seen in the previous chapter (see fig. 4.9), he designed a house with an original and complex plan: the entry route leads anticlockwise through porch, vestibule and hall and continues up the stairs in a spiral (fig. 5.48).[102] The three principal downstairs rooms are arranged in an L around the stair hall, and the stair itself is expressed on the outside by a large mullioned window. What is remarkable about this house in comparison to Pugin's work, however, is the fact that Teulon has retained characteristic elements of Tudor-gothic: gables sitting above parapet shoulders, a brick pinnacle, and a central gablet decorated with a lozenge. One finds there too the mannerisms of the previous generation of picturesque parsonage builders – a mullioned bay window to the drawing room, a window in a chimney shaft – but the architect has begun to mould these into a coherent style which is derived from the plastic form of these elements

5.45 (above, left)
Red House, Bexley Heath, Kent by Philip Webb (1859): the west front. The house's distinct character may well be the result of a successful mixture of motifs from Pugin, Street and Butterfield in a single building. Photographed in November 1998.

5.46 (above, right)
Red House: the entrance (north) front. Photographed in July 1990.

5.47 (right)
The Watermen's Company almshouses at Penge, Surrey, by George Porter (1840–1). Porter's lively and confident version of the Tudor-gothic style evidently influenced his pupil Samuel Sanders Teulon.

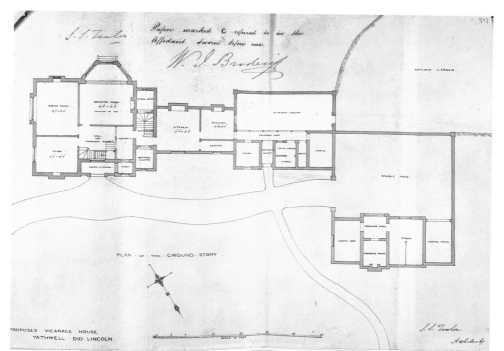

5.48
Tathwell, south of Louth,
Lincolnshire, by Teulon (1849).
The entrance route spirals
anticlockwise from the entry
door to the upper floor –
a Puginian device in an L-plan
house. The external detailing
was idiosyncratic. See fig. 4.9.
[*Lincolnshire Archives,
MGA 338*].

rather than their detail. In a sense, Teulon is the mannerist architect of the gothic revival, working with the forms themselves in an original way by resolving the use of materials to the Tudor-gothic styling, rather than the other way around; it is a shame that Gottfried Semper, in England after 1848, is not known to have turned his attention to Teulon. The Tathwell house marks an important intermediate stage between pre and post-Pugin work in a way that suggests knowledge of Pugin's work, but is also original. And yet in even slightly later houses Teulon reverted to simple old plans. Steeple Barton vicarage of 1855 has an L-corridor plan, albeit with a large central hall;[103] and so does West Grimstead, of 1857. This house, like Wyatt's Alderbury vicarage located close to St Marie's Grange, has a Tudor-gothic gable-and-bay elevation animated by strange brick patterning of almost pagan appearance (fig. 5.49).[104]

The two other leading eccentrics of the time remained in many respects Regency architects too, piling up their wild detailing on plans which represented only slight experimentation. Henry Woodyer designed at least seven new or mainly new parsonages up to the end of the 1850s, and attracted the attention of the *Ecclesiologist* for the one at Marchwood in Hampshire.[105] This was the house that had that 'peculiar character' which the magazine left undetermined, although it added

5.49

A simple house with brick decoration of almost pagan appearance: West Grimstead, just to the east of Alderbury, Wiltshire, by Teulon (1857). Teulon's work was often very strange and not particularly gothic [*Wiltshire & Swindon Record Office, D1/11/131*].

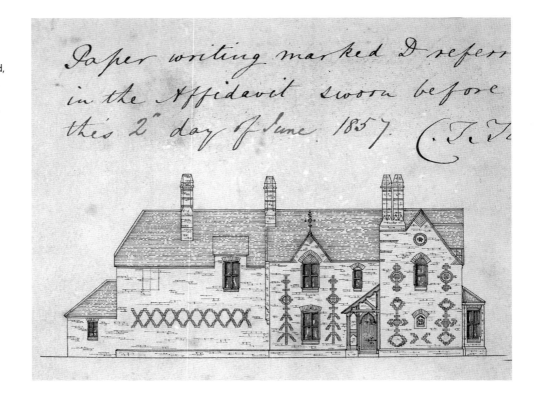

gnomically that 'its dining room [was] adapted to receiving poor people'.[106] Presumably the implication of the *Ecclesiologist*'s comments is that the dining room, rather than the study, was arranged so that parishioners could reach it without going through the main entrance of the house. If this was considered desirable, it would explain why many houses had their dining room, rather than their drawing room, furthest from their kitchen, a recurrent feature in many contemporary parsonages. The house was extended by William White in 1862, so its original layout has been obscured.[107] A slightly later house by Woodyer at Coldwaltham in Sussex was essentially a typical back-corridor plan, but with the sequence of principal reception rooms varied in form and in their fenestration in the way that Butterfield was designing them (fig. 5.50). The lengthy specification for the house includes small freehand sketches showing Pugin-like chamfering of the exposed joists, a useful indicator of the way in which Pugin's details were passed on: no doubt the builder, William Smart of Arundel, used them later in projects where there was no architect to instruct him otherwise.[108] At Cove in 1845 Woodyer designed a brick house with diaper patterning and large picturesque chimneys in what was basically a variation of an L-corridor plan, except that the front door

EAST

was in the stair part of the L rather than at the opposite end, thus forming a very modest staircase hall.[109] The real concession to the gothic revival was that the house was split into two parallel ranges, so the double gable on the end wall, with its imposing bay window on the drawing-room side, provided the requisite expression of the form and structure of the house from outside. E. B. Lamb, possibly the best-known of the other 'rogue' architects, in many respects remained a Regency gothic architect throughout his life; his parsonage at Wheatley, Oxfordshire, of 1850, adopts only timidly a staircase hall, no larger than 13 feet by 10 feet, from the Pugin repertoire; another of his houses, at Copdock in Suffolk (1858), strung the main rooms out along a large hallway, but the stairs were relegated to the side (fig. 5.51). In both these houses his style although mainly gothic was eclectic and picturesque; it stayed that way throughout his career.[110] Why have these eccentrics always been relegated to the second division of the gothic revival, in spite of the English penchant for the picturesque? Was it because the planning of their small houses was conventional? Even William White's splendid parsonages have escaped the interest they deserve, and the reason might well be that their internal layouts, behind their richly fashioned exteriors, were rarely original or unusual.[111]

5.50
The east elevation of Henry Woodyer's parsonage at Coldwaltham, between Horsham and Chichester, West Sussex (1848). The use of the back-corridor plan enabled gothic-revival enthusiasts to arrange the principal rooms in a row with changing types of windows to suit the different uses of the rooms. In this case they indicated (from left to right) the drawing room, dining room, and study (with the traceried window) [*West Sussex Record Office, EPI/41/72 part 2*].

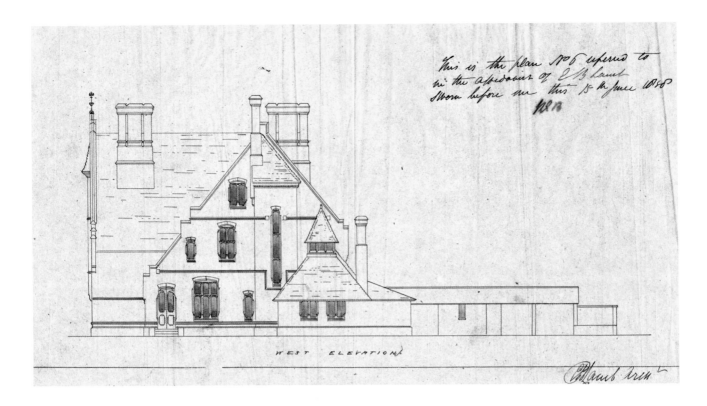

WEST ELEVATION

5.51
Copdock rectory, near Ipswich,
Suffolk, by Edward B. Lamb
(1858). Lamb's unusual
composition and idiosyncratic
detailing are not usually as
successful as this. Just as the
irregular entrance elevations
of back-corridor plans
heralded the emergence of the
asymmetrical gothic-revival
house, the back and side
elevations of high gothic
houses begin now to hint at
Queen Anne or arts and crafts
designs [*Suffolk Record
Office, Ipswich, FF1/24/1*].

Higher things

It was Jane Austen's Mr Elton who introduced us to the sorry state of
the village parsonage in the 1810s, and the serious discrepancy between
its physical condition, and the social standing of its residents. By the
1840s, the whole process of the arrival of a new type of parson, and a
dignified house to suit, was already being described by novelists.
Writing from personal experience in mid decade, Anne Brontë
introduces us to Mr Weston, the young clergyman who comes to
redeem her heroine Agnes Grey from the life of drudgery that has
befallen her since her father, a parson himself, lost his money in
unwise investments and died bereft of all. He also comes with 'certain
reforms' to redeem his new parish from the likes of Mr Hatfield,
a cold, snobbish rector of the old school.[112] Early in the story,
Mr Weston has '*no home*' – Brontë's italics, and there to stress the
importance that her heroine has attached all her life to a comfortable
and secure house.[113] At the end of the tale, we can guess that they are
both happily settled in a comfortable parsonage with his wife and
children, for at the time of writing one of the first things that a new
reforming clergyman would turn his attention to was the provision
of a parsonage that matched his station.

In Chapter One we also had a glimpse of Mr Miller, sitting in his study at Walkeringham, and toasting some muffins before the fire. By mid century there were plenty of clerical writers with ideas for how he should be better spending such spare time as they might have allowed him. In 1845, a popular devotional writer called W. E. Heygate, one of many to criticise the squarson, the hunting, shooting, fishing parson who sat on the local magistrates' bench, quoted the words of George Herbert on a parson's daily life with approval: "The furniture of his house is very plain, but clean, whole and sweet...His fare is plain and common, but wholesome, what he hath is little".[114] To this, Heygate added the following recommendation of his own:

> There is a straightness and an harmony, and a symbolism, which should cling to every external portion of the priest and of his house. A priest's dress, a priest's house, a priest's table, a priest's conversation, should all be sacerdotal.[115]

One of the characteristics of the new architecture was that every detail had to be consistent with the whole; there was no longer any back elevation, or any shabby workmanship that could be covered up with stucco; and one of the characteristics of the new religion was that there was to be no hiding from it in any room of the house. In the privacy of his den a newly-ordained young parson might soon find it hard to ignore voices like that of the best-selling author and preacher Ashton Ovenden, whom we met at Barham in Kent. Following Heygate, Ovenden wrote in 1857 that

> now I speak of the minister's *Study*. And should not this be almost a sacred spot? Here, if he would feed his people with food convenient for them, he must lay in ever-increasing stores of mental and spiritual food. The public fountain will soon fail, if there is no hidden source from whence the supply may flow in...The Clergyman's Study should be hallowed also to increasing prayer.[116]

And as for the house as a whole

> The Parsonage should be a kind of pattern house. There should be an air of neatness, sobriety, and cheerfulness about it, but nothing like

extravagance, or needless display. It may well be questioned whether some of our Parsonages of the present day are not of too pretending a character — whether they are not, in many cases, both too large and too luxurious...a lordly Parsonage is not only inconsistent with our character who comes not to be ministered unto but to minister, and hurtful to our own Spirit as men of another world; but it will have this bad effect too — it will repel rather than invite, our humble parishioners to come to us. They will feel that he who lives in so rich a mansion can hardly desire their company.[117]

Have we found something else that Pugin did for architecture? Did he make a kind of building that tried to determine the behaviour of those that live there? If so he, and his admirers, were simply providing the clerical revival with the visual imagery they wanted and needed to make their campaign a success. Architectural determinism is out of fashion nowadays; but if we too disapprove of it, we cannot of course blame architects, for they derive their language from what they see and hear all around them. The bossy building is the fault of the English who tend to see architecture in terms of something else: keeping up with the Joneses; sentiment; literature; politics; morality; sociology; economics; religion. Anything but what a building actually looks like. And so however brilliant and original it was, the architects' new passion for raising houses rationally, expressively, and consistently would have been nothing had it not provided the imagery sought by the swelling wave of educationalists and moralists; by the reforming writers and political poets; by the early dawn and the cold showers of the rebuilt public schools. Everything must be consistent with everything; everything must speak of the truth; nothing must be hidden. As with Pugin, as with Philip Webb and the others, every last detail down to the furniture and the silver and glassware on the table is designed to convey the same message as the house itself – a brilliant, exhilarating idea! So appropriate for the reforming parson bringing morality and education into a poor, straggling, illiterate village.

The days of a comfortable, unpretentious house like Miller's at Walkeringham, a practical investment, are gone.

The Pastor's Home! we must now leave him there. That home may be sweet and peaceful. It may be endeared to him by a thousand ties.

The hours spent there may for many years have been full of enjoyment and full of usefulness. But it is not his resting-place. He must never forget that he is but a stranger and a pilgrim here. His real, his true Home is above. He must live on earth as one hastening onwards to the many mansions of his father's house.[118]

A parsonage had ceased to be an ordinary home in a village, a little better appointed perhaps than its humbler neighbours, but an ordinary home just the same: a house that met the practical needs of living comfortably; two or three fine rooms; a hearth; a kitchen court; a stable; a cellar for beer and cider as well as for wine. It had become a spiritual necessity, a devotional aid; to cross its doorstep was to set foot on the road to salvation. The symbols were there from the doorknobs to the cutlery. But will the Regency hedonism of our own time also lead on to such an invigorating future?

Epilogue

'*Real, simple,* and religious' – that was how the 'eminent church architect' writing in 1849 to the Architectural and Archæological Society for the County of Buckinghamshire had described his ideal parsonage. It is perhaps a significant statement, and one which draws the history of the design of the parsonage into the much wider field of social history, laying the clues for why the story of these houses may be of interest beyond the realm of architecture.

I questioned above whether the words chosen by that 'eminent church architect' would have been understood by all of his audience in the same way. 'Realism' in particular seems then to have been used as a term without a precise definition. Adrian Forty's *Words and buildings* provides however two meanings for the word as it might then have been deployed by architects: the revelation by the form of a building of the real nature of a community or activity housed; and, more traditionally, the blatant expression of the constructional characteristics of building in the way that Pugin was now doing.[1] In other words, it was at least partly a term drawn from what we would now call sociology as from the technical language of the architectural profession.

And 'religious' – that too may have carried more specific meanings than seems obvious today; as a kind of inverse to 'real', it was evidently mainly a social term but one which carried an architectural connotation. It sounds primarily as if it should mean 'devotional', and Anglican writers such as Heygate and Ovenden, wanting to avoid any suggestion that 'religious' might imply a mere popish ceremonialism, appear to conflate the two. They evidently believed that anyone following a religious life should always act in an outwardly devotional way. It seems logical to suppose that for an architect the word 'religious' when applied to buildings meant a form of construction that determined or emphasised that devotional way of life. In other words, 'religious architecture' actually meant at this time 'realist architecture for religious people'. And that, it seems to me, is precisely the key to what was happening in parsonage architecture in the years following the launch of Pugin's career.

An important question then for those who pressed for ecclesiastical reform was how to determine what that religious life should consist of; and in a parallel fashion to all that we have heard here about the architectural profession, church reformers were also trying to standardise their own profession, and in a similarly technical and 'scientific' way. Indeed, architects and churchmen were going hand in hand. The period was one when the daily life and ritual of churchmen was being defined in a manner that was unprecedented in England since the middle ages; in the case of Roman Catholics, new foundations of monasteries and convents from the late 1830s made the circumscription of daily life a priority. The creation of mediaevalising 'Rules' along the lines of those of monastic orders was a significant feature of the new religious life, especially in the light of the reappearance of the twelfth-century *Chronicle* of Jocelyn de Brakelond, the basis of Thomas Carlyle's *Past and present* in 1843 and published in translation in 1844.[2] These new 'Rules' required different codes of behaviour for different places, and architects – especially Pugin – seem to have designed buildings that exaggerated that differentness for the various areas of a religious institution.[3]

During Pugin's working life, however, there was as yet no 'Rule' that applied to the daily life and living conditions of the Roman Catholic priest; and what happened in the Church of England was a matter of individual discretion. In these situations Pugin seems to have provided his clients with a kind of house that met their expectations. He demonstrated realism by his demand that each room be separately articulated according to its function, as realised in the pinwheel plan houses; he thus created an external manifestation of the real nature of the activities within but balanced by architectural control expressed for example through his continuous ridge heights, so different from the happy variety of the picturesque. Each of Pugin's three major rooms, typically study, library and dining room, has a distinct external presence because of the pinwheel plan and the gabled arrangement of the roofs – a design that contrasts with classical-Georgian convention and with Loudon's preferred solutions, which were also intended to be primarily practical and functional, but which were typically organised to form a simple geometrical shape that could be easily and cheaply roofed. Pugin's houses were also distinct from the rarer L-plan type houses, because in these the principal rooms were tucked into a simple geometrical shape rather than fully expressed externally. The fact that he was aware of the importance of what he was trying to do is clearly indicated by the fact that after its construction he drew the Grange, the first of the pinwheel plans, with the south library wall projecting southwards from the face of the dining-room wall, even though in reality it was flush with it.[4]

Pugin may have been drawn to these designs for architectural reasons; but their attraction for religious people, looking for an architecture which expressed time of day, uniqueness of place, and changes of mood and movement between different spaces can be easily understood. So in this way his architecture was 'religious' too, because it varied from one part of a house to the next; the character of each place was modified according to the expected activity in it and the full value of a building is experienced by moving from room to room, in sequence, according to a regular timetable. Procession and formal movement between rooms reappear in the pious Victorian household. If the 'real' building reflects the needs of the occupants, the 'religious' building imposes on the occupants what their needs should be and 'tells' them how to behave in it. To achieve this, religious architecture acts as a prompt and a tool for measuring something that was otherwise hard to judge: the different behavioural response of a person according to the situation he or she is in. People will have known, as they still do, in which room to drop their voices without being told, and Pugin's cloisters and corridors provided appropriate transitional areas. The dynamism of the pinwheel house plans is the key to the layout. The stair at the centre of the house acts as a hub; the rooms are, as it were, thrown outwards from it, each one distinct and yet clearly part of a whole. In the past I have put it like this: architects before Pugin made a plan into a diagram, because they made an arrangement of rooms and then fitted it somehow into a simple shape dictated by convention and economy; Pugin on the other hand turned a diagram into a plan: he mapped out the various spaces and the relationships between them the way he wanted them, and then froze this into a plan.[5] Some of the very odd and technically inefficient plans of his institutional buildings seem to have been devised this way. At the same time, as George Gilbert Scott observed, Pugin remained enough of an artist to ensure that his buildings remained visually coherent.[6] That central stair hall and that strong geometrical form provided coherence. By the 1850s, what gothic architects are primarily trying to do is to balance the variety they wanted across their facades with an overall form that asserted the required architectural discipline. Pugin had shown them how.

But it is the fact that Pugin designed a kind of architecture that met these demands not only to architects but to a large group of politically and socially influential people such as theologians, reformers and preachers who really had no idea about what a modern house should look like is what has assured him of his central role in this book. He is part of a general phenomenon which one can see spread right across the society of his day. Forty's first definition of realism – that of form representing the real nature of use – was shared, in Pugin's working life, by creative artists in other fields, by rational thinkers such as Loudon who were struggling to create technical definitions for vague ideas, and by the new emerging sciences, such as sociology, which, like Britton's contemporary *Architectural antiquities*, strove to make scientific judgments from apparently irrational phenomena.[7] Pugin himself borrowed realist devices from non-architectural sources such as these early on in his career, for example from Walter Scott whose shadow hangs over the whole of the popular artistic world of the 1820s and 1830s. Scott created realistic figures inhabiting realistic settings, meticulously described. In *Kenilworth* (1821), Countess Amy's apartments at Cumnor Place are arranged in a series of rooms, each leading from the next, each with its own design identity, and with the most intimate of the chambers placed at the deepest point.[8] The significance of Scott's description is that the rooms do not only have a merely metaphorical quality that expresses the events happening inside in the manner of a didactic, romantic or picturesque fable, but are clearly 'real' rooms with highly detailed architecture. As we have seen, Pugin reproduced Scott's Cumnor Place in the arrangement of rooms at St Marie's Grange in 1835: the three rooms on the principal floor lead off from one another without a corridor, a plan entirely unlike any new architect-designed house of similar scale of the period, and indicating the literal way in which an ambitious architect hungry to realise his ideas can translate a literary conceit into an architectural one.

Indeed Pugin also closely echoed the foremost realist writer of his period, the French novelist Honoré de Balzac. Balzac's novels presented rooms in an anthropomorphic or symbolic way that had long been characteristic of novel writing.[9] Unlike his predecessors, however, he described architectural settings to a degree of precision that suggests that they *are* real, a sense of reality far enhanced above that of Scott by the contemporary context of the stories. The descriptions of the house forming the claustrophobic setting for *Eugénie Grandet* (1833) are so detailed that is possible to work out even the relationship between the doors of rooms. Strikingly, Balzac described his *Père Goriot* (1834-5) as a meditation 'upon natural principles' wherein he will see 'Societies depart from or approach "the eternal rule, the true, the beautiful"' (in Balzac's own words, *la règle eternelle, le vrai, le beau*)[10] – an announcement echoed only a few years later by Pugin's declaration that 'the Beautiful and the True' be the watchwords of architecture.[11] Unlike the case of *Kenilworth*, I am not suggesting that Pugin was familiar with Balzac's writing; but the coincidence in the phrasing is remarkable. Since architects are not generally particularly deft with words, it seems very likely that Pugin was picking up on phrases and ideas that were going around at the time and appealed to him. And if the realist novel writer allows every detail to build up a consistent picture of a realistic whole, which is in itself part of the portrayal of a good or bad character, the realist architect designs a building such that each part of it both expresses the activity within, but is also utterly consistent with the whole and in its details – a process that has a parallel both in the reforming construction industry of Bartholomew's day but also in the new medical and pseudo-medical sciences in that all were concerned with making distinctions between different types of human behaviour ever more precise.

As Walter Scott was enjoying his public success, from the 1820s and at least until the conclusion of Pugin's working life, a major international movement established throughout Europe a link between two-dimensional diagrams – plans – and personal behavioural traits in public perception: phrenology. Franz Josef Gall, the 'inventor' of phrenology, visited Britain in 1823, and his associate Spurzheim based himself in London from that time onwards. When pointing out the vast sales of George Combe's phrenologically orientated 'Constitution of Man', which had sold over 80,500 copies in Britain by 1847, Roger Cooter in his comprehensive study of the subject remarks that Combe was attempting 'a demonstration of morality as a science' – in other words, that it was possible to translate abstract behavioural qualities into finite analytical diagrams.[12] Cooter provides the following gloss on Combe's theories of rationally derived happiness: 'For happiness, all that was required was that people come into harmony with and abide by the natural laws of mind and morality'. These natural laws were derived from a supposedly rational analysis of the physical form of the skull. 'In a way that would appeal to a Dickensian character, all was made plain: The mind was no longer "chaos of Passion all confus'd," it was a set of physiological structures functioning in an orderly way'.[13] The cranial map that phrenology used and widely publicised was a translation of behavioural attributes to a two-dimensional plan draped across a skull. Pugin's translation of the behavioural expectations of a modern religious life into an architectural diagram – and then a house or convent plan – is undoubtedly part of a similar manoeuvre. One sees there too an attempt not only to categorise and to rationalise indistinct information, but also to represent it in two and three-dimensional form. Looking at this absorption of a general principle into the very specific world of early Victorian design, one might conclude that a distinguishing characteristic of the kind of Victorian architecture practised by Pugin and his admirers was that it mapped out the mind and the mind's perceived division into distinct behavioural characteristics. A room for praying; a room for thinking; a room for eating; a room for marital relations – and all with precise physical relationships to one another. In that way it seems to me – as I have also suggested elsewhere – that the kind of Victorian architecture exemplified by our parsonages marks a distinct contrast to the popular idea, much rehearsed by its adherents, that a classical building is meant in some way to be a representation of the physical characteristics of the body, a matter of external balance and hierarchy.[14]

In fact, once one starts to look one finds other links between contemporary popular culture and the apparently elevated and restricted writings of church and social reformers. Here we are properly in the territory of the social or political historian; but the architectural historian too soon finds valuable leads. For example, there is clearly a strong link between the gothic revival and a significant characteristic of phrenology: social dissent. Pugin's approving view of the feudal past is not to be confused with an acquiescence with the social and political *status quo*: in the wake of the Great Reform Act and the long period of ineffectiveness of the Tory party and the landed aristocracy that dated from Lord Liverpool's government, he was as opposed to contemporary Toryism as was, say, the author of *Coningsby*; and his strong belief that the primary distinction in worship should be between the clergy and their lay congregation, rather than between the different social layers of the congregation alone – an idea expressed emphatically in his championing of the revival of the rood screen in Catholic churches in the late 1840s – is a example of how his traditionalism opposed contemporary practice.

It was a primary goal of the ecclesiological movement to end the social hierarchies inherent within congregations in the rented pew system in English churches. It is an important issue, because it addresses the desire of the reformers to break down the private sphere of life – in this case the comfy rented box with its curtains, like the Ovendens' at Barham – and amalgamate it with the public one. It was the central theme of more than one of the pamphlets of the leading ecclesiologist J. M. Neale, and also an incidental one both in his widely circulated *A few words to churchwardens* and in his novel *Ayton Priory* (1843), the story of a landed family that returns their property to the church, and thus reverses England's post-Reformation settlement.[15] *A few words to churchwardens* reached its fourteenth edition within a few years of its first publication. William Butterfield, the ecclesiologists' primary designer after the death of R. C. Carpenter, introduced benches for common use to replace pews whenever he could, and he was widely imitated.[16] The degree to which this blatantly anti-establishment aspect of ecclesiology was successful in Pugin's work can be gauged from this late nineteenth-century description of the congregation of one of his churches:

> There were rags and satins, moleskins and patent kids, corduroys and smooth broad black cloths, silks and cottons, with every style of fashion, from the old-fashioned frill cap, to the most exalted chignon, from the common plaid shawl to the very antipodes of dress *a la mode*; all this could be seen at St. Mary's Catholic Chapel, Norton Road, Stockton-on-Tees, in the County of Durham.[17]

This architecturalisation of social dissent was not confined to churches. George Roberts' anonymous publication *Speculum episcopi* ('The mirror of a bishop') (1848), which was widely reviewed, including in the *Dublin review*, was principally an attack on the way in which the contemporary Anglican bishop was isolated in his palace from his clergy; the author pointed out that amongst Roman Catholics bishops and priests are, because of the way they live together, in 'continual intercourse' with each other.[18] The plans of Pugin's large clergy houses, with their common staircases and long narrow corridors that contrast so starkly with the central staircases and formal arrangements of contemporary new bishops' palaces, make contact between the clergy inevitable. Indeed at Birmingham, the most prestigious of all these houses, the bishop is required to walk almost the longest distance possible through his house if he is to reach its major public space from the front door. It could even be said that Pugin's simple architrave joinery, which did not distinguish between the rooms of clergymen and their servants, also has a social aspect to it: in other architects' houses, superior rooms were always marked by grander architraves and that is why the Hansoms, T. H. Wyatt and Fowler restricted the use of the simple kind, when they borrowed it for private residences, to attic and service rooms. What distinguishes Pugin from all the gothic-revival architects of his generation is not only the fact that he was in many respects the first to create a coherent new architectural style of form and detail; it is also that wherever one looks one sees that the connotations of his work correspond to more and more aspects of contemporary society in general; and time and time again one sees too that the new rectories he designed, and the many he inspired, play a role in more than just the history of an architectural style.

There is a limit to the extent that a single architect can influence the course of architecture, but by way of conclusion it has seemed to me that the prevalence of Pugin and Puginite ideas in the latter part of this book has required some further justification. A change in English domestic architecture as dramatic as that from the simple and elegant Georgian house to the complex, even tortured, Victorian one – a place that was never intended to be conventionally beautiful – so completely, and in so short a period of time, can only have come from the unusual coincidence of a politically strong social movement with a clear set of ideas and needs on the one hand, and on the other, an architectural visionary of unparalleled creative power.

Many of the ideas raised briefly here in this Epilogue deserve fuller treatment: it is unwise for an architectural historian to immerse himself in subjects that have been better and more appropriately presented by the historians of the various fields. But there are places where the study of architecture has more to offer than may at first be obvious. It was the design of the parsonage, the place where the technical world could interfere in the religious, and the religious in the technical, that fused disparate elements together so powerfully. Pugin's knowledge of gothic and his many thousands of designs created an architectural realism which was without precedent in English architecture; it was his ability to transform what had previously only existed as theoretical concepts into a vocabulary of detailed, reliable and comprehensive design that marked him out from every other gothic architect of his generation. He combined, however, the world of the realist with that of the fantasist, possessed of an architectural vision that went beyond what had become standard architectural questions of style and layout, and which was much more closely related to abstract literary concepts of imaginary worlds in which every action had its appropriate place and method. His constant repetition, in different ways, of a series of very few historical sources and the presentation of ideas that had possessed him since his earliest childhood all testify to an easily identifiable personal vision of great power. When Loudon, with customary foresight, had suggested in 1833 that prospective architects should be tested upon phrenological principles for their suitability for their intended profession, he would have been correct in implying that only someone of very unusual character and imagination could have brought about the transformation in English architecture that many sought.[19]

Abbreviations

'Autobiography' The autobiography of A.W.N. Pugin, published in Wedgwood 1985

BAA Birmingham Archdiocesan Archives, Birmingham

BIUY Borthwick Institute, University of York

CCA Canterbury Cathedral Archives, Canterbury

CERC Church of England Record Centre, Bermondsey, London

CKS Centre for Kentish Studies, Maidstone

CUL Cambridge University Library, Cambridge

CRO County record office

DRO Devon Record Office, Exeter

'Diary' The diary of A.W.N. Pugin, published in Wedgwood 1985

GL Guildhall Library, London

Hants RO Hampshire Record Office, Winchester

Herefs RO Herefordshire Record Office, Hereford

HLRO House of Lords Record Office, London

LMA London Metropolitan Archives, London

LA Lincolnshire Archives, Lincoln

MBEC Minutes of the board of the Ecclesiastical Commissioners, at CERC

MCEC Minutes of the committees of the Ecclesiastical Commissioners, at CERC

MCO Magdalen College, Oxford

MGQAB Minutes of the meetings of the governors of Queen Anne's Bounty, at CERC

NRO Norfolk Record Office, Norwich

ODNB *Oxford dictionary of national biography*, Oxford, 2004

ORO Oxfordshire Record Office, Oxford

PAG *Pevsner architectural guides*

QAB Queen Anne's Bounty

RIBA Royal Institute of British Architects

RIBALDC Royal Institute of British Architects' Library Drawings Collection, at the V&A

RIBAJ *Journal of the Royal Institute of British Architects*

SRO Somerset Record Office, Taunton

SROB Suffolk Record Office, Bury St Edmunds

SROI Suffolk Record Office, Ipswich

Surrey HC Surrey History Centre, Woking

V&A Victoria and Albert Museum, London

W Sussex RO West Sussex Record Office, Chichester

WSRO Wiltshire & Swindon Record Office, Trowbridge

Notes to Chapter One

For clarity in the case of CERC records I have given first a description (usually MGQAB or MBEC), the volume number or file name in the case of a distinct collection of papers, and then the CERC reference number. Anyone looking for these documents is advised to have all this information to hand. Note in particular that MBEC volumes started again at volume i after volume iii.

1 Hogg 2003, *passim*. Clarence House, now much changed, was first built to Nash's designs from 1825–8.

2 Hammond 1977, ch 3 pp 44–71; Bax 1964, *passim*; Savidge 1964, *passim*.

3 Austen 1966, p 108; the book was written in 1814 and published two years later.

4 Virgin 1989, p 147.

5 Mitford 1836, 'Tom Cordery', pp 79–80.

6 Britton 1849, pp 23; 46.

7 NRO, DN/DPL1/4/72; application of 1838.

8 Austen 1966, p 113 (chapter 10).

9 Austen 1972, p 213 (chapter 26).

10 Virgin 1989, p 116.

11 Virgin 1989, pp 158–9; Scott's act was 43 Geo III cap. 84.

12 These were the Commission to inquire into the state of the Established Church, with reference to ecclesiastical duties and revenues; and the Commission to inquire into the revenue and patronage of the Established Church. Both reports are included in Parliamentary Papers 1835 (xxii).

13 1&2 Vict cap. 106.

14 Both 1777 and 1778 saw the passing of a great deal of building and paving legislation: 17 Geo III cap. 72–111, and 18 Geo III cap. 76–116, were all concerned with allowing it.

15 The term 'Gilbert's Acts' has a different connotation elsewhere in the field of social history, for Gilbert also promoted two acts sometimes known by that name in 1782 which aimed at reforming houses of correction, and relief and unemployment measures (22 Geo III cap. 64; 22 Geo III cap. 83).

16 According to Virgin 1989, p 64, when the Bounty was established in 1704 the annual income from these sources was around £17,000. Henry VIII's act of confiscation was 26 Hen VIII cap. 3 (1534); Anne's redisposal was 2&3 Anne cap. 11 (1703).

17 21 Geo III cap. 66; forms: sec. ii.

18 43 Geo III cap. 84, sec. xxv.

19 43 Geo III cap. 107, sec. iii. The Mortmain Act was 9 Geo II cap. 36.

20 CERC, QAB/7/6/1680; letter to Edward Legge, Bishop of Oxford, dated 7.4.1819 referring to plans approved by the Bounty two weeks later.

21 43 Geo III cap. 108, sec. v.

22 W Sussex RO, Ep/I/41/69. The drawings were prepared for him by Charles Bowman of Arundel.

23 See Virgin 1994, ch 9 & 10, for a detailed description of the house and Smith's relationship with it.

24 Hodgson 1826, p 53.

25 *Idem.*

26 1&2 Vict cap. 23, sec. vii. The act also (at sec. v) allowed Oxford and Cambridge colleges, as patrons of benefices, to advance or lend money for the improvement and building of parsonages.

27 MBEC, vol ii, 1.2.1842, item 15; 2.8.1842, item 7 (CERC, ECE/2/1/1/5). One of the eventual aims in establishing the Commissioners (by an act of parliament of August 1835 called the Established Church Act, 6&7 Will IV cap. 77) was to improve the lot of the poor parson. In practice the funds to do this came about when the Cathedral Act of 1840 (3&4 Vict cap. 113) and an amending act (4&5 Vict cap. 39) suppressed various sinecures and cathedral positions; by a further act (6&7 Vict cap. 37), the QAB could lend the Commissioners money. The conditions for grants towards house-building were published by the Commissioners in their 'Resolutions respecting grants in augmentation of livings' of 27.2.1844 (filed at CERC with 'Benefices – parsonage houses – general file 8129 – pt i', ECE/7/1/8129/1); where a house was in public patronage they paid half; where it was in private patronage they paid two fifths of the cost. In both cases the maximum house-building sum allowed was £1,000. See also Best 1964, p 351–4. For Railton, see Chapter Four above.

28 These refer to ways of financing a new house for an existing church: in addition the Church Building Commissioners were from 1818 building new churches that required new residences to go with them. The original act of this sequence was 58 Geo III cap. 45, which allowed, at sec. xxxiii, for up to ten acres for a parsonage house, garden, and 'appurtenances'. Some houses were financed by the Ecclesiastical Commissioners, who from August 1842 were doing this on the basis of their augmentation duties, although entirely new ones were very rare. In addition, once freed from the restriction of the Mortmain Act, the church could accept benefactions for new churches together with parsonages from individuals. Port 2006 provides an incomparable description of the work of the Church Building Commissioners.

29 After the passing of the Tithe Act 1836, 6&7 Will IV cap. 71. See Ward 1965. Tithes were commuted into land which raised rent for the incumbent. Legislation did not apply to current incumbents; tithes in kind were more prevalent in poor areas.

30 Eliot 1998, p 18. The 'Curates Act' was 53 Geo III cap. 149. It required incumbents to appoint curates in certain circumstances and fixed a sliding scale of minimum payment.

31 Summarising costs is difficult because of the variety in the size of house, and because the submitted estimated prices do not necessarily include reused materials; but as a rule of thumb it can be said that that just under half of a sample of 271 parsonages for which estimated building or remodelling costs were submitted up to the 1860s were due to cost between £200 and £1,000, and the other half between £1,000 and £3,000.

32 The value of such materials was generally very low, but the house at Portesham, Dorset, by T. H. Harvey in 1841, is an exception: it reused some £385, probably at least a third of the cost of the new house. CERC, QAB/7/6/E43.

33 A rare example of significant reuse is Richard Carver's stylish proposal for the new vicarage at East Brent in Somerset,

which employed £30 worth of timber from the glebe. SRO, D/D/Bbm/71. Thomas Rickman's house at Soham, Cambs, made use of 'one old walnut tree': SROB, 806/2/21. Ewan Christian, conscientious chap that he was, found £13 worth of old timber for his vicarage at Acton in Suffolk (CUL, EDR/G3/41 MGA/SUFF/19).

34 SROB, 806/2/21.

35 17 Geo III cap. 53, sec. 1.

36 CCA, DCb/DC/S28/1; governors' approval, *ibid*, U163/4.

37 For example Thomas Fox, incumbent at Abbas Combe in Somerset, clearly sought approval of his bishop first, and his file includes a letter which sets out his claim to a mortgage: SRO, D/D/Bbm/62.

38 CCA, DCb/DC/B11A/1.

39 These standards are set out in Hodgson 1826, pp 57–64, about which more in Chapter Four above. The QAB set out various rules for approving sums for applying augmentation funds to parsonage building: MGQAB vol xxiii, 6.2.1840, item 5.4; and 22.5.1845, item 18 (CERC, QAB/2/1/23).

40 I would here like to thank Professor M. H. Port for allowing me to see his notes on the holdings of the CERC, and also the Centre's Mrs Sarah Duffield who kindly provided me with samples of material from the archive.

41 There are, of course, plenty of designs for parsonages by architects in other collections, such as the Bodleian Library, the British Library, the V&A, and, principally, the RIBA LDC: these are generally from bequests by the architects themselves, and so they are not accompanied by the procedural requirements that the legislation of the various ecclesiastical reforms demanded; therefore they are without working specifications, estimates, or other information. In some cases, such as William Donthorn's design for remodelling Rushbury rectory of 1852, there is a set in the local CRO, and a further, neater, set in the RIBA LDC: Herefs CRO, HD 10/6 1853; RIBA LDC, Donthorn [Rushbury] 1. Applicants were advised by the secretary to the governors of the Bounty in 1826 to keep their own set of drawings (Hodgson 1826, p 61); there is little evidence that they did.

42 SRO, D/D/Bbm/33.

43 SROI, FF1/44/1, affidavit of 23.10.1812. For Catt, see Brown, Haward & Kindred 1991, pp 63–4; Colvin 1995, p 235.

44 At Wantage in 1849; ORO, MS. Oxf. dioc. papers b.80.

45 At Tydd St Giles, Cambs, in 1863: CUL, EDR/G3/39 MGA/91; specification, p 4.

46 CCA, DCb/DC/M20/1.

47 It was Edmunds' quay, adapted from an original design by John Rennie, that was to provide the plinth for the proposed new 'Turner Contemporary' gallery, designed by Messrs Snøhetta, the Norwegian architects, in collaboration with the British architect Stephen Spence; it sadly proved unequal to the task. Edmunds also designed a Commissioners' church in the town, the very fine Holy Trinity; built in 1825–8 (Port 2006, Appendix I, p 334), it was unfortunately not rebuilt after bomb damage in 1943. I am very grateful to Mr Mick Twyman of the Margate Historical Society for allowing me access to his researches.

48 As was the case at Broughton under Blean in Kent, in 1854: CCA, DCb/DC/B17/1.

49 The set of drawings of 1840 by Robert Wallace of Westminster for the imposing new rectory at Stourmouth near Canterbury includes details both of a well-equipped stable and farm yard and of the whole of the site, indicating a neighbouring meadow for annexation. CCA, DCb/DC/S37/1.

50 For his rectory at Rampisham, Dorset; WSRO, D28/6/11, for which see Chapter Three, pp 153–7 above.

51 See figs. 1.7–1.10. I found no other reference to the architect, S. H. Turner of St Marychurch.

52 MGQAB, vol xxiv, 3.4.1849 (CERC, QAB/2/1/24).

53 Very few Gilbert's Acts application drawings are marked for approval with a bishop's signature, although some dioceses seem to have done this.

54 W Sussex RO, Ep/I/41/66. Quotations from reports by Jackson Bale, 20.6.1821; William Frivett, 15.6.1821; B. Phipps (about Hunston barn), 19.7.1821.

55 W Sussex RO, Ep/I/41/66, report by H. J. Grace of Levington, 18.6.1821.

56 The documents for the rectory at Kingsdon, for example, include a full measured plan of the old house: SRO, D/D/Bbm/66, of 1836. There is more on this characteristic feature of the diocese in Chapter Four above.

57 The *First report of the commissioners on the state of the Established Church, with reference to duties and revenues*, published in Parliamentary Papers 1835 (xxii) details, at Section II, the net income of the dioceses on three years' average ending 31 December 1831. Canterbury's income was the highest at £19,182, for 343 parishes and a population of 402,885; at Oxford it was £2,648 for 209 parishes and 139,581. The total income of the 20 dioceses was £151,737. Table no iv, pp 98 ff, gives the details of the averaged revenues for all the parishes in England.

58 LA, MGA 220: correspondence of 16.5.1837 and 3.6.1837. The house has been demolished.

59 Some parishes in the diocese were transferred to Rochester in 1841; some were transferred back again in 1845; and various other exchanges between the two have been made since. It is not clear what has happened to some of the records of the parishes that changed hands, and in any case most of Rochester's mortgage records are unfortunately largely untraceable or currently inaccessible. So there may possibly have been a small number of additional new parsonages in the Canterbury diocese during this period. I am referring here to retained mortgage files in diocesan collections, but it may be possible, although it is unlikely to be particularly rewarding, to discover the exact answer by combing through the MGQAB.

60 CCA, U163/4, Hawkstead bundle.

61 CCA, DCb/DC/S42/1 (1833).

62 CCA, DCb/DC/S28/1.

63 CCA, DCb/DC/S35/1. See Chapter Four, p 192, above.

64 CCA, DCb/DC/W24/1.

65 SROB, 806/2/18; CCA, DCb/DC/R13/1; DCb/DC/L2/1; DCb/DC/L3/4.

66 That appears to be the situation from MBEC, vol x, 19.7.1849, no 25, and 26.7.1849, no 19 (CERC, ECE/2/1/1/13).

67 CKS, P157B/3/2; draft letter dated 20.9.1850.

68 MBEC, vol iii, 4.7.1843, item 2, first records the Commissioners' involvement (CERC, ECE/2/1/1/6). Further details of this project and its outcome appear in Chapter Five above.

69 CKS; p157B/3/2; contemporary copy of letter dated 21.8.1850. The various documents in the file do not have separate numbers.

70 CKS; p157B/3/2; report dated 4.4.1853.

71 There is an album of Roos' decorative sketches, nearly all classical, at the RIBA LDC: Roos [2].

72 MBEC, vol x, 24.5.1849, item 25 (CERC, ECE/2/1/1/13).

73 MBEC, vol i, 7.9.1841 (CERC, ECE/2/1/1/4). Lord Duncannon's extensive career in building works is discussed in detail in Crook & Port 1973, at pp 181 n5 and 189–94 *i.a.* He was First Commissioner of the Board of Woods and Works from 1831–4 and 1835–41; he succeeded his father to become 4th Earl of Bessborough in 1844.

74 See for example MBEC, vol i, 13.7.1841 (CERC, ECE/2/1/1/4). This must have been Richard Pope, District Surveyor in Bristol from 1831–72, who early in his career had acted as clerk of works on local projects for London architects, and who was here working with Decimus Burton.

75 Trubshaw's life and works are described in detail in Bayliss 1978, which also describes the personal link between builder and client. See also *ODNB.*

76 His drawings and specification are included in the file in the BIUY, MGA 1823/5.

77 Dearn 1807, p 7.

78 *Ibid*, p v.

79 *Ibid*, p 9, pls x–xii.

80 For example, Dearn 1807, pl i.

81 See the reference to Lugar at Yaxham, pp 44–5 above.

82 See Cobbett 1853, pp 53–4. The *Rural rides* were first published in 1830.

83 Virgin 1989, p 122.

84 Not all records were accessible during 2004 when I checked them, and in some cases it has not been possible to ascertain whether applications referred to anything more than very minor alterations, but the following figures for the Norwich diocese give an overall picture. NRO has records accumulated from various sources for the following number of Gilbert's Acts applications: pre-1811: 12; 1811–19: 9; 1820s: 12; 1830s: 32; 1840s: 125; a total of 194 houses, almost a third of the total number of parishes in the county, up to mid century. SROB has as follows: pre-1811: 2; 1811–19: 8; 1820s: 8; 1830s: 6; 1840s: 1; a total of 25; and SROI: pre-1811: 2; 1811–19: 5 (excluding the purchase of an existing house); 1820s: 4; 1830s: 17; 1840s: 28; a total of 56. The third CRO in the diocese, at Lowestoft, has no diocesan collection. The total number of records for new or substantially new parsonages for the diocese up to 1850 is therefore 206. By comparison, the Canterbury diocesan records at CCA have retained records for only 28 houses over the same period. By searching through the MGQAB and the MBEC it would be possible to build up an alternative set of figures, so these are a guideline only – but they certainly show that there was a great deal of parsonage building going on in East Anglia during the period. It is worth stating in my defence that there is little evidence for administrative efficiency for the period in which the applications were lodged.

85 NRO, DN/DPL1/1/10; the affidavit is signed by Francis Stone and dated 27.7.1805. The value of the building works was estimated at £2,079.2.4; the actual cost to the client was £1,779.2.4 after deduction of the value of old materials and taking into account monies for dilapidations that had already been received.

86 SROB, 806/2/4.

87 SROB, 806/2/9. The house was altered in 1854, for which see Chapter Four, p 224, above.

88 SROB, 806/2/23. A rather later house which is also essentially still a central-corridor type and with a grand central axis, was applied for by William Hinsbey, at Bramerton in 1838 (NRO, DN/DPL1/1/11).

89 SROB, 806/2/10. Browne designed his house in an ambitious Tudor-gothic style, simultaneously rustic and castellated, but the house may well have been executed as it currently appears, in a conventional vernacular classical–Georgian. There are still substantial outbuildings there, but unfortunately not as Browne designed them.

90 Lugar 1828, pls xiii-xiv.

91 NRO, DN/DPL1/4/75.

92 The only other classical houses in the book are a small and plain Grecian farmhouse near Belfast (pls viii and ix) and an unexecuted remodelling of a pre-existing classical house called The Tor, at Warley near Birmingham (pls xxxvi-xxxviii), the client of which eventually chose a new house in Lugar's gothic style.

93 Lugar 1811, pls vii–ix.

94 Lugar 1828, preface p ix.

95 Lugar 1828, facing pl xiv.

96 Johnson was a cousin of William Cowper, and had known Blake since he had been himself a student in the 1790s; there is some description of him in Bentley 2001 (and a portrait as a young man, *ibid*, pl 90). The paintings are described in the *PAG Norfolk NW & S*, p 809.

97 ORO, MS. Oxf. dioc. papers b.103/2d. See Hinde 1984, p 76.

98 ORO, MS. Oxf. dioc. papers b.106/2.

99 See Mansbridge 1991, pp 136–7.

100 CCA, DCb/DC/K3/2.

101 CERC, QAB/7/6/E32.

102 CCA, DCb/DC/N1/1.

103 SROI, FF1/17/2. The house was lengthened on the garden front, probably following an application of 1874 (which was inaccessible for consultation in 2004).

104 SROI, FF1/57/1. The house was replaced by the current gothic structure in the 1850s.

105 Herefs RO, HD 8/18 1843.

106 CERC, QAB/7/6/E57.

107 SRO, D/D/Bbm/76; D/D/Bbm/82.

108 RIBA LDC, Donthorn [Moulton St Michael] 1.

109 RIBA LDC, Donthorn [Moulton St Michael] 4.

110 BIUY, MGA 1838/2.

111 BIUY, MGA 1841/4. Pritchett's buildings include the neo-classical Huddersfield railway station.

112 NRO, DN/DPL1/3/52. See Chapter Two, pp 105–6, above.

113 Galby (architect, William Parsons): LA, MGA 153; Dallinghoo (William Bilby): SROI, FF1/29/1; Nacton (John Whiting): SROI, FF1/62/1.

114 According to an assessment carried out for recent owners. They may of course have been reused from a house on the site that was earlier still.

115 Nacton rectory survives much as Whiting left it (although one wall of the new central corridor has been taken down), but sadly Galby rectory has been de-gothicised.

116 WSRO, D1/11/77.

117 SROB, 806/2/21.

118 SRO, D/D/Bbm/88.

119 17 Geo III cap. 53, sec. x.

120 CCA, DCb/DC/T4/2.

121 Austen 1966, p 275 (chapter 32).

122 ORO, MS. Oxf. dioc. papers b.105/6.

123 Launton: ORO, MS. Oxf. dioc. papers b.104/1; South Weston: ORO, MS. Oxf. dioc. papers b.106/5.

124 ORO, MS. Oxf. dioc. papers b.102/7.

125 ORO, MS. Oxf. dioc. papers b.104/5.

126 ORO, MS. Oxf. dioc. papers b.102/4.

127 Hants RO, 16M70/27/1–6.

128 The Northallerton house was demolished in 2001, just before I managed to see it. Allibone 1988 describes it.

129 LA, MGA 260.

Notes to Chapter Two

1 For Ormesby, now demolished, see J. P. Neale 1824. Edward, 1st Baron Thurlow of Ashfield, and 1st Baron Thurlow of Thurlow, rumbustious Tory Lord Chancellor from 1778–92, presided over the trial of Warren Hastings; he died in 1806 and was succeeded by his nephew Edward, who took the second peerage only. It was this younger Edward's brother Thomas who built Boxford rectory. The third Edward Thurlow, the incumbent at Lound, was the son of another of 1st Lord Thurlow's nephews. They were an East Anglian clerical family. Eminent families in the area tended to patronise the same architect when repeatedly building parsonages.

2 NRO, DN/DPL1/3/38.

3 SROB, SO6/2/3. This splendid house survives with few alterations.

4 Surrey HC, 472/12/1–4. Moberly, rather than Ware, signed the drawings.

5 LA, MGA 153.

6 RIBA LDC, J. Trubshaw [2].

7 Lugar 1828, pl xv.

8 There are nice descriptions of this process in Mandler 1997 ch i pp 21–69, and Brooks 1999, pp 129–52.

9 Nash: Mandler 1997, pp 41–5; Brooks 1999, pp 192–3; Coningsby: Disraeli 1844, vol iii pp 114–5.

10 Some detailed comparison is made in Sweet 2004, pp 266–7. The most comprehensive study of John Britton's work still appears to be Crook 1968.

11 Britton 1814, preface.

12 Britton 1826, preface p i.

13 *Ibid*, p iii.

14 Britton 1838, p 283.

15 In vol ii (Britton 1809).

16 Britton 1826, preface.

17 Britton & Boutell 1846. The other examples are Tudor or later.

18 Parker's list of 1840, Parker 1840, recognises the true nature of the building.

19 Britton & Boutell 1846, p 5.

20 See for example 'Normandy – Architecture of the Middle Ages', *Quarterly review*, vol xxv, April 1821, p 126: 'Our old dwelling–houses are usually composed of timber frames, filled in with plaster'.

21 Habershon 1839, Preface, p xiii; Gwilt 1842, §393 p 170.

22 Cotman & Turner 1822, p 67.

23 *Ibid*, pp 67–8. The spelling 'Winwal' is Turner's.

24 In addition to the two examples mentioned in Chapter One above, at Abbotskerswell in Devon, and the 'ancient structure' that John Whichcord surveyed in Warehorne, Kent, there were many others.

25 Papworth 1818, p 37; p 45.

26 This partial list is derived from Taylor's friend Britton; see Britton's *Autobiography*, Britton 1849, p 240.

27 Hunt 1827b, preface p 5.

28 Whitaker's book is entitled, *An history of the original parish of Whalley and honor of Clitheroe, in the counties of Lancaster and York*, Blackburn, 1801. Quoted in Hunt 1827b, pp 29–30. Hunt drew on Whitaker a little later in his *Exemplars of Tudor architecture* of 1830, in which Whitaker describes Whalley Grange as being 'a valuable specimen' because 'by no other means that I know of [have we] been able to form a guess at the accommodation of the next inferior rank'. Hunt 1830, p 72. Writers tended to latch on to a single example that appealed to them.

29 *E.g.*, his commentary to pl vi, design iv (Hunt 1827b).

30 Hunt 1827b, pl ix, design v; pl xviii.

31 Hunt 1830, pl x; section iii p 45.

32 C. Parker 1833.

33 Exning: SROB, 806/2/6; the house was subsequently extended. Uphaven: CERC, QAB/7/6/E36. The son, who signed himself J. Henry Hakewill, was a good stylist; he designed a small rectory at Crowmarsh Gifford in Oxfordshire in 1846 in an unusually authentic domestic Tudor, rather than Tudor–gothic, style: ORO, MS. Oxf. dioc. papers b.107/8.

34 'Old English Domestic Architecture', *Quarterly review*, vol xlv, July 1831, pp 471–2. The reviewer has been identified by the *Wellesley index*.

35 In particular, in the additions he made entitled 'The rental dwelling' and 'The house and artistic culture' to the second edition of his *Stilarchitektur und Baukunst*: Muthesius 1903 (see Muthesius 1994, pp 95–7).

36 Old English Domestic Architecture', *Quarterly review*, vol xlv, July 1831, p 474.

37 *Ibid*, p 480.

38 *Idem*; *ibid*, p 484.

39 The political, religious and social history of this era is wonderfully recorded in Hole 1989, *passim*.

40 Loudon (1783–1843) awaits the biography he deserves. In the meantime, see Colvin 1995, pp 623–4; and also Gloag 1970.

41 Loudon 1806, vol i, p 14; p 15; p 16.

42 *Ibid*, p 68.

43 *Ibid*, p 26; p 35; p 39.

44 *Ibid*, vol ii, p 407.

45 *Ibid*, p 604.

46 *Ibid*, p 612; vol i, p 112; p 160.

47 *Ibid*, vol i, p 156.

48 Loudon 1833, p 1.

49 *Ibid*, p 2.

50 See, for example, Dearn 1807, p vii; Elsam 1816, p viii.

51 The correspondence of beauty to use – which derives perhaps initially from Horace – was a common theme in mid-17th-century poetry, and was identified in particular with Pope, for which see Barrell 1972, pp 61; 73.

52 Loudon 1833, §366 p 183.

53 *Ibid*, §29 p 15.

54 *Ibid*, §1652 p 773; §1654 p 774.

55 Loudon 1812.

56 Loudon 1833, design xvi pp 65–7; pls 114, 115.

57 *Ibid*, design ix, §1772–5, pp 853–4.

58 *Ibid*, §1833, p 897.

59 *Ibid*, §1878 p 928.

60 *Ibid*, §1888 p 935.

61 *Ibid*, §2195 p 1112; §2198 p 1112.

62 *Ibid*, §2198 p 1113.

63 From November 1837, under the *nom-de-plume* Kata Phusin.

64 The standards Loudon proposed for housing the very poor must have been well known among professionals by the time that Edwin Chadwick completed his *Report on the sanitary condition of the labouring population* in 1842.

65 Loudon 1833, §1331 p 628.

66 *Ibid*, §1652 p 773.

67 *Ibid*, §1875 p 927.

68 'Old English domestic architecture', *Quarterly review*, vol xlv, July 1831, p 487. The quotation is derived from William Mason's *The English garden* of 1772; it should read 'Beauty scorns to dwell/ where Use is exiled'.

69 *Ibid*, p 492.

70 *Ibid*, p 493.

71 *Ibid*, p 500.

72 The attribution and date are from Colvin 1995, p 82. Colvin also points out that it was Atkinson who had provided that early benefactor of Gilbert's Acts, Sydney Smith, with an unexecuted rectory design for Foston.

73 Later buildings in Minster Yard, by Pritchett and others in the 1830s, were more explicitly gothic, with castellations and pointed windows: see the former St Peter's School by Watson & Pritchett (1829), and 8–9 and 12 Minster Yard, by Pritchett, (1837–8 and 1830s respectively). The attributions for the first two are in Colvin 1995, pp 785–6; the third is from *PAG York & East Riding*.

74 DRO, Chanter 1190; Fowler's drawings are missing from the file.

75 A.W.N. Pugin 1843a, p 14, n 10.

76 RIBA LDC; the plans are seen best in the *Survey of London*: London County Council 1951, pp 100–1, pls 62, 80.

77 V&A print room, 8732 1–10; RIBA LDC, Blore [St Asaph].

78 The attribution to Wyatt is in *PAG Clwyd etc*, p 440. For more on extending old buildings, see Chapter Four above.

79 He was thus echoing a characteristic feature of the Jew's House in Lincoln well before A.W.N. Pugin did.

80 Habershon 1839, dedication.

81 *Ibid*, preface p vi.

82 Both the Great Snoring rectory and East Barsham Manor, referred to in the text of 1831 as 'Wolterton' house, were illustrated in the first volume of A.C. Pugin & Willson's *Examples of gothic architecture*. The plates are dated 1829. Pugin & Wilson 1828–31, pp 60–2; 49–58.

83 Habershon 1839, pl 2.

84 Jones 1977, p 116; Colvin 1995, p 464. Keble's sermon was delivered on 14.7.1833, just after the new rectory was completed; the meeting convened there between 25–9.7.1843.

85 With the deanery at Hadleigh one of the very few parsonages outside London from the early nineteenth century visited during my research (2000–4) actually still functioning as such. The mortgage application and drawings are in the LA, MGA 171.

86 Gore & Carter 2005, pp 96–8. Repton thought at the time of writing, probably some time before 1811, that it was unlikely that any of it survived.

87 Colvin 1995, p 515.

88 My attribution is from Colvin 1995, p 563.

89 NRO, DN/DPL1/2, 29. This was the third of the three Joseph Stannards mentioned by Colvin (Colvin 1995, p 915).

90 SROI, FF1/62/1.

91 NRO, DN/DPL1/4/58. The character assessment is in Colvin 1994, p 975.

92 SROI, FF1/85/1.

93 ORO, MS. Oxf. dioc. papers b.103/2; the details of Underwood's career are from Colvin 1994, p 1001.

94 Habershon 1839, p 18. The drawings and mortgage application file are at LA, MGA 208, dated 12.4.1837.

95 NRO, DN/DPL1/3/52; see Chapter One, p 53, above.

96 NRO, DN/DPL1/3/53.

97 CUL, EDR G3/39 MGA/44.

98 ORO, MS. Oxf. dioc. papers b.102/2b. Greenshields went on to design the more logical house at Swilland, p 104 above, but others never seem to have learnt the lesson.

99 Herefs RO, HD8/15 1840.

100 ORO, MS. Oxf. dioc. papers b.106/8.

101 East Bilney: NRO, DN/DPL1/1/9; architect, Arthur Browne. East Brent: SRO, D/D/BbM/71; architect, Richard Carver.

102 Little Melton: NRO, DN/DPL1/3/39; Little Glenham: SROI, FF1/39/1.

103 This attribution from Colvin 1995, p 882.

104 Paterson's was not an entirely new building, as Colvin 1995, p 742, implies. BIUY, MGA 1838/1.

105 See Chapter One, pp 50–3, above.

106 See LA, MGA 225.

107 LA, MGA 220, and see Chapter One, pp 29–30, above.

108 WSRO, D1/11/83.

109 WSRO, D1/11/77. More on Ferrey in Chapter Four above. His building suffered badly from damp, and was rebuilt in 1871 on a higher site to a design by G.R. Crickmay: WSRO, D1/11/203.

110 ORO, MS. Oxf. dioc. papers b.103/2b. See Colvin 1995, p 257; according to Colvin, Cockerell's diary recorded that he designed a Tudor parsonage at North Weald Basset in Essex of 1828–9 (ibid, p 261).

111 Herefs RO, HD8/10 1834–5.

112 CCA, DCb/DC/S37/1.

113 CERC, QAB/7/6/E52. It was cheap, too, at £630.5.9³⁄₄.

114 NRO, DN/DPL1/1/2; demolished.

115 My attribution is from Colvin 1995, p 1026.

116 The Chevalier lived in London from the 1760s, dying as late as 1810. He was buried in St Pancras' churchyard.

117 Shinfield: ORO, MS. Oxf. dioc. papers b.108/3; Turweston: ORO, MS. Oxf. dioc. papers b.109/5. Freeman seems never to have learnt that big central bays and Tudor-gothic styling mix only with difficulty. New Radnor: Herefs RO, HD 10/4 1851 (2).

118 Loudon 1833, pl 137.

119 Lancaster 1938, p 50. But what has actually come blundering out of it, after an interval of some 170 years, is the new Tudor-gothic architecture of the speculative developers of the present day.

Notes to Chapter Three

1 Saint 1975, p 1.

2 Phoebe Stanton's doctoral thesis, Stanton 1950, provided some description of many of Pugin's smaller houses, but the first comprehensive study of them as a group can be found in Wedgwood 1994. Alexandra Wedgwood's contribution to Pugin scholarship, through her published catalogues of his drawings and her other writings, and her encouragement of the highest standards from all that work in the Pugin field, have brought about a transformation in Pugin studies over recent decades. My own doctoral dissertation, Brittain-Catlin 2004a, examined Pugin's residential architecture as a whole, and the analysis of his houses that is summarised here was first presented there.

3 Pevsner 1943, especially at p 34, which refers to 'the theory of functionalism' as Pugin's 'great discovery'.

4 A.W.N. Pugin 1841a, p 1.

5 A.W.N. Pugin 1843, pp 38; 39.

6 Stanton 1971, pp 180–4.

7 This, it seems to me, was the message behind the 'Pugin: a gothic passion' exhibition at the V&A in 1994.

8 See Chapter Five, p 279, above.

9 I am including his various ideal schemes, as well as some of the most minor projects. He designed over thirty domestic projects (that is, substantial alterations and new houses for clergy and private individuals but excluding a school, a monastery, a number of convents and various other institutional communal residences) that were actually built.

10 Wedgwood 2006, a first-hand account by John Hardman Powell, Pugin's son-in-law and only in-house professional assistant, describes his daily life in some detail.

11 G. Scott 1995, p 88.

12 A.W.N. Pugin 1841a, p 76.

13 Forty 2000, pp 289–303, traces the history of the word and its evolving meaning across the eighteenth and nineteenth centuries, claiming that Pugin 'imported the new terminology of structural truth into the English language' (p 297).

14 Palgrave: 'Normandy – Architecture of the middle ages', Quarterly review, vol xxv, April 1821, p 117. The identity of the writer is derived from Shine & Shine 1949; Willson: A.C. Pugin & Willson 1831, p vii.

15 Ezekiel ch xiii vv 10–1 (Authorised Version).

16 Bartholomew 1840, I-XXXII-§302. This notoriety dates at least from the problems associated – not always fairly – with the case of John Nash, who had been humiliated when his practices had fallen under public scrutiny since the Select Committees of 1828–31.

17 Bartholomew 1840, I–XLII–§384.

18 Robison 1822, vol i, §554; quoted in Bartholomew 1840 at I-LVIII.

19 Bartholomew 1840, Preface §XXI.

20 Ibid, I-CX-§901; and see Belcher 1987, D227; D659.

21 Loudon 1806, vol i p 45.

22 Ibid, p 31.

23 Loudon 1833, §476 p 237 and §1434–7.

24 Actually, James Lowther, Some thoughts on building and planting, to Sir James Lowther, of Lowther Hall, Bart, probably of 1755.

25 Loudon 1833, §1886 p 938; italics in the original.

26 Bartholomew viewed Pugin's rise with some jealousy, believing that he himself had been the first to identify gothic architecture with structural purity (Bartholomew 1840, I-LII-§470); the reference to 'a silent voice giving previous utterance' to some of Pugin's claims for the gothic, in a review of The present state in the Builder, vol i, no vi (18.3.1843), is surely to himself.

27 Gwilt 1842, §437 p 195.

28 Bartholomew 1840, I–LXVIII–§623.

29 Dickens 1994, p 507 (chapter 53).

30 Dickens 1999, pl p 776 (chapter 65).

31 Dickens 2000, p 548 (chapter 72); pp 553–4 (chapter 'the last' [73]); p 550 (chapter 'the last'[73]).

32 Rudd 2004 gives some enjoyable examples of the former.

33 Stanton 1951, passim.

34 Pugin had drawn the 'Abbot's Kitchen' at Glastonbury in 1833 when preparing the third volume of the Examples (1836–40): letter of 26.2.1833 to E. J. Willson: Belcher 2001, pp 14–5.

35 'Autobiography', 3.3.1831. Pugin told Powell 'he was very fond of Walter Scott's writings': Wedgwood 2006, p 47.

36 Most of A.C. Pugin's books were sold on his death, but A.W.N. Pugin kept this book and Nodier's second volume all his life. See Brittain-Catlin 2001; Brittain-Catlin 2002a.

37 Reproduced in Ayling, 1865. The location of the original is unknown.

38 Clues can be found in surviving characteristic Pugin details such as his familiar door architraves which can be seen facing outwards towards the new stair hall.

39 'New churches', *British critic*, vol xxviii, October 1840, p 513. According to Margaret Belcher, the writer was probably Thomas Mozley, J. H. Newman's brother-in-law.

40 A rumour recorded by the *British critic* writer suggested that it was for Nicholas Wiseman as coadjutor to the vicar for the Midland district. *Ibid*, p 516.

41 'Myers family album', p 30 item 57.

42 The fact that Pugin's plan for the presbytery includes the plan of the church in some detail, as well as of the unexecuted house on the other side of it, implies that the presbytery was designed together with the church even if its execution followed sometime thereafter.

43 The *British critic* thought that the result of such cheap materials was that the presbytery 'greatly sets off its fair unearthy looking neighbour'. However he did comment that the house was 'comfortable and handsome'. 'New churches', p 516.

44 I found a rare example at Withermarsh Green, close to Giffords Hall at Stoke by Nayland in Suffolk, probably dating from the later 1820s. It is an unassuming cottage in the classical-Georgian style, directly attached to the crude Tudor-gothic chapel.

45 A detailed description of Pugin's planning of long corridors in the context of his institutional planning appears in Brittain-Catlin 2006, and some of the information in this chapter has appeared there.

46 Wedgwood 1977, [5] 75 v.

47 The drawings are in St Louis Public Library, Missouri, cat no 1032129 and ref 723.5.

48 In at least one case, at William Faber's community at Cotton on the Shrewsbury estate, the Shrewsburys were complicit with the design of corridor routes which were redundant in practical terms, for Lady Shrewsbury herself funded the ambulacrum there, part of the series of corridors that connect the residential building with the church. Brompton Oratory Archives, Correspondence vol 27, letter 37, 25.8.1847. See Brittain-Catlin 2006, p 368.

49 His stage machinery drawings can be seen in a sketchbook of c1835 in the V&A: Wedgwood 1985, 107 ff 44v–56; he drew nautical scenes in many of his sketchbooks throughout his life.

50 Keighley: RIBA LDC [73] 2 (then unidentified); Uttoxeter: Research Library, The Getty Research Institute, Los Angeles, California (870366).

51 Unfortunately the staircase and the areas beyond it were rebuilt later in the nineteenth century.

52 There is a fairly dry description of it in A.W.N. Pugin 1842, p 101–3.

53 *Ecclesiologist* (vol v, no 7, January 1846, pp 10–6); *Tablet* (vol vii, no 30 (31.1.1846), p 69.

54 In the meantime, he had made various other presbytery designs which are now untraceable. According to a letter to his friend the Oxford don J.H. Bloxam of 13.9.1840, Belcher 2001, p 142, he designed a presbytery in the Norman style for his church of St James in Reading. He claimed, in A.W.N. Pugin 1842, p 29 n, that a new presbytery for his church of St Mary & St Thomas at Dudley was currently being built, but there is no evidence that it was ever executed. According to *ibid*, p 31 n 1, supported by Duffield 1850, p 132, he designed an executed house for the church of St Wilfred, Hulme, Manchester; this was evidently subsequently altered, and there does not now appear to be any record of its original appearance and plan. He probably also designed the presbytery at St Mary, Stockton-on-Tees, at this period or soon after. This house incorporated parts of an earlier Tudor-gothic house of soon after 1832; only small fragments survived a rebuilding of 1909, and the few photographs available are insufficient to reconstruct the building.

55 The screen is Andrew Saint's interpretation. There have been minor alterations both inside and out of the building.

56 It is unlikely that he actually designed the two Brewood school buildings in detail, but according to a letter of 5.1.1849 by a later incumbent he had certainly anticipated them, designing the whole group of church buildings as a single scheme: BAA, B1386. Pugin's perspective drawing for the Fulham presbytery has recently been uncovered in the collection of the Order of the Visitation, Waldron, East Sussex, and at the time of writing seems likely to be transferred to the RIBA LDC.

57 In his letter to Bloxam, of 26.9.1843, referring to the purchase of the plot at Ramsgate, Pugin drew a sketch of his design approximately as it was eventually built: Belcher 2003, p 110.

58 In the summer of 1843 Pugin began work on the design of an orphanage in Liverpool, and it is probably this that brought him into contact with Sharples, a stalwart of the Catholic community there and a benefactor of several of its institutions. Pugin's diary first recorded a meeting with Sharples in February 1844, and it seems likely that this was the point at which their direct and fruitful working relationship started. Belcher 2003, p 101; 'Diary', 16.2.1844.

59 V&A, E.78(6)–1970; Wedgwood 1985, 236.

60 4.10.1845: Belcher 2003, pp 116–7.

61 The current restoration by the Landmark Trust, advised by Paul Drury, has restored this fireplace which was lost during remodellings by later members of the Pugin family.

62 CCA, DCb/DC/H8/1.

63 CCA, DCb/DC/E7/1.

64 ORO, MS. Oxf. dioc. papers b.108/5.

65 SROB, 806/2/7.

66 SROI, FF/27/1.

67 CUL, EDR/G3/39 MGA/38.

68 CCA, DCb/DC/R14/1.

69 Rooke recorded the total cost upon completion in a diary kept with the parish records. The application is at WSRO, D28/6/11.

70 This was Charles Eastlake's criticism. Eastlake 1970, p 164. See also Brittain-Catlin 2004b for further comments on the house.

71 'Autobiography', 8.10.1829.

72 A.W.N. Pugin 1841a, p 63.

73 This is what Professor Crook glosses as 'ornament expressing structure', in Crook 2003, p 37.

74 In all A.W.N. Pugin's drawings of the Ramsgate house that followed its construction, he drew it with the library gable projecting; he also unfailingly drew the house aligned orthogonally with the adjoining church, which it is not.

75 As in his second scheme for Magdalen College School, Oxford of 1843: I reproduced this plan in Brittain-Catlin 2002b, p 32. The set of drawings is kept at the school, and catalogued as no 603 in R.White & Darwall-Smith 2001.

76 In a letter to Bloxam, 7.12.1845?: Belcher 2003, pp 482–3.

77 The mortgage was reported as paid by the Bounty, in mid June 1847: MGQAB, vol xxiv, 15.6.1847, item 33/3 (CERC, QAB /2/1/24). Possibly the documents are amongst those currently inaccessible in the CERC. Pugin had earlier offered the working drawings to Bird for £36; letter of 1.2.1846, MCO MS 528/65.

78 11.11.1845; Belcher 2003, pp 476–7.

79 He used the same pinwheel layout on two further occasions – for an ambitious and large house for William Leigh at Woodchester Park, which was never built; and for his last executed private house design, at Wilburton between Cambridge and Ely.

80 Again, see Brittain-Catlin 2006.

81 Processions appear also in Nodier 1820, for example in plate 8, where one is seen within the ruins of the abbey church at Jumièges; for Pugin's use of Nodier's plates, see Brittain-Catlin 2001; Brittain-Catlin 2002a.

82 Much of the daily ritual at the house was described by his assistant John Hardman Powell (Wedgwood 2006).

83 So he told John Bloxam on 3.3.1840: Belcher 2001, p 133.

84 According to the 'Diary', Pugin visited Scott-Murray on 15.10.1844.

85 A direct connection with Ludlow Castle cannot be proved, but Pugin knew Kenilworth well: he himself had drawn there for the second volume of his father's *Examples* (1831–6), and he designed a chapel for the village in 1841.

86 An undated and unreferenced quotation reproduced in Stanton 1950, p 346.

87 At the Grange and Oswaldcroft, although apparently not at either of the two rectories, the valley formed at the centre of the house over the hall and between the pinwheel ridges was used for water storage.

88 He had drawn the Vicars' Close for the third volume of *Examples,* published 1836–40.

89 A.W.N. Pugin 1841a, p 1.

90 As he wrote in both the first and second editions of *Contrasts*, a builder must share 'the ancient feelings and sentiments' of the mediaeval builders: A.W.N. Pugin 1836, p 22; A.W.N. Pugin 1841b, p 43. There are many references to 'feelings' in both editions of this book.

91 Ferrey 1861, p 225.

92 There is certainly a strong resemblance at Lanteglos to the type of detailing one sees in the many Tudor-gothic parsonages of George Wightwick, who worked in Cornwall in the 1830s and 40s. Chapter Four above describes some of these houses.

93 There is here, too, an inexplicable exception, this time in the case of his own house at Ramsgate, which has occasional horizontal courses of a bluer brick on the south and west walls. Perhaps he made use of some irregular bricks that arrived on site.

94 Pugin distinguished himself from classical-Georgian architects in that he almost always used stone for window quoins and other dressings; it seems to be Butterfield, amongst the gothic revivalists, who reverted to using brick for these too, probably first at his Avington parsonage of 1847. Pugin did in fact design a very small number of windows like this – at Handsworth and at his schoolmaster's house in Spetchley, Worcs, of 1841 – and, surprisingly, they have secret lintels.

95 Or, conceivably, Wiseman, who was vicar apostolic of the central district at the time of the completion of St Barnabas. Willson was E. J. Willson's brother, priest at Nottingham from 1825 until 1842, when the church was in early stages of construction, and when he was transferred to Tasmania to become Bishop of Hobart.

96 A.W.N. Pugin 1841a, p 1.

97 As his friend Etty noted in 1845: see Belcher 2003, p 368 n 5. Pugin's surviving specifications require clear varnish finishes for internal timberwork.

98 Scarisbrick lodge: RIBA LDC, A.W.N. Pugin [64] 80. The Handsworth convent was designed in 1840.

99 In the case of the upper floor library and chapel of the Bishop's House in Birmingham he 'cheated', devising an open duopitch roof to sit below a monopitch forced on him, very probably, because of the need to avoid an eaves gutter along the party wall at the site boundary. BAA, APD/P1/9.

100 A.W.N. Pugin 1843, p 38.

101 Wedgwood 2006, p 14.

102 Dickens 1999, p 679 (chapter 55).

103 There are several examples of an array of building facades drawn at obtuse angles to each other, particularly in a sketchbook of 1831–2, Wedgwood 1977, [17] ff 5, 14, 16, 18 (dated 1832), and 30v.

104 Donaldson 1842, p 33.

Notes to Chapter Four

1 ORO has records of 35 Gilbert's Acts applications for the 1840s, of which 28 are for new or rebuilt houses; it has a total of 4 from 1800–11 (including 1 new house); 8 for 1811–19 (6 new); 10 for the 1820s (4 new); and 15 for the 1830s (10 new). See Chapter One, note 84, for details of the Norwich holdings. Other dioceses also show an increase, although in general less marked.

2 Wightwick's account of Soane was printed in Bolton 1927, but is nicely recalled in context in Darley 1999, especially at p 284; for draughtsmanship see Britton & A.C. Pugin 1825–8; Wightwick 1827.

3 Colvin 1995, p 1049.

4 MGQAB vol xxiii, provides the dates for the houses at St Dominick, Pelynt, and Probus given below (CERC, QAB/2/1/23). The application papers for houses in what was at the time part of the Exeter diocese ought to be at the Devon RO, but there is no trace of them either there or at the Cornwall CRO at Truro.

5 St Dominick's: RIBA LDC, Wightwick [120] 3; the executed building appears to vary slightly from the drawings. Probus: RIBA LDC, Wightwick [119] 1.

6 The appearance of a blind lancet on a chimney gable on Pugin's rectory at Lanteglos, together with the plaster groining in the hall and the Georgian joinery suggests that this might have been built by builders familiar with Wightwick's work. Liskeard is RIBA LDC, Wightwick [47] 1.

7 Wedron: RIBA LDC, Wightwick [148] 1; St Ives: [122]. Other examples in RIBA LDC are Lanreath: Wightwick [40]; and Morval: Wightwick [53].

8 RIBA LDC, Donthorn [Moulton St Michael] 4; [Oundle] 1.

9 RIBA LDC, Donthorn [Thrapston] 1.

10 RIBA LDC, Donthorn [Weybridge] 1; [Fontmell] 1.

11 RIBA LDC, Donthorn [Dummer] 2.

12 Herefs CRO, HD 10/6 1853; further set, RIBA LDC, Donthorn [Rushbury] 1.

13 And, ungenerously, A.C. and A.W.N. Pugin seem to be conflated in his bibliography. Habershon's *Ancient timber houses* is mentioned but not A. W. N. Pugin's *Details of antient timber houses of the 15th and 16th century* of the same year. Gwilt 1842, section IV.

14 *Ibid*, §2496 p 674.

15 Donaldson 1842, p 29.

16 The obligations upon an architect when a building was to be submitted for contracting in gross is referred to on pp 198–200 above.

17 Bartholomew 1840, preface §III; I–XIX–§72.

18 It occurs to me that Bartholomew's combination of general moral outrage but precise building instructions is revived at the present time in the various manuals on the subject of 'sustainable' architecture. Very rational thinkers are not easily appreciated, it seems.

19 Bartholomew 1840, II–XXIII and II–XXXIV.

20 *Ibid*, II–XXIII–§§2644–64.

21 *Ibid*, II–XXIII–§2671.

22 BIUY, MGA 1841/4; and see Chapter One, pp 53–5, above.

23 Bartholomew 1840, II–XXIII–§2680.

24 *Ibid*, II–XXIII–§§2684–2690; II–XXIII–§2675; II–XXIV–§2796.

25 *Ibid*, II–XXIV–§2794; §2858.

26 *Ibid*, II–XXIII–§2722; II–XXII–§2532, §2534; II–XXI–§2444; II–XXII–§2530. In a rare reference to a technical specification, the MBEC record approving the use of cement instead of battening for waterproofing, following the application to that end by the Rev. William Coombs of Scholes, Wigan; 7.2.1850, item 11 (CERC: ECE/2/1/1/14). That probably marks the point at which it became standard practice.

27 Bartholomew 1840, II–XXIII–§2738; notes–§4741; II–XXIV–§§2838–9.

28 NRO, BN/DPL1/4/58, drawing of 23.6.1840. There do, admittedly, appear to have been three other submitted documents, but these are missing from the file which contains only one slightly later set of revised plans. According to Sir Howard Colvin, Thompson was 'ingenious but dubious', something of a contrast to our other Thompson, Mark, who was clearly most industrious. Colvin 1995, p 975.

29 Theydon Bois: CERC, QAB/7/6/E29.

30 Hants RO, 16M70/29/1–59.

31 Letter of 9.5.1816 from Richard Burn, Bounty secretary 1790–1822, to the incumbent Thomas Lancaster; CERC, QAB/7/6/E89.

32 Hodgson 1826, p 61.

33 MGQAB, vol xxiii, 6.2.1840, item 8 (CERC, QAB/2/1/23).

34 *E.g.*, the Rev Mr Copleston of Lamyat in Somerset in 1833: SRO, D/D/Bbm/63.

35 Hodgson 1826, p 60.

36 This was during Burns' watch in 1820, and he replied laconically that the governors were 'unlikely to object': CERC, QAB/7/6/E1680.

37 Bedingham: NRO, DN/DPL2/1/24; Isle Brewers: SRO, D/D/BbM/96.

38 W Sussex RO, Ep/I/41/69; Ep/I/41/83.

39 All this is described with characteristic aplomb by G. F. A. Best, at Best 1964, pp 225–6.

40 Blore's drawings for 3 Dean's Yard (which also show 3A) are in the V&A Prints & Drawings Study Room, 8745.1–5, and his accounts are at CUL, MS. Add. 3955.

41 MGQAB, vol xxiv, 3.4.1849 (CERC, QAB/2/1/24).

42 The word 'vespasian' appears to derive from a contemporary jocular French expression, *colonne vespasienne*, meaning a public lavatory, in honour of a tax imposed by the eponymous Roman emperor on such conveniences.

43 Hepworth: SROB, 806/2/10 – see Chapter One, pp 43–4, above; Potton: CUL, EDR/G3/40 MGA/BED/10.

44 At East Brent: SRO, D/D/Bbm/71.

45 Not that there is anything exclusively nineteenth-century about that. The architect Ulrik Plesner tells me that he was first employed by the famous Celanese Modernist Minette de Silva in the 1950s in order to sort out the detailing of the more complicated parts of her buildings that she hid, on drawings, behind renditions of lush greenery.

46 CUL, EDR/G3/39 MGA/58.

47 At Boxford: SROB, 806/2/3; Hartest: SROB, 806/2/9; and Bures: SROB, 809/2/4.

48 CCA, Dcb/DC/B1/1.

49 CCA, DCb/DC/S35/1.

50 LA, MGA 338.

51 SRO, D/D/Bbm/107.

52 Application of 1823; ORO, MS. Oxf. dioc. papers b.106/4.

53 ORO, MS. Oxf. dioc. papers b103/1A/B.

54 WSRO, D1/11/83.

55 Milton: CCA, Dcb/Dc/M15/1.

56 WSRO, D1/11/246. See also Chapter Five, pp 284–8, above.

57 W Sussex RO, Ep/I/41/77.

58 Report by Archdeacon Charles Webber of Boxgrove, 17.7.1821: W Sussex RO, Ep/I/41/66.

59 NRO, DN/DPL1/4/75; DN/DPL1/1/11.

60 NRO, DN/DPL/1/4/58, document 5 (1840).

61 WSRO, D28/6/11 (1846).

62 Lytton: SRO, D/D/Bbm/86; Wantage: ORO, MS. Oxf. dioc. papers b.80. There is no real evidence of Belcher's own designing skills in this archive beyond a very small plain and simple classical-Georgian extension to a parsonage at Denchworth, so it is fair to assume that he was not at all involved in the design of Street's house.

63 CERC, QAB/7/6/E43.

64 SROB, DN/DPL1/2/29.

65 For example, Kaye 1960 and Jenkin 1961; and see the following footnote.

66 The processes and their historical development in the late eighteenth and early nineteenth centuries are described in Cooney 1955–6; and Port 1967. A useful aphorism is provided in the latter by Professor Port: 'if, as Cooney argues, the development of contracting may have contributed to the rise of the master builders, it seems more likely that the rise of the master builder encouraged the use of contract in gross': Port 1967, p 109.

67 From the meticulous daybooks kept by John Soane's office, in Sir John Soane's Museum, it is possible to gauge the considerable number of man-hours required for this process.

68 See Cooney 1955–6, p 175.

69 Port 1967, p 110.

70 MBEC, vol iii, 8.8.1843 (CERC, ECE/2/1/1/6). This is the same John Clutton who founded the business that works today for the Church Commissioners. He soon moved into 8 Whitehall Place, close to the Commissioners, and alongside their architect Ewan Christian, who took up offices eventually in the stable yard behind at 8a. *ODNB* adds that Clutton's work for the Commissioners came as a result of the introduction of the 1842 Ecclesiastical Leases Act.

71 Bartholomew 1840, I–IV–§13 and II–I–§986 reinforce this point. At I–IX–§22 he warns of the dangers of contracts being signed with insufficient or inadequate specifications.

72 W Sussex RO, Ep/I/41/71, 1843.

73 The National Archives, ref. WORK 29/64.

74 The Nelson Monument was won in competition in 1839, and was slowly erected from 1843; the shaft went up that year, but it was not completed until 1850 (*Builder*, vol i, no 37 (21.10.1843), p 446; vol viii, no 375 (13.4.1850), p 169). John Britton had been amongst the competitors, submitting a low gothic tabernacle.

75 Original application: MBEC vol ii (first series), 15.2.1838 (CERC, ECE/2/1/1/2); Ripon competition and Riseholme: *ibid*, 3.4.1838; Stapleton, MBEC vol iii (first series), 26.2.1840 (CERC, ECE/2/1/1/3).

76 The goings-on are well described in Best 1964, pp 363–5.

77 MBEC, vol ii, 1.2.1842, item 15 (CERC, ECE/2/1/1/5).

78 MBEC, vol ii, 2.8.1842, item 7 (CERC, ECE/2/1/1/5).

79 MBEC, vol iii, 27.3.1844, item 21 (CERC, ECE/2/1/1/6).

80 Benefices – parsonage houses – general file 8129 pt i, 'Resolutions respecting grants in augmentation of livings'

27.2.1844, Rules and Instructions no 3 (CERC, ECE/7/1/8129/1). The estimated total cost for houses was £1,000 – in fact, not far off: a table of 2.3.1846 gives an average of £1074.5.10 for the 64 houses built to date and a further 6 tenders received (see *ibid*, pt ii).

81 RIBA LDC, Railton, [5] London, St James Muswell Hill; [6] London, Rotherhithe. The plans are undated, but there are clues in MBEC: the land for the Muswell Hill church was bought in 1845 (MBEC, vol v, 26.11.1845, item 15 (CERC, ECE/2/1/1/8)).

82 RIBA LDC, Railton, [1] Bristol, St Barnabas; [2] Carisbrooke (Isle of Wight); [3] Churchstow (Devon); [4] Coningham (Lincs).

83 CERC, QAB/7/6/E12.

84 Loudon, incidentally, had made the point more than once that it was because the English landscape was so dull that it needed a fancy style of architecture to enliven it: Loudon 1833, §1678 p 792, *i.a.*

85 *Ecclesiologist*, vol ii, June 1843, p 146.

86 Benefices – parsonage houses – general file 8129 pt i, 'Minutes of evidence taken before the Ecclesiastical Commissioners', 30.7.1845, p 86 (CERC, ECE/7/1/8129/1). He reiterated this view a year later, in the case of the house at Mathon discussed below: *ibid*, pt ii, 'Printed evidence, report of the Parsonage House Committee', 26.6.1846.

87 Benefices – parsonage houses – general file 8129 pt i, 'Minutes of evidence taken before the Ecclesiastical Commissioners', 30.7.1845, p 14 (CERC, ECE/7/1/8129/1).

88 *Ibid*, pp 11–2; 22–5.

89 *Ibid*, p 86.

90 *Ibid*, p 19.

91 *Ibid*, pp 32–4.

92 *Ibid*, pp 36–7; pp 45–6.

93 *Ibid*, pp 9–10; 60–5; 88; 97; 107–8.

94 *Ibid*, pp 60–1; 103–4.

95 *Ibid*, p 88.

96 *Ibid*, pp 104–5.

97 *Ibid*, pp 103–4; 109–110.

98 *Ibid*, pp 45–8. Chalk explained here his connection to Railton thus: 'He was originally introduced to my brother by a Gentleman who is a near Connection of the Bishop of Ripon who recommended him to my brother to alter his house, and he did it so well that I afterwards became acquainted with Mr Railton, and I recommended him to send that plan here. There were other plans sent in, and his was adopted as being the best'.

99 This is summarised from the 'Report of Select Committee parsonage houses': Ecclesiastical Commissioners for England, Committees, minutes, vol i, 30.7.1845 (CERC, ECE/2/4/1).

100 MBEC, vol v, 22.7.1845, item 16 (CERC, ECE/2/1/1/8).

101 Benefices – parsonage houses – general file 8129 pt ii, 'Report of the Parsonage House Committee' 26.6.1846 (printed evidence) (CERC, 7/1/8129/2).

102 MBEC, Parsonage House Committee Report, 26.6.1846; read at the General Meeting, MBEC, 1.7.1846, vol vi, p 215 (CERC: ECE/2/1/1/9).

103 Benefices – parsonage houses – general file 8129 pt ii, 'Report of the Parsonage House Committee' 26.6.1846 (printed evidence) (CERC, ECE/7/1/8129/2).

104 Upleadon vicarage files, 6804, pt i (CERC, ECE/7/1/6804/1). This is referred to in the printed version of the correspondence there, and also in the same file, in Morris' report of 31.12.1846.

105 *Ibid*, Sayers' letter to the Commissioners' offices of 28.2.1846; Morris' report, 31.12.1846; note from Murray (as Commissioners' treasurer) of 31.8.1846.

106 *Ibid*, Sayers' letters to the Commissioners' offices of 28.8.1846; 14.11.1846; 7.12.1846.

107 *Ibid*, Morris' report of 31.12.1846.

108 *Ibid*, Sayers to Chalk, 29.1.1847; Chalk to Sayers, 30.1.1847; Robertson to Chalk, 9.2.1847.

109 *Ibid*, letter from Bishop of Gloucester & Bristol to Sumner, 19.2.1847; to Sayers, 20.2.1847; Sayers to the Commissioners, 22.2.1847.

110 *Ibid*, letter from Farmar to the Commissioners, dated February 1847.

111 Upleadon vicarage files, 6804, pt ii, 'book of evidence taken before the Ecclesiastical Commissioners', 9.3.1847 (CERC, ECE/7/1/6804/2). Sayers and Chalk had been interviewed beforehand on 4.3.1847.

112 MBEC, vol vii, 10.6.1847, item 11; resolved, 17.6.1847, item 3 (CERC, ECE/2/1/1/10).

113 For example that at Homerton, MBEC, vol vi, 2.8.1846, item 17 (CERC, ECE/2/1/1/9).

114 MBEC, vol ix, 11.5.1848 (CERC, ECE/2/1/1/12); the patron of Little Milton was actually the vicar of Ashfield – and it was his patron that was the bishop.

115 MBEC, vol ix, 20.7.1848, no 33 (CERC, ECE/2/1/1/12).

116 MBEC, vol ix, 30.11.1848, no 5 (CERC, ECE/2/1/1/12).

117 MBEC, vol x, 8.2.1849, item 22 (CERC, ECE/2/1/1/13).

118 MBEC, vol x, 11.1.1849, item 34 (CERC, ECE/2/1/1/13).

119 MBEC, vol x, 22.2.1849, item 20; 15.3.1849, item 15 (CERC, ECE/2/1/1/13).

120 MBEC, vol x, 10.5.1849 (CERC, ECE/2/1/1/13); and see Chapter One, pp 31–3, above.

121 At Byers Green. MBEC, vol x, 7.6.1849, item 21 (CERC, ECE/2/1/1/13).

122 According to his obituary in the *Builder*, vol xxxix, 3.9.1880, pp 281–3. The building was designed as a combined home for the National Gallery and the Royal Academy: all this is recounted definitively in Crook & Port 1973, pp 461–70.

123 *ODNB*.

124 *Builder*, vol xxxix, 4.9.1880, pp 281–3.

125 WSRO, D1/11/77.

126 WSRO, D28/6/12.

127 SRO, D/D/Bbm/93. This parsonage was omitted from Ferrey's *Builder* obituary.

128 ORO, MS. Oxf. dioc. b.109.

129 ORO, MS. Oxf. dioc. c.1540.

130 See Adkins 1911.

131 *Ibid*; and *ODNB*; the illustrations were for Habershon 1839, for which see Chapter Two, pp 97–100, and fig. 2.43 above.

132 MBEC, vol xii, 7.11.1850, item 25 (CERC, ECE/2/1/1/15).

133 In addition to the cases mentioned in this chapter, Ferrey had also found himself on the opposing side to Railton in the case of the restoration of the bishop's palace at Wells, which in the event was restored by him rather than by Railton.

134 I am indebted to Mr Chris Morley for sharing his researches on his former house with me. According to the *Clergy list* for 1849, Bevan was actually rector of Burton Latimer, several hundred miles away, at the time.

135 Acton: CUL, EDR/G3/41 MGA/SUFF/19; Salisbury: WSRO, D1/11/270.

136 Adkins 1911, p 728.

137 *Ibid*, p 725.

138 This and the outlines of his successors are from *ODNB*.

139 This and the following diocesan statistics are derived from the table in Appendix VI of Best 1964; it should be remembered that there were several alterations made to the boundaries of the dioceses during the first decades of the nineteenth century.

140 Dividing the income by the number of benefices does not give an accurate impression of the overall wealth of the diocese, because the income was not distributed equally between them; but by way of comparison, Bath & Wells had this 'average' income of £13.12.7 per benefice, whereas Canterbury, with the highest net income, had an average of about £65.0.7 for a similar size population and a slightly smaller number of benefices.

141 The second volume of A.C. Pugin & Willson's *Examples* (published as a book in 1836), to which A.W.N. Pugin contributed, had illustrated the deanery house and bishop's palace in Wells, and two houses and two monastic buildings in Glastonbury. The third volume (completed in 1840) included the Vicars' Close in Wells.

142 SRO, D/D/Bbm/62.

143 Holford, 1833, by Richard Down & Son of Bridgwater: SRO, D/D/Bbm/61.

144 Charlecombe, 1834, by G.P. Manners of Bath: SRO, D/D/Bbm/64.

145 SRO, D/D/Bbm/40.

146 SRO, D/D/Bbm/60.

147 SRO, D/D/Bbm/71.

148 SRO, D/D/Bbm/73.

149 At East Coker: SRO, D/D/Bbm/65.

150 SRO, D/D/Bbm/69.

151 SRO, D/D/Bbm/76.

152 SRO, D/D/Bbm/109.

153 Compare the original application, SROB, 806/2/9 of 1821, with the alterations shown in CUL, EDR/G3/41 MGR/SUFF/25. An additional floor was added at the same time. The second application was the work of Thomas Farrow, surveyor of Diss.

154 SRO, D/D/Bbm/97; 1846.

155 By Samuel Tripp, 1848, in a relaxed Tudor-gothic style; SRO, D/D/Bbm/102.

156 SRO, D/D/Bbm/54 (Wainwright, 1827); D/D/Bbm/98 (Gane, 1846). Colvin 1995, p 107, points out that George Basevi made an unexecuted design for Dinder that was reproduced in *Country life*, 20.10.1977, p 1104, fig 2; and that Basevi also designed a rectory at Coulsdon.

157 Respectively, at Lamyat in 1833 (SRO, D/D/Bbm/63); and East Pennard, a standard L-corridor, Tudor-gothic house, in 1841 (SRO, D/D/Bbm/81).

158 SRO, D/D/Bbm/74. I see from Colvin 1995, p 577, that Kempthorne also designed two churches in Somerset, at Haselbury Plucknett and Misterton, at the same period.

159 SRO, D/D/Bbm/101.

160 SRO, D/D/Bbm/82.

161 Ovenden 1891, p 40. It was Ashton Ovenden, of whom more later, who described Howley as 'high and dry' (*idem*).

162 But not to the vicarage house that stands there today, for that was designed by Lewis Wyatt for Lord Augustus Fitz Clarence, the son of William IV and Mrs Jordan, in 1831. It has an unusual early staircase hall. The patron of the living was Eton College. ORO, MS. Oxf. dioc. papers b.104/2.

163 *Dictionary of national biography*, first edition 1898, vol 55, p 169.

164 Some of the parsonage building plans are kept separately from the main collection, (Dcb/Dc), in bundles numbered U/163/3–4; they may have been built under augmentations rather than Gilbert's Acts' legislation.

165 CCA, U163/4.

166 The attribution is from Colvin 1995, p 1041.

167 CCA, Dcb/DC/S24/1.

168 CCA, Dcb/DC/H8/1.

169 Warehorne: CCA, Dcb/DC/W24/1; Newchurch: CCA. Dcb/DC/N1/1.

170 The attribution is again from Colvin 1995, p 1041.

171 CCA, Dcb/DC/B13/1.

172 It should be added that there were examples of this type of composition, but without a bay, previous to the Grange in Ramsgate, such as at Rockland St Peter, in Norfolk, in 1840 – for which see Chapter Two, p 105, above.

173 No executed house by Pugin has either of these elements.

174 A.W.N. Pugin 1841a, p 1.

175 According to Dixon & Muthesius 1978, p 269, John Whichcord junior later designed the Grand Hotel at Brighton (1862–4).

176 Ovenden 1891.

177 *Ibid*, p 7. He meant, of course, Anglican churches; there were many more of other denominations, in addition to Pugin's St Augustine's, not least for the seaside tourists.

178 *Ibid*, p 13.

179 *Ibid*, p 39.

180 *Ibid*, pp 54–5.

181 *Ibid*, p 7.

182 The attribution to Vulliamy for the two Bethnal Green houses is from Colvin 1995, p 1013, and from *PAG London 5: East*, pp 552, 555: I found no contemporary mortgage records for them. It is fair to say that there are certain similarities here with the slightly earlier (1837) brick Roman Catholic presbytery designed by J. J. Scoles in Colchester, adjoining his Norman style church of St James. Pugin's church of St James in Reading was (uniquely, for him) Norman too. Why, I wonder, should St James be associated with the Romanesque style? Vulliamy's St James the Less church has been rebuilt after bombing but for the tower.

183 In the final volume of his *Architectural antiquities* (Britton 1826); and see above Chapter Two, figs. 2.17–8.

184 Some changes have taken place on the south, main, entrance elevation, and Vulliamy's original intentions are unclear. The church itself is built of flint and is less grand than St James the Less was.

185 The plan is traceable through existing situation plans prepared by Henry Letts Pridmore to accompany his application to alter the building in 1903. GLL, 19,244/600.

186 NRO, DN/DPL2/2/216. A tablet set into the wall gives the date as 1840.

187 CUL, EDR/G3/39 MGA/40.

188 In other words, it was similar to the Barham parsonage referred to above.

189 For which see Chapter Three, p 124, above.

190 RIBA LDC, Roberts. See Curl 1983, p 20, for further discussion of this house in the context of Roberts' career. Neither Professor Curl nor I have been able to locate this building in either of the Kentish Southboroughs.

191 CERC, QAB/7/6/E58.

192 See Curl 1983, p 24, pl 32.

193 Surrey HC, 472/23/2/2–4; and see Curl 1983, p 35. The house has been demolished.

194 For anxiety about missionaries, see for example Merewether 1845; Lapley: J Watson, c1840 (Colvin 1995, p 1026).

195 See Chapter One, pp 29–30, above.

196 CERC, QAB/7/6/E1740.

197 LA, MGA 153; and see Chapter One, p 56, and Chapter Two, pp 69–70, above.

198 Aylestone (1838): LA, MGA 225/1838; Thurmaston (1837): LA, MGA 220/1837.

199 These are given in Colvin 1995, p 882. Colvin lists the classical rectory at Tenbury of 1843 as being Smith's, but the plans in the Herefs RO, HD8/18 Benefice 1843, are signed by Harvey Egerton of Worcester, who was an architect. It is certainly a good deal more sophisticated than Smith's work.

200 There is no record at Herefs RO of an application: the attribution is from Colvin 1995, p 882. See Chapter Two, p 108, above.

201 Stokesay: Herefs RO, HD/44 1839; Wheathill: Herefs RO, HD10/6 1853 (*sic*).

202 Herefs RO, HD10/4 1851 (2).

203 See Hussey 1966.

204 According to Colvin 1995, p 139.

205 I am indebted to Peter Meadows of CUL for sharing with me his researches on this house. Mr Meadows kindly showed me his copy of plans and elevations of the house that had been reproduced in an unpublished album entitled *Mrs Ignatius' Bonomi's album, 1832*. The house was heavily altered and extended later in the nineteenth century.

206 Britton 1814.

207 Mackenzie & Ross 1834, vol ii, p 435.

208 Both houses were designed in partnership with J. A. Cory: Colvin 1995, p 140. This gives the date of 1844 for Wilton. A mortgage of £1,146 for the Loftus house was noted in the MGQAB for 4.5.1843, item 14/6 (CERC, QAB/2/1/23); and Mr Meadows tells me that he has in the past found the application documents for it in the collection now housed in the CERC, although if there now they are currently untraceable.

209 His National School at Croft in the North Riding of Yorkshire of 1844–5 was 'Tudor-gothic': Colvin 1995, p 140.

Notes to Chapter Five

1 WSRO, D1/11/250.

2 CUL, EDR/G3/40 MGA/BED/16. Parsonage files usually include archaic parish names, and from this one I discovered that Leighton Buzzard was at the time also called Leighton Bosard and, exotically, Leighton Beaudesert.

3 A.W.N. Pugin 1842, pl 11.

4 See Wedgwood 2006, p 22.

5 Photocopy of letter at HLRO, PUG/3/2/110, undated. Scott was working at St Mary's in 1842–4.

6 Only one letter of Pugin's directly refers to the presbytery at Cheadle, and it is undated, but is probably from November 1842 (or possibly 1843). It was a remodelling of an old house, with a new block at the rear, a new bay window, and an entry passage from the street. See Belcher 2003, pp 131–2.

7 The incumbent was Dr Samuel Edmund Walker: Chadwick 1966, p 220. I am indebted to Dr Gill Hunter for identifying the source of this story. Walker's travails were reported in the *Times* newspaper, 3.3.1845, p 7.

8 W. White 1851; W. White 1853. As a further example, Peter Howell tells me that the Oxford Architectural Society papers show that Pugin's name was erased from their record of Dorchester Abbey.

9 Milton: CCA, DCb/DC/M15/1, 1855; demolished.

10 Hansom's obituary in the *Builder* reported that the partnership, from 1862–3, 'had a disagreeable termination'. Oh dear! – so much did, where E.W. Pugin was involved. Joseph Hansom also worked in partnership with his son, from 1859–62. *Builder*, vol xliii, no 2057 (8.7.1888), p 44.

11 Letters from Pugin to John Hardman, 25.6.1845 and 9.7.1845 (in Belcher 2003, pp 410 and 412), refer to a 'Dr W', probably Wiseman, having made this complaint. Leetham 1950, a history of Ratcliffe College, suggests that Rosmini, the client, fell out with Pugin: pp 12; 17–8.

12 Quoted from a letter, probably mid-1846, to Shrewsbury in Ferrey 1861, p 133.

13 In a letter to Hardman of October 1849, HLRO, PUG/1/966: I am enormously grateful to Dr Margaret Belcher for finding me this and the following quotation which will appear in letters included in her forthcoming volumes of Pugin's correspondence. This one this seems to have been in relation to the priory church of Our Lady of the Annunciation at Woodchester, Gloucestershire, which C. Hansom designed from 1846.

14 HLRO, PUG/1/411.

15 The very few and partial views of Pugin's obliterated presbytery at St Mary, Stockton-on-Tees, suggest that this house had a similar west elevation. Harrison 1975 has one such photograph.

16 In an article entitled 'A few remarks on gothic ecclesiastical building, and its cost', in the *Rambler*, vol v, January 1850; quoted in Belcher 1987 at E64.

17 An impression long since corrected now by Evinson 1980.

18 For which latter subject see the excellent Andrews 2001 and Andrews 2002, and the work of Ursula de Jong.

19 Herefs RO, HD8/15 1840 (both refs).

20 CUL, EDR/G3/39/ MGA 50.

21 For details, see Girouard 1958.

22 The most comprehensive description of Salvin's work can be found in Allibone 1988.

23 LMA, ACC 1083/3. It has also been demolished.

24 WSRO, D1/11/112.

25 WSRO, D1/11/113.

26 Burston: Norfolk CRO, DN/DPL2/6/216; Horringer: SROB, FM500/1/6, of May 1871. The style of this latter house is a little odd – perhaps American-looking.

27 LA, MGA 315.

28 MGQAB vol xxiv, 26.3.1846, item 13; 1.7.1846; 16.3.1848, item 104/47 (CERC, QAB/2/1/24).

29 It is now part of Lincoln Minster School.

30 As Andrew Saint records, in Saint 1975, pp 3–5, Burn soon employed two fervent young Puginites in his office: Norman Shaw from 1849, and soon afterwards Shaw's future partner Nesfield, who later moved to Salvin. Much later Shaw designed one small house which has a plan very similar to that of Rampisham: the Corner House, of 1872: *ibid*, pl 89 p 106.

31 It seems possible that Charles Fowler junior (c1823–1903) may have been involved in the design. The drawings are in DRO.

32 W Sussex RO, Ep/I/41/88, 1853. Clarke produced many designs for parsonages in later years.

33 Hants RO, 16M70/16/1–8.

34 *Ecclesiologist*, vol ii, June 1843, p 145.

35 Savidge 1964, pp 133–4, identified this as Wordsworth's *The excursion*, Book VIII.

36 *Ecclesiologist*, vol ii, June 1843, p 146.

37 *Ibid*, p 147.

38 *Idem*.

39 By Butterfield, Carpenter and Daukes respectively; *Ecclesiologist*, vol iv, July 1845, p 189.

40 *Ibid*, vol vi, December 1846, pp 238–9.

41 *Ecclesiologist*, vol ii, June 1843, p 147.

42 Hants RO, 16M70/19/1–2.

43 Shinfield: see Chapter Two, p 116.

44 *Ecclesiologist*, vol viii, February 1848, p 258.

45 *Ibid*, vol viii, April 1848, p 321. See pp 276–8 above.

46 *Ibid*, vol viii, February 1848, p 249. It is very likely that the minutes of other county architectural societies, such as that at Oxford, could yield a great deal more interesting information about contemporary parsonages.

47 *Ibid*, vol ix, April 1849, p 328.

48 *Ibid*, June 1849, p 402.

49 *Ibid*, vol x, August 1849, pp 57–8. The meeting had been held the previous June.

50 Scott certainly read at least one paper (on the subject of church restoration) before the Society, referring to it in his *Recollections*: G. Scott 1995, p 149.

51 *Builder*, vol xxxvi, 1878, p 360. As with Ferrey's obituary, this list is not completely trustworthy – it does not include the clergy house at St Giles, Camberwell, for example.

52 G. Scott 1995, pp 157–64.

53 G. Scott 1857, p 241.

54 This was Pevsner's expression, in *PAG Staffs*, p 97.

55 There seems to be no record of Scott's house in the ORO. Drawings there of an extension of 1866, MS. Oxf. dioc. papers c.1656, appear to refer to a different building.

56 WSRO, D1/11/90. The plans are signed by Moffatt, on behalf of the partnership. Butterfield later made further additions, in effect converting the house into a more conventional central-corridor plan type (D1/11/215).

57 There is a partial view in Thompson 1971, p 348.

58 ORO, MS. Oxf. dioc. papers b.103/7.

59 GL, Ms 19224/455.

60 CUL, EDR/G3/39 MGA/91.

61 LMA, ACC 1083/² (cc no 1704).

62 At Tydd St Giles the study was reached from the corridor that leads from the front door.

63 ORO, MS. Oxf. dioc. papers c.1479.

64 For which see Stamp 2002, particularly pp 38–63.

65 A.W.N. Pugin 1841a, p 60; pp 1–2.

66 See for example Belcher 2003, p 153 n 3. Carpenter may have seen St Augustine's from the outside in 1845: Belcher 2003, p 330 n 4.

67 The MGQAB (vol xxiii) recorded a mortgage of £1,500 on 16.5.1844, item 12/1 (CERC, QAB/2/1/23). Elliott 1995, a doctoral dissertation, is the most comprehensive work on Carpenter to date, and his chapter 6 describes Carpenter's parsonages in detail. Brasted is referred to at pp 140–1. There are no files on his three major parsonages – Brasted, Kilndown and Monkton Wyld – in the relevant diocesan collections, but it seems possible that application details for some houses may one day be found somewhere in the CERC.

68 The flat, angular tracery of the windows of Wenlock Priory made other appearances in Carpenter's work; Pugin himself used it at least once, at Alton Castle which was probably also designed in 1843.

69 SRO, D/D/Bbm/61. Richard Down & Son were architects practising from Bridgwater. Ferrey, not an imaginative planner, used it himself very soon after Carpenter, at his 1844 vicarage at Midsomer Norton (SRO, D/D/Bbm/93).

70 See Chapter Three, pp 162–3, above.

71 *Ecclesiologist*, vol viii, April 1848, p 321.

72 Ferrey 1861, p 225.

73 Elliott 1995 has further details on Carpenter's domestic architecture. See Chapter One, pp 31–3, above for details of the angry correspondence between Harrison, the incumbent, the architect Roos, and Christian.

74 It appears that Carpenter's house incorporated some fragments of Roos', for there is a pre-extant brick-built wing on the south side of the house that suffers from the damp that had earlier plagued Harrison.

75 According to the MBEC vol iii, 4.7.1843, item 2 (CERC, ECE/2/1/1/6), the benefaction came from all three members of the family. They put up £600 for the land, and the Commissioners agreed to meet this with a grant of a further £400 (*ibid*, 27.6.1843). After Lady Beresford's death in 1851, and until he himself inherited the estate in 1854, Beresford-Hope managed his stepfather's affairs (*ODNB*). Lord Beresford told the Commissioners that he intended to spend £3,000 on this house – the same cost as the grand deanery in Lincoln mentioned above: MBEC vol viii, 25.11.1846, item 23 (CERC, ECE/2/1/1/11). From the first there were problems: his solicitors were unable to establish title on the piece of land he had in mind, and after a long delay he had to settle for a site half the size: MBEC vol ix, 9.12.1848 (CERC, ECE/2/1/1/12). Then came the protracted calamity of Roos' house. As Christian put it when describing the latter, 'it is greatly to be regretted that in a case like this where the provision of a complete and comfortable residence was desired irrespective of cost, the design of the Founder should have been so thwarted by the persons employed to make it so' (CKS, P157B/3/2: report of 4.4.1853).

76 He may in addition have built or remodelled the vicarage opposite his church of St John at Bovey Tracey in Devon, which has Puginesque joinery inside.

77 Cotes Heath: Elliott 1995, pp 208–9; Little Cornard, *ibid*, p 209.

78 Photocopy: HLRO, PUG/1/582, not dated; Birmingham City Library History Centre, Hardman Collection, Pugin Correspondence, 1847–1852 box; a letter dated by Pugin 'August 1851' includes 'I send you some rough sketches of seals that may do to show Mr Butterfield the sort of thing he could have more or less ornamented'.

79 Habershon 1839, *passim*, in succession to many picturesque and Tudor-gothic architects, had seen half-timbering as 'English'.

80 Carpenter may have designed the Brasted house as early as 1843, but he had earlier blotted his copybook somewhat with his feeble designs for terraces in Islington, designed from 1839 onwards in classical-Georgian and Tudor styles.

81 The interior has been remodelled by the opening up of the first reception room to the entrance corridor; see Savidge 1964, p 135 fig 49. The plan before this alteration was redrawn by M.G. Clens for the National Monuments Record in 1965: BB66/2602. There are other alterations from the original plan.

82 Thompson 1971, p 85, makes this latter point.

83 Although see Chapter Three, fn 94 above.

84 WSRO, D1/11/206.

85 Thompson 1971, fig 60 p 152. Pugin designed further square-sectioned, rectangular bays like this for his work at the Cheadle presbytery and at Cotton Hall some time soon after September 1846.

86 *Ibid*; see particularly pp 356–60.

87 Street 1883, p 13.

88 ORO, MS. Oxf. dioc. papers b.80. The hall has been compromised by modern subdivision.

89 According to Hammond 1977, p 45. Beeson 2004, pp 86–95, provides an enjoyable description of Butler's time at Wantage.

90 Quoted in Street 1883, p 15.

91 Savidge 1964, pp 139–43, provides good examples of the kind of derision I am referring to.

92 ORO, MA. Oxf. dioc. papers c.1789.

93 A.W.N. Pugin 1843, p 39.

94 Rather in the manner of what Lutyens was to do at Whalton Manor in Northumberland in 1908–9, although on a much smaller scale; ORO, MS. Oxf. dioc. papers c.1718.

95 WSRO, D1/11/246.

96 Hants RO, 16M70/29/1–59. The file is an interesting one however because of the interference of Christian, for the Ecclesiastical Commissioners, who asked Street to add 'protection' above window heads and other openings. It was here that the bishop himself, Samuel Wilberforce, added a water closet. Street was obliged to reduce costs by making the whole of the new part of the house slightly smaller.

97 Professor Crook has long ago noticed this joint parentage, in Eastlake 1970, preface p 14. Webb's hipped dormers had been previously used by S. S. Teulon, in his design for his parsonage, c1846, at Kirmington, Lincs (RIBA LDC, Teulon [10]).

98 Kirk 2005, pp 20–35; 92.

99 SROI, FF1/106/1; dated 19.3.1844.

100 SROI, FF1/47/1.

101 This was the style for parsonages including Creake (c1845), Potters Bar (not dated), Roade (not dated), and Wetheringsett [1844]: RIBA LDC, Teulon [3]; [12]; [15]; [17]. An undated scheme probably from the mid-1840s in the same sketchbook, [19], is in an Italianate style. The design there for 'Hollesby' (Teulon [9]) must refer to 'Hollesley'.

102 LA, MGA 338.

103 ORO, MS. Oxf. dioc. papers c.1721.

104 WSRO, D1/11/131.

105 Elliott & Pritchard 2002 includes a gazetteer of Woodyer's work, although omits the parsonage at Cove.

106 *Ecclesiologist*, vol vi, December 1846, pp 238–9.

107 The only file in Hants RO relating to the building is for White's extensions, and includes no original plan: 16M70/22/1–30.

108 W Sussex RO, Ep/I/41/72.

109 Hants RO, 16M70/10/1–21.

110 Wheatley: ORO, MS. Oxf. dioc. c.2066. The house, now substantially altered, was built in mirror image to how it had been drawn in the mortgage application. Ferrey's obituary in the *Builder* (vol xxxix, 4.9.80, pp 281–3) incorrectly lists this as his. Copdock: SROI, FF1/24/1.

111 This is particularly true of the house at St Ive, near Callington, Cornwall, with its sweeping roofs and sculptural forms. Dr Hunter's forthcoming work on this architect will at last provide a worthy appraisal of his work. See in the meantime Hunter 2006.

112 Brontë 1994, p 113.

113 *Ibid*, p 291.

114 Heygate 1845, p 51, quoting from Herbert's *Priest to the Temple* of 1671, cx.

115 Heygate 1845, p 50.

116 Ovenden 1857, pp 293–4.

117 *Ibid*, p 270.

118 *Ibid*, pp 298–9.

Notes to the Epilogue

1 Forty 2000, pp 109–10.

2 Brakelond 1844.

3 Brittain-Catlin 2006 discusses this in detail.

4 Drury 2001, §1.4 p 55.

5 Brittain-Catlin 2006, p 372.

6 G. Scott 1857, p 120.

7 The pioneering work of sociology, Auguste Comte's *Course of positive philosophy*, was published in 1830–42.

8 W. Scott 1999, pp 46–8.

9 This is discussed extensively in Auerbach 1953, p 468 ff.

10 Quoted in *ibid*, p 477.

11 The concluding words of A.W.N. Pugin 1841a.

12 Cooter 1984, p 124.

13 *Ibid*, p 119.

14 Brittain-Catlin 2006, p 372.

15 References to pews include J.M. Neale 1841; J.M. Neale 1843, pp 208–9; J.M. Neale; 1846, p 10 (*i.a.*).

16 Thompson 1977, pp 37–8.

17 *Stockton critic*, no 4, 15.2.1876, pp 50–1; the description, by 'Criticus', is of the Palm Sunday service of 1875.

18 *E.g.* Roberts 1848, pp 136–7.

19 Loudon 1833, §353 p 179.

Bibliography

This is a list of all publications and unpublished manuscripts or typescripts referred to in this book. Very long book titles have been shortened for convenience unless the full title is of intrinsic relevance.

The edition given here is that referred to in the text above. Where relevant, the original date and/or place of publication is given in brackets after its name.

An author's publications are listed chronologically. The Pevsner architectural guides are listed after the main list and by county. I have used the new term 'PAG' also in respect of titles previously published as part of the 'Buildings of England' series.

I have adopted the use of lower-case initials in accordance with British Library current practice.

Raleigh Addington 1974 *Faber, poet and priest: selected letters by William Frederick Faber 1833–1863*, Cowbridge & Bridgend.

J. Standen Adkins 1911, 'Ewan Christian, a memoir', *RIBA journal*, vol xviii, 30.9.1911, pp 711–30.

Edmund Aikin 1808 *Designs for villas and other rural buildings*, London.

Jill Allibone 1988 *Anthony Salvin, pioneer of gothic revival architecture, 1799–1881*, Cambridge.

Brian Andrews 2001 *Australian gothic: the gothic revival in Australian architecture from the 1840s to the 1950s*, Melbourne.

Brian Andrews 2002 *Creating a gothic paradise: Pugin at the Antipodes*, Hobart.

William Atkinson 1805, *Views of picturesque cottages*, London.

Paul Atterbury & Clive Wainwright 1994 (eds) *Pugin: a gothic passion*, New Haven & London.

Jane Austen 1966 *Emma* [first published 1816], Harmondsworth.

Jane Austen 1972 *Northanger Abbey* [first published 1818], Harmondsworth.

Eric Auerbach 1957 *Mimesis,* translated by W. Trask, New York.

'Autobiography', in **Wedgwood 1985**, pp 24–31.

Stephen Ayling 1865 *Photographs from sketches by A.W.N. Pugin*, London.

John Barrell 1972 *The idea of landscape and the sense of place 1730–1840*, Cambridge.

Alfred Bartholomew 1840 *Specifications for practical architecture, preceded by an essay on the decline of excellence in the structure and in the science of modern English buildings; with the proposal of remedies for those defects*, London.

B. Anthony Bax 1964 *The English parsonage*, London.

Anne Bayliss 1978 *The life and works of James Trubshaw (1777–1853): Staffordshire builder, architect and civil engineer*, Stockport.

Trevor Beeson 2004 *The deans*, London.

Margaret Belcher 1987 *A.W.N. Pugin: an annotated critical bibliography*, London & New York.

Margaret Belcher 2001 *The collected letters of A.W.N. Pugin, vol i: 1830–1842*, Oxford.

Margaret Belcher 2003 *The collected letters of A.W.N. Pugin, vol ii: 1843–1845*, Oxford.

G.E. Bentley Jr 2001 *The stranger from paradise: a biography of William Blake*, New Haven & London.

G.F.A. Best 1964 *Temporal pillars, Queen Anne's Bounty, the Ecclesiastical Commissioners, and the Church of England*, Cambridge.

A.T. Bolton 1927 *The Portrait of Sir John Soane RA*, London.

Jocelin of Brakelond 1844, *Monastic and social life in the twelfth century as exemplified in the chronicle of Jocelin of Brakelond, with notes, introduction, &c by T.E. Tomlins*, London.

Timothy Brittain-Catlin 2001 'A.W.N. Pugin and Nodier's Normandy'; in *True principles* (the newsletter/journal of The Pugin Society), vol ii, no 3, Winter 2001, pp 3–6.

Timothy Brittain-Catlin 2002a 'La Normandie de Nodier; L'Angleterre de Pugin'; in **Meade, Szambien & Talenti 2002**, pp 149–54.

Timothy Brittain-Catlin 2002b 'It all melts away: A.W.N. Pugin in Oxford'; in *True principles* (the newsletter/journal of The Pugin Society), vol ii, no 4, Summer 2002, pp 32–4.

Timothy Brittain-Catlin 2004a 'A.W.N. Pugin's English residential architecture in its context' [PhD thesis, Cambridge University].

Timothy Brittain-Catlin 2004b 'Pugin's perfect priestly palaces', *Country life*, vol cxcviii, no 8 (19.2.04), pp 68–71.

Timothy Brittain-Catlin 2006 'A.W.N. Pugin's English Convent Plans', *Journal of the Society of Architectural Historians* [of the US], vol 65 no 3, September 2006, pp 356–77.

John Britton 1807–26 *The architectural antiquities of Great Britain represented and illustrated in a series of views, elevations, plans, sections, and details, of various ancient English edifices: with historical and descriptive accounts of each* [as published as books]:

John Britton 1807 *The architectural antiquities of Great Britain, vol i*, London.

John Britton 1809 *The architectural antiquities of Great Britain, vol ii*, London.

John Britton 1812 *The architectural antiquities of Great Britain, vol iii*, London.

John Britton 1814 *The architectural antiquities of Great Britain, vol iv*, London.

John Britton 1826 *The architectural antiquities of Great Britain, vol v*, London.

John Britton 1832 *Descriptive sketches of Tunbridge Wells and the Calverley Estate*, London.

John Britton 1838 *A dictionary of the architecture and archaeology of the Middle Ages: including words used by ancient and modern authors in treating of architectural and other antiquities: with etymology, definition, description, and historical elucidation: also, biographical notices of ancient architects*, London.

John Britton 1849 *The autobiography of John Britton FSA*, London.

John Britton & Charles Boutell 1846 *Illustrations of the early domestic architecture of England; drawn and arranged by John Britton, Esq. FSA. &c. with notices, descriptive and historical by the Rev. Charles Boutell M.A.*, London.

John Britton & A.C. Pugin 1825–8 *The public buildings of London*, vol i 1825; vol ii 1828, London.

John Britton, A.C. Pugin, and John and Henry Le Keux 1828 *Historical and descriptive essays accompanying a series of engraved specimens of the architectural antiquities of Normandy*, London.

Anne Brontë 1994 *Agnes Grey* [first published 1846], London.

Chris Brooks 1999 *The gothic revival*, London.

S.H. Brooks 1839 *Designs for cottage and villa architecture; containing plans, elevations, sections, perspective views and details for the erection of cottages and villas*, London [not dated – plates are 1839].

Cynthia Brown, Birkin Haward & Robert Kindred 1991 *Dictionary of architects of Suffolk buildings 1880–1914*, Ipswich.

Owen Chadwick 1966 *The Victorian church*, London.

William Cobbett 1853 *Rural rides* [first published 1830], London.

Howard Colvin 1995 *A biographical dictionary of British architects* 1600–1840, 3rd ed, New Haven & London.

E.W. Cooney 1955–6 'The origins of the Victorian master builder'; in *Economic history review* (2nd series), vol viii, pp 167–76.

Roger Cooter 1984 *The cultural meaning of popular science: phrenology and the organization of consent in nineteenth-century Britain*, Cambridge.

John Sell Cotman & Dawson Turner 1822 *Architectural antiquities of Normandy, by John Sell Cotman; accompanied by historical and descriptive notices by Dawson Turner FR and AS*, London & Yarmouth.

J. Mordaunt Crook 1968 'John Britton and the genesis of the gothic revival'; in **Summerson 1968,** pp 98–119.

J. Mordaunt Crook 2003 *The architect's secret*, London.

J. Mordaunt Crook & M.H. Port 1973 *The history of the King's Works, vol vi, 1782–1851*, London.

James Stevens Curl 1983 *The life and work of Henry Roberts, 1803–1876*, Chichester.

Gillian Darley 1999 *John Soane: an accidental Romantic*, New Haven & London.

T.D.W. Dearn 1806 *Sketches in architecture; consisting of original designs for public and private buildings*, London.

T.D.W. Dearn 1807 *Sketches in architecture; consisting of original designs for cottages and rural dwellings, suitable to persons of moderate fortune, and for convenient retirement; with plans and appropriate scenery to each*, London.

'Diary', in **Wedgwood 1985** pp 32–100.

Charles Dickens 1994 *Oliver Twist* [completed 1839], London.

Charles Dickens 1999 *Nicholas Nickleby* [completed 1839], London.

Charles Dickens 2000 *The old curiosity shop* [completed 1841], London.

Benjamin Disraeli 1844 *Coningsby, or the new generation*, London.

Roger Dixon & Stefan Muthesius 1978 *Victorian architecture*, London.

Thomas Leverton Donaldson 1842 *Preliminary discourse pronounced before the University College of London, upon the commencement of a series of lectures in architecture*, London.

Paul Drury 2001 'The Grange, Ramsgate, Kent: conservation plan – sixth and final draft', London, February 2001.

H.G. Duffield 1850 *The strangers guide to Manchester, containing information on every subject interesting to residents or strangers. Chronological, historical and descriptive derived from the most authentic sources*, Manchester.

Charles Eastlake 1970 *The gothic revival* [first published 1872]; annotated edition, ed J. Mordaunt Crook, Leicester.

George Eliot 1998, *Scenes of clerical life* [first published 1857], London.

John Patrick Elliott 1995 The architectural works of Richard Cromwell Carpenter (1812–55), William Slater (1819–72) and Richard Herbert Carpenter (1841–93)' [PhD thesis, Royal Holloway College, University of London].

John Elliott & John Pritchard 2000 (eds) *Henry Woodyer: gentleman architect*, Reading.

Richard Elsam 1816 *Hints for improving the condition of the peasantry in all parts of the United Kingdom*, London.

Denis Evinson 1980 *Pope's corner*, Hammersmith.

Benjamin Ferrey 1861 *Recollections of A.W.N. Pugin and his father Augustus Pugin*, London.

Adrian Forty 2000 *Words and buildings: a vocabulary of modern architecture*, London, 2000.

Joseph Gandy 1805a *The rural architect, consisting of various designs for country buildings*, London.

Joseph Gandy 1805b *Designs for cottages, cottage farms, and other rural buildings including entrance gates and lodges*, London.

Mark Girouard 1958 'Horsted Place, Sussex', in *Country life*, vol cxxiv, no 3212 (7.8.1958), pp 276–9; no 3213 (14.8.1958), pp 320–3.

John Gloag 1970 *Mr Loudon's England*, Newcastle upon Tyne.

Ann Gore & George Carter 2005 *Humphry Repton's* Memoirs, Wilby.

Joseph Gwilt 1842 *An encyclopædia of architecture, historical, theoretical and practical*, London.

E. Gyfford 1806 *Designs for elegant cottages and small villas*, London.

E. Gyfford 1807 *Designs for small picturesque cottages and hunting boxes*, London.

M. Habershon 1839 *The ancient half-timbered houses of England*, London.

Peter C. Hammond 1977, *The parson and the Victorian parish*, London.

Francis E. Harrison 1975, 'A history of Stockton-on-Tees' [tss], Stockton [there is a copy at Stockton Local History Library, ref 942851 Q9495351].

W.E. Heygate 1845 *Probatio Clerica, or aids in self-examination to candidates for holy orders, or for those of the clergy who may desire them*, London.

Thomas Hinde 1984 *A field guide to the English country parson*, London.

Christopher Hodgson 1826 *An account of the augmentation of small livings by the* "governors of the Bounty of Queen Anne, for the augmentation of the maintenance of the poor clergy" *and of benefaction by corporate bodies and individuals, to the end of the year 1825; also the charters, rules and acts of parliament by which the proceedings of the governors are regulated. To which are prefixed, practical instructions for the use of incumbents and patrons of augmented livings, and of other interested parties, on various subjects relating to Queen Anne's Bounty*, London.

Min Hogg 2003 'Clarence House'; in *The world of interiors*, October 2003, pp 190–9.

Robert Hole 1989 *Pulpits, politics and public order in England 1760–1832*, Cambridge.

T.F. Hunt 1827a *Architetture campestre: displayed in lodges, gardeners' houses, and other buildings, composed of simple and economic forms in the modern or Italian style; introducing a picturesque mode of roofing*, London.

T.F. Hunt 1827b *Designs for parsonage houses, alms houses, etc. etc. with examples of gables, and other curious remains of old English architecture*, London.

T.F. Hunt 1830 *Exemplars of Tudor architecture adapted to modern habitations, with illustrative details, selected from ancient edifices; and observations on the furniture of the Tudor period*, London.

Gill Hunter 'An examination of the work of William White FSA, architect (1825–1900)' [PhD thesis, University College London].

Christopher Hussey 1966 'Lambton Castle, County Durham'; in *Country life*, vol cxxxix, no 3603 (1966), pp 664–7; and no 3604 pp 726–9.

Frank Jenkin 1961 *Architect and patron: a survey of professional relations and practice in England from the sixteenth century to the present day*, London.

W.A.B. Jones 1977 *Hadleigh through the ages*, Ipswich.

Barrington Kaye 1960 *The development of the architectural profession in Britain*, London.

Sheila Kirk 2005 *Philip Webb*, Chichester.

Osbert Lancaster 1938 *Pillar to post, or the pocket-lamp of architecture*, London.

C.R. Leetham 1950 *Ratcliffe College 1847–1947*, Leicester.

London County Council 1951 'South Bank & Vauxhall part i', *Survey of London*, vol xxiii, London.

J.C. Loudon 1806 *A treatise on forming, improving, and managing country residences*, London.

J.C. Loudon 1812 *Observations on laying out farms in the Scotch style, adapted to England*, London.

J.C. Loudon 1833 *An encyclopaedia of cottage, farm, and villa architecture and furniture*, London, Paris & Strasburg, Edinburgh, New York, Boston, Philadelphia, Sydney, Hobart Town.

James Lowther 1755 [?] *Some thoughts on building and planting, to Sir James Lowther, of Lowther Hall, Bart*, Whitehaven.

Robert Lugar 1805 *Architectural sketches for cottages, rural dwellings, and villas*, London.

Robert Lugar 1806 *The country gentleman's architect*, London.

Robert Lugar 1811 *Plans and views of buildings executed in England and Scotland in the castellated and other styles*, London.

R. Lugar 1828 *Villa architecture*, London.

E. Mackenzie & M. Ross 1834 *An historical, topographical and descriptive view of the County Palatine of Durham, etc.*, Newcastle upon Tyne.

James Malton 1798 *An essay on British cottage architecture*, London.

Peter Mandler 1997 *The fall and rise of the stately home*, New Haven & London.

Michael Mansbridge 1991, *John Nash*, London.

Martin Kew Meade, Werner Szambien & Simona Talenti 2002 (eds) *L'architecture normande en Europe, identités et échanges*, Marseilles.

Francis Merewether 1845 *A pastoral address to the inhabitants of Whitwick, Leicestershire, on the opening of a monastery within the limits of that parish: with a supplement*, Ashby-de-la-Zouch.

Mary Russell Mitford 1936 *Our village*, [originally published in the *Lady's Magazine*, 1824–32], London.

'The Myers family album', in a private collection.

Hermann Muthesius 1903, *Stilarchitektur und Baukunst* [first published 1902], 2nd edition, Mülheim an der Ruhr.

Hermann Muthesius 1994 *Style–architecture and building–art* [first published in German, 1902/1903], introduced and translated by Stanford Anderson, Santa Monica.

Joseph Nash 1839–1848 *Mansions of England in the Olden Time*, London.

J.M. Neale 1841 *The history of pews; a paper read before the Cambridge Camden Society*, Cambridge.

J.M. Neale 1843 *Ayton Priory; or the restored monastery*, London.

J.M. Neale 1846 *A few words to church wardens on churches and church ornaments, part I suited to country parishes*, 14th ed, London.

J.P. Neale 1822–3 *Views of seats*, vol iii, London.

Charles Nodier, I. Taylor & Alph. de Cailleux 1820 *Voyages pittoresques et romantiques dans l'ancienne France*, vol i, Paris.

Ashton Ovenden 1857 *The pastoral office: its duties, difficulties, privileges, and prospects*, London.

Ashton Ovenden 1891 *The history of my life*, London.

J.B. Papworth 1818 *Rural residences*, London.

Charles Parker 1833 *Villa rustica selected from buildings and scenes in the vicinity of Rome and Florence; and arranged for lodges and domestic dwellings. With plans and details*, London.

J.H. Parker 1840 *A glossary of terms used in Grecian, Roman, Italian and gothic architecture* [first published 1836], 3rd ed, Oxford.

Nikolaus Pevsner 1943 'A short Pugin florilegium'; in *Architectural review*, vol xciv, August 1943, pp 31–4.

John Plaw 1795 *Rural architecture*, London.

John Plaw 1800 *Sketches for country houses, villas and rural dwellings*, London.

William Pocock 1807 *Architectural designs for rustic cottages, picturesque dwellings, villas, etc.*, London.

M.H. Port 2006 *Six hundred new churches: the Church Building Commission 1818–1856* [2nd edition], Reading.

M.H. Port 1967 'The Office of Works and Building Contracts in early nineteenth-century England'; in *Economic history review* (2nd series), vol xx, pp 94–110.

A.C. Pugin 1821–5, *Specimens of gothic architecture*, as books:

A.C. Pugin 1821 *Specimens of gothic architecture, vol i*, London.

A.C. Pugin 1825 *Specimens of gothic architecture, vol ii*, London.

A.C. Pugin & E.J. Willson 1828–31 *Examples of gothic architecture, vol i*, London.

A.C. Pugin, A.W.N. Pugin & E.J. Willson 1831–6 *Examples of gothic architecture, vol ii*, London.

A.C. Pugin *Examples of gothic architecture, vol iii*: see **A.W.N. Pugin & T.L. Walker 1836–40** below.

A.W.N. Pugin 1836 *Contrasts: or, a parallel between the noble edifices of the fourteenth and fifteenth centuries, and similar buildings of the* *present day; showing the present decay of taste: accompanied by appropriate text*, Salisbury.

A.W.N. Pugin 1841a *The true principles of pointed or Christian architecture*, London.

A.W.N. Pugin 1841b *Contrasts*, 2nd edition, London.

A.W.N. Pugin 1842 'On the present state of ecclesiastical architecture in England' [part II], *Dublin review*, vol xii February 1842, pp 80–183; [published anonymously].

A.W.N. Pugin 1843 *An apology for the revival of Christian architecture in England*, London.

A.W.N. Pugin & T. L. Walker 1836–40, *Examples of gothic architecture, vol iii*, London.

George Richardson 1792 *New designs in architecture*, London.

George Roberts 1848 *Speculum episcopi, the mirror of a bishop* [published anonymously], London.

John Robison 1822 *A system of mechanical philosophy*, Edinburgh.

Andrew Rudd 2004 'Gothic horror versus gothic revival: Protestant visions of Catholic society'; in *True principles* (the journal of The Pugin Society), vol iii no I, Summer 2004, pp 48–50.

Andrew Saint 1975 *Richard Norman Shaw*, New Haven & London.

Alan Savidge 1964 *The parsonage in England: its history and architecture*, London.

George Gilbert Scott 1995 *Personal and professional recollections* [first published 1879], annotated and extended edition, Gavin Stamp (ed), Stamford.

George Gilbert Scott 1857 *Remarks on secular and domestic architecture, present and future*, London.

Walter Scott 1999 *Kenilworth* [first published 1821], 'Edinburgh Edition', Harmondsworth.

Hill Shine & Helen Chadwick Shine 1949 *The* Quarterly review *under Gifford, identification of contributors 1809–1824*, Chapel Hill.

R.J. Smith 1987 *The gothic bequest: medieval institutions in British thought, 1688–1863*, Cambridge.

Gavin Stamp 2002 *An architect of promise: George Gilbert Scott Junior (1839–1897) and the late gothic revival*, Donington.

Phoebe Stanton 1950 'Welby Pugin and the gothic revival' [PhD thesis, Courtauld Institute, University of London].

Phoebe Stanton 1951 'Pugin at twenty-one'; in *Architectural review*, vol cx, September 1951, pp 187–90.

Phoebe Stanton 1971 *Pugin*, London.

A.E. Street 1888 *Memoirs of G. E. Street RA*, London.

John Summerson 1968 (ed), *Concerning architecture*, London.

Rosemary Sweet 2004 *Antiquaries: the discovery of the past in eighteenth-century Britain*, London.

Paul Thompson 1971 *William Butterfield*, London.

Peter Virgin 1989 *The Church in an age of negligence: ecclesiastical structure and problems of church reform 1700–1840*, Cambridge.

Peter Virgin 1994, *Sydney Smith*, London.

W.R. Ward 1965 'The tithe question in England in the early nineteenth century', in *Journal of English history* 16.

Alexandra Wedgwood 1977 *Catalogue of the drawings collection of the Royal Institute of British Architects, the Pugin family*, London.

Alexandra Wedgwood 1985 *Catalogue of drawings in the Victoria & Albert Museum, A.W.N. Pugin and the Pugin family*, London.

Alexandra Wedgwood 1988 (ed) 'Pugin in his home', a memoir by J.H. Powell; in *Architectural history*, vol 31, 1988, pp 171–205.

Alexandra Wedgwood 1994 'Domestic architecture', in **Atterbury & Wainwright 1994**, pp 42–61.

Alexandra Wedgwood 2006 (ed) 'Pugin in his home', two memoirs by J.H. Powell, Ramsgate (updated version of **Wedgwood 1988**).

Thomas Whitaker 1801 *An history of the original parish of Whalley and honor of Clitheroe, in the counties of Lancaster and York*, Blackburn.

Roger White with the assistance of **Robin Darwall-Smith 2001** *The architectural drawings of Magdalen College, Oxford*, Oxford & New York.

William White 1851 'Upon some of the causes and points of failure in modern design'; in *Ecclesiologist*, vol xii, no lxxxvii (October 1851), pp 305–13.

William White 1853 'Modern design'; in *Ecclesiologist*, vol xiv, no xcviii (June 1853), pp 313–30.

George Wightwick 1827 *Select views of Roman antiquities*, London.

Pevsner architectural guides

The following are the editions referred to in footnotes:

PAG Clwyd etc.
Edward Hubbard *The buildings of Wales [vol 2], Clwyd, Denbighshire and Flintshire*, Harmondsworth, 1986.

PAG London 5: East
Bridget Cherry, Charles O'Brien & Nikolaus Pevsner *The buildings of England, London 5: East*, London, 2005.

PAG Norfolk NW&S
Nikolaus Pevsner & Bill Watson *The buildings of England, Norfolk North West & South*, 2nd ed, London, 1999.

PAG Staffs.
Nikolaus Pevsner *The buildings of England, Staffordshire*, Harmondsworth, 1974.

PAG York & East Yorks.
Nikolaus Pevsner & David Neave *The buildings of England: Yorkshire: York & the East Riding*, 2nd ed, Harmondsworth, 1995.

Acknowledgments

This book owes its existence, and such value as it has, to Andrew Saint, who as my supervisor for my doctoral dissertation on A.W.N. Pugin's domestic architecture at Cambridge University between 2000 and 2003 and subsequently never tired of directing, advising, correcting and inspiring my writing on Victorian and pre-Victorian architecture. I need hardly add that any errors of fact or conclusion, especially the more far-fetched of the latter, are entirely my responsibility. I am but a humble foot soldier in Andrew's war against 'meaning', and it must sometimes have appeared that I, like Joyce Emily in *The prime of Miss Jean Brodie*, have been marching towards the sound of gunfire that was emanating from the wrong direction.

I have received generous funding for this book in three invaluable stages. The basic kernel of information grew out of my doctoral research at Cambridge University, which itself received generous support from the Hyam, the Rouse Ball and the Eddington Funds of Trinity College, and I am enormously grateful to my tutor David McKitterick for his interest and support. Secondly, this book was largely written during the course of the summer of 2004 with the help of a most generous scholarship from the Harold Hyam Wingate Foundation. Alongside these, my loyal patron Rupert Thomas, the editor of *The world of interiors*, has thoughtfully kept me going with commissions for interesting and enjoyable work, and has also added his personal support to the realisation of the project. Finally, generous funding has also been received from the donors listed at the front of the book which has enabled it to be illustrated as it should be, both with considerable reference to the archival sources that form the basis of the story, but also with outstanding new photography by Martin Charles. Throughout the long route to publication I have received invaluable advice and support from Peter Blundell Jones for which I am particularly grateful. In addition, this book has become a reality thanks to the generous and far-sighted interest in the project from Geoff Brandwood and John Elliott at Spire Books, who received critical support from English Heritage's Historic Environment Commissions scheme. In addition, I am personally grateful to Allon Kaye for the book's elegant design.

I have along the way received much friendly help and advice from Alexandra Wedgwood, Roderick O'Donnell, and Joseph Sharples; from Desmond Day; from Michael Port, who kindly gave me impromptu tutorials on church legislation, nineteenth-century professional practice, and much other useful advice; from Peter Virgin, the author of the wonderful *The church in an age of negligence*; from Gill Hunter; from Martin Goalen; from Margaret and Ray Honey; from David Watkin; and from Catriona Blaker, Sarah Houle, and my many friends in The Pugin Society. Margaret Belcher, the editor of Pugin's published collected correspondence, has very generously helped me with material from her forthcoming volumes. I have also been much encouraged by my old friend Mark Bostridge, and by Irénée Scalbert. Like many others I owe a great deal of my interest in this subject to the influence of reading Mark Girouard's books at an impressionable age, and if Andrew Saint's *Richard Norman Shaw* was, as its author suggests, one of Girouard's sons, then this book is undoubtedly one of his grandsons, albeit somewhere far down the cadet line.

I would like in particular to thank those at the Architectural Association who provided invaluable help: Sarah Franklin, for a great deal of her time in working on the images; the librarian, Hinda Sklar; the photo librarian, Valerie Bennett, and the photographer Sue Barr. I would also like to thank the independent photographers who carried out work for me at the various record offices: Glynn G. Burrows (Norfolk Record Office); Nick Cistone of Preservation Photography (Oxfordshire Record Office); Derek James (Herefordshire Record Office); and Derek Parker (Wiltshire & Swindon Record Office). It has been a pleasure to work with the many county and diocesan archivists, their assistants and their technical staff who have often been generous and patient in dealing with my endless enquiries. In particular I would like to thank Sara Slinn of the Borthwick Institute, University of York; Mark Bateson, Paul Blewitt, David Pilcher, Peter Whitehead and Cressida Annesley of Canterbury Cathedral Archives; Sarah Duffield, Paul Kendall and Philip Gale of the Church of England Record Centre; Clare Brown, Cristina Henshaw, Rachel Cosgrave, Sarah Drewery and Tim Pye of Lambeth Palace Library; at Cambridge University Library: Godfrey Waller, superintendent, and Peter Meadows (Keeper of Ely Diocesan Records, and in charge of an exemplary collection) and their staff at the

Department of Manuscripts; Anne Taylor and the staff of the Map Room; the staff of the Rare Books Room; and Patricia Killyard, Gerry Bye and Lynda Unchern of Imaging Services. John Draisey and Renee Jackaman of Devon Record Office; Eleanor John and Mandy Williams of the Geffrye Museum; Julio Sims of The Getty Research Institute; Stephen Freeth, Claire Titley and Seamas McKenna of the Guildhall Library, London; Sarah Lewin and Linda Champ of Hampshire Record Office; Elizabeth Semper of Herefordshire Record Office; Adrian Wilkinson of Lincolnshire Archives; Howard Doble of London Metropolitan Archives; Jennifer Broomhead of the State Library of New South Wales; Jonathan Butler of the English Heritage Photo Library; Natalie Hill and the staff of the National Monuments Record in Swindon; Edwin King of Norfolk Record Office; Dorothy Ritchie of Nottingham City Local History Library; Mark Priddey, Rosemary Hamilton, Karen Garvey and Timothy Xu of Oxfordshire Record Office; Nick Tomlinson of picturethepast.org.uk; Robert Elwall and Valerie Carullo of the RIBA Library Photographs Collection; Liz Grant of Somerset Record Office; Sheila Reed of Suffolk Record Office, Bury St Edmunds; Bridget Hanley and Sue Lodwick of Suffolk Record Office, Ipswich; Teresa Gray, Carole Garrard and Mary Mackey of Surrey History Centre; Richard Childs and David Milnes of the West Sussex Record Office; and John d'Arcy and Martyn Henderson of Wiltshire & Swindon Record Office. My sincere apologies if I have left anyone out.

In addition, I would like to thank the following for their kind help and in some cases a good deal of their time: Julie Allinson of Stockton-upon-Tees Public Library; Caroline Armstrong-Wilson; Alexandra Armstrong-Wilson; Paul Barton; Susan Bates of the Department of East Asian Studies, University of Durham; Ben Blackburn; Rod Boucher; Alex Bremner; Michael Bresalier; James Campbell; Fr Ronald Creighton-Jobe; Robin Darwall-Smith of Magdalen College, Oxford; Chris Davies; the Squire de Lisle; Tim den Dekker; Canon Anthony Dolan; Paul Drury; Robert Fairbairn; Francis Fawcett; Fr Norbert Fernandes; Geoffrey Fisher of the Conway Library, Courtauld Institute; Fr Michael Fisher; Robert and Patsy Floyd; Brian Galway; Patrick Galvin; Fr Sean Gilligan; Michael Hall; Fr Pat Hartnett; Peter and Gina Higgins; Boyd Hilton; Lynne Jackson; Hilary Kent; Fr David Lannon; Timothy McCann; Monsignor McGovern;

Irene MacNamara of Keighley Public Library; Mr and Mrs William McPherson; Duncan Mather; Jane Martineau; Rose Luckman and the community of Monkton Wyld Court; Chris Morley; Jeremy Musson; Paul Pollock; Fr Michael Scanlon; Fr John Sharp of Birmingham Archdiocesan Archives; Fr Fred Sheldon; Catherine Slessor; Patricia Spencer-Silver; Fr David Standen; Mr and Mrs Robin Stow; Sir Conrad Swan; Mick Twyman of the Margate Historical Society; Fr Bede Walsh; Sally Watson, Catriona Cornelius, and the staff of RIBA Library Drawings Collection at the Victoria and Albert Museum; Rev John Weir; Mr and Mrs D.A. Whittle; Martin Williams; and the staff of the RIBA Library at 66 Portland Place. And of course I thank the many residents of parsonages whom I disturbed at their homes when I turned up unexpectedly, and who were invariably generous with their time. On behalf of both Martin Charles and myself I would further like to thank those residents of former parsonages who have allowed photography of their homes for this book.

Finally, I would like to thank my dear friend Assaf Krebs for his continued enthusiastic encouragement and support; and Hillel Helman, whom I first met 12 years ago on the top floor of the Bezalel Academy on Mount Scopus above Jerusalem (and thus at the closest place on earth to heaven); this book is dedicated to him and his family, with endless love.

Illustration credits

New photography
All recent photography of buildings is, unless otherwise noted in the caption, by Martin Charles and was photographed from January to November 2007 especially for this book. © Martin Charles.

New plans
The following plans were drawn by the author: 1.16, 1.28, 1.29, 3.9, 3.14, 3.20, 3.22, 3.24, 3.27, 3.30, 3.32, 3.34, 3.35.
© Timothy Brittain-Catlin.

Archival illustrations:
A note on the reproduction of archival drawings

This book is as much about the actual drawings found in diocesan collections as it is about their content and for that reason it has been important to reproduce them faithfully and without succumbing to the temptation of improving their clarity through digital manipulation. In most cases the drawings were photographed or scanned directly from the original; with others, there was necessarily an intermediate printed stage. These reproductions, however they are achieved, inevitably give a slightly distorted appearance to an image: a fold or crease in the paper, for example, will be much more prominent in the reproduction than it appears when looking at the original document itself; and the contrast between line and background appears less marked in a reproduction than it is in reality. Distortions such as these, arising from the reproduction process itself, have been therefore reduced as far as is reasonable. The rule of thumb in any case has been that the reproduction on the page should resemble the original item as much as possible. All the work of preparing images for publication from digital files received from archives and from my original drawings was done professionally by Assaf Krebs. I am also very grateful to Sarah Franklin of the Architectural Association Photo Library for help with the transfer of images.

Credits

French and German summaries

L'histoire du presbytère anglais victorien fait partie de l'histoire bien connue du néogothique, mais l'histoire du presbytère du début du dix-neuvième siècle est tout autre chose.

A partir de 1810 l'administration du Queen Anne's Bounty, la caisse de l'église anglicane, établie pour aider les membres du clergé dans le besoin, commençait à distribuer des emprunts logements pour des presbytères neufs, une fois que la procédure de demande était complète. Cette procedure obligeait l'architecte ou l'entrepreneur du curé à présenter les desseins entiers et une spécification à l'évêque du diocèse pour son approbation. Résultat : il existe des centaines de demandes détaillées, ce qui est sans égal pour d'autres types de bâtiments dans les archives diocésaines.

D'un côté, ces collections donnent un commentaire continu au sujet des changements professionnels et techniques des architectes pendant la phase critique de leur passage de géomètres et entrepreneurs (pendant les années 1810 et 1820) au statut d'architectes et membres de l'Institut des Architectes Britanniques [Institute of British Architects] (pendant les années 1830 et 1840). Ces collections donnent donc une illustration très nette du procès de rationalisation et de réglementation du dix-neuvième siècle. D'un autre côté, bien entendu, l'évolution du style des maisons montre exactement quand et comment le néogothique est arrivé. Ces bâtiments de charme, bien aimés de ceux qui apprécient tout ce qui est beau dans les villages typiques anglais, sont originaux et fascinants.

A. W. N. Pugin est le personnage central dans cette deuxième histoire. Très souvent il apparaît dans l'histoire de l'architecture soit comme le dernier, soit comme l'initiateur d'une tradition. D'autre part, il est quelquefois traité essentiellement comme quelqu'un d'exceptionnel qui, avec ses singularités diverses, ne supporte aucune comparaison facile avec d'autres architectes de sa génération. En fait, la période la plus intense de sa vie active, les années 1840, était une période de transition pour la profession d'architecture anglaise, et cette étude des presbytères de cette époque essaie de mettre Pugin dans le contexte des dessinateurs contemporains qui faisaient face aux même problèmes que lui. Les riches réserves de documentation détaillée nous permettent de voir exactement comment son travail différait de celui de ses collègues et comment ces idées radicals ont eu très vite des répercussions dans les œuvres des architectes vers la fin du dix-neuvième siècle.

La vraie gloire de cette histoire se trouve dans des centaines de maisons elles-mêmes, toujours sur place, souvent peu changées, dans l'attente d'être redécouvertes, prêtes à raconter leur histoire étonnante, celle d'une grande révolution dans l'architecture domestique britannique.

Traduction: Heather Pickford

Die Geschichte des Pfarrhauses im viktorianischen England ist ein weit bekannter Teil der neugotischen Architekturgeschichte, aber der Hintergrund des Pfarrhauses im frühen 19. Jahrhundert ist eine ganz andere Angelegenheit.

Ab dem Jahre 1810 fing das Direktorium der «Queen Anne's Bounty» damit an, nach ausführlichem Antragsverfahren Hypotheken für den Bau von Pfarrhäusern zu erlassen. Bei der «Queen Anne's Bounty» handelte es sich um einen Unterstützungs-fond, benannt nach der damalig herrschenden Königin Anne, der für den verarmten Klerus von der englischen Staatskirche eingerichtet worden war. Das Verfahren erforderte die Vorlage von Zeichnungen, Lageplänen des vom Pfarrer beauftragten Architekten oder Bauherrn, und die Spezifikations-zustimmung des Bischofs. Als Resultat dessen gibt es nun hunderte von Anträgen in diözesanen Archiven, die von unvergleichlichem Ausmaß zu anderen Bauweisen sind.

Einerseits stellen diese Ansammlungen einen lückenlosen Kommentar auf fachliche und technische Änderungen zur Verfügung, die englischen Architekten während der kritischen Phase ihrer Umwandlung vom Vermesser und Bauherrn (von 1810 bis in die 20iger Jahre) zum Architekten und Mitglied des Instituts der britischen Architekten [Institute of British Architects] (in den 30iger und 40iger Jahren des 19. Jahrhunderts) erfuhren. Folglich liefern sie eine lebhafte Darstellung der bekannten Entwicklung der Rationalisierung und der staatlichen Beeinflussung der Architektur im frühen 19. Jahrhundert. Andererseits gibt der sich ändernde Stil der Häuser einen Einblick, wo und wann genau die gotische Erneuerung (Neugotik) geschah. Die Gebäude selbst sind oft bezaubernd, faszinierend und originell. Deshalb sind sie sehr beliebt bei denjenigen, die die Schönheiten eines typischen englischen Dorfes zu schätzen wissen.

A. W. N. Pugin ist der Mittelpunkt dieser zweiten Geschichte. Sehr häufig erscheint er in architektonischen Berichten als der Anfang oder das Ende einer Tradition. Außerdem wird er manchmal biographisch in erster Linie als einzigartig behandelt, da er mit seinen verschiedenen Eigenheiten nicht leicht mit anderen Architekten seiner Zeit verglichen werden kann. Tatsächlich sind die 40iger Jahre, die die intensivste Periode seines Berufslebens darstellten, eine entscheidende Übergangsphase der englischen Architektur. Diese Studie der Pfarrhäuser aus dieser Zeit zielt darauf hin, Pugin in den Kontext zu Architekten seiner Zeit, die ähnlichen Aufgaben gegenüberstanden, zu setzen. Das enorm reichhaltige Angebot von ausführlichen Unterlagen macht es möglich, genau zu sehen, wo sich seine Arbeit von der seiner zeitgenössischen Kollegen unteschied, und, wie es dazu kam, dass, sich seine radikalen Ideen bald darauf in Werken von Architekten des späten 19. Jahrhunderts widerspiegelten.

Die eigentliche Pracht dieser Entwicklungsgeschichte jedoch sind die Hunderte von Häusern selbst. Oftmals sind sie kaum umgebaut, auf Wiederentdeckung wartend und bereit, die erstaunliche Revolution der englischen Architekturgeschichte zu erzählen.

Übersetzung: Manuela Joynes

Index

Place names are given twice: once by name, and once by county name at the time of building. Where the latter has changed; the new ceremonial county (or preserved county, in Wales) is given in brackets. Publications are listed following the name of author. Numbers in bold refer to illustrations – the figure, rather than the caption, page is given.